CONTENTS

Introduction

The Rough Guide Portuguese phrasebook is a highly practical introduction to the contemporary language. Laid out in clear A-Z style, it uses key-word referencing to lead you straight to the words and phrases you want – so if you need to book a room, just look up 'room'. The Rough Guide gets straight to the point in every situation, in bars and shops, on trains and buses, and in hotels and banks.

The main part of the Rough Guide is a double dictionary: English-Portuguese then Portuguese-English. Before that, there's a section called The Basics, which sets out the fundamental rules of the language, with plenty of practical examples. You'll also find here other essentials like numbers, dates, telling the time and basic phrases.

Forming the heart of the guide, the English-Portuguese section gives easy-to-use transliterations of the Portuguese words wherever pronunciation might be a problem, and to get you involved quickly in two-way communication, the Rough Guide includes dialogues featuring typical responses on key topics – such as renting a car and asking directions. Feature boxes fill you in on cultural pitfalls as well as the simple mechanics of how to make a phone call, what to do in an emergency, where to change money, and more. Throughout this section, cross-references enable you to pinpoint key facts and phrases, while asterisked words indicate where further information can be found in The Basics.

In the Portuguese-English dictionary, we've given not just the phrases you're likely to hear (starting with a selection of slang and colloquialisms), but also various labels, instructions and other basic words you may come across in print or in public places.

Finally the Rough Guide rounds off with an extensive Menu Reader. Consisting of food and drink sections (each starting with a list of essential terms), it's indispensable whether you're eating out, stopping for a quick drink, or browsing through a local food market.

boa viagem!

have a good trip!

Basics

Pronunciation

In this phrasebook, the Portuguese has been written in a system of imitated pronunciation so that it can be read as though it were English, bearing in mind the notes on pronunciation given below:

a	as in h**a**t
ay	as in m**ay**
eh	as in g**e**t
g	as in **g**oat
i	as in **i**t
ī	as the 'i' sound in m**i**ght
J	as the 's' sound in plea**s**ure
o	as in n**o**t
oh	like the exclamation **oh**
oo	as in b**oo**t
ow	as in n**ow**

In words such as **não** [nowng] and **bem** [bayng], the final 'g' in the pronunciation signifies a nasal sound and should barely be sounded.

Letters given in bold type indicate the part of the word to be stressed.

Abbreviations

adj	adjective
f	feminine
fam	familiar
m	masculine
pl	plural
pol	polite
sing	singular

Nouns

All nouns in Portuguese have one of two genders: masculine or feminine. Generally speaking, those ending in **-o** are masculine:

o sapato
oo sap**a**too
the shoe

Nouns ending in **-or** are masculine. To make the corresponding feminine, add **-a**:

o professor	**a professora**
oo proofes**oh**r	a proofes**oh**ra
the (male) teacher	the (female) teacher

Nouns ending in **-a**, **-ade** or **-ão** are usually feminine (although there are exceptions):

a cama	**a cidade**	**a pensão**
a k**a**ma	a sid**a**d	a payns**ow**ng
the bed	the city	the boarding house

A small number of nouns ending in **-a** and **-e** (usually professions) can be either masculine or feminine:

o/a guia	**o/a intérprete**
oo/a g**ee**-a	oo/a int**eh**rprit
the tourist guide	the interpreter

Plural Nouns

The plurals of nouns are formed according to the rules below.

For nouns ending in a vowel, add **-s**:

a empregada	**as empregadas**
a aympreg**a**da	az aympreg**a**dash
the waitress	the waitresses

To obtain the plural of nouns ending in **-ão**, remove the **-ão** and add **-ões**:

a pensão	**as pensões**
a payns**ow**ng	ash payns**oy**ngsh
the guesthouse	the guesthouses

To obtain the plural of nouns ending in **-l**, remove the **-l** and add **-is**:

o hotel	**os hotéis**
oo oht**eh**l	ooz oht**eh**-ish
the hotel	the hotels

To obtain the plural of nouns ending in **-m**, remove the **-m** and add **-ns**:

o homem	**os homens**
oo **oh**mayng	ooz **oh**mayngsh
the man	the men

For nouns ending in other consonants, the plural is formed by adding **-es**:

o condutor	**os condutores**
oo kondoot**oh**r	oosh kondoot**oh**rish
the driver	the drivers
uma mulher	**umas mulheres**
ooma mool-y**eh**r	**oo**mash mool-y**eh**rish
a woman	some women

Articles

The words for articles in Portuguese depend on the number (singular or plural) and gender of the noun.

The Definite Article

The definite article (the) is as follows:

	singular	plural
masculine	**o** [oo]	**os** [oosh]
feminine	**a** [a]	**as** [ash]

o livro
oo **lee**vroo
the book

os livros
ooJ **lee**vroosh
the books

a piscina
a pishs**ee**na
the swimming pool

as piscinas
ash pishs**ee**nash
the swimming pools

When the definite article is used in combination with **a** (to), **de** (of), **em** (in, on) or **por** (by), it changes as follows:

	o	**a**	**os**	**as**
a +	**ao** ow	**à** a	**aos** owsh	**às** ash
de +	**do** doo	**da** da	**dos** doosh	**das** dash
em +	**no** noo	**na** na	**nos** noosh	**nas** nash
por +	**pelo** p**i**loo	**pela** p**i**la	**pelos** p**i**loosh	**pelas** p**i**lash

vamos ao museo
v**a**mooz ow moos**ay**-oo
let's go to the museum

perto do hotel
p**eh**rtoo doo oht**eh**l
near the hotel

The Indefinite Article

The indefinite article (a, an, some) also changes according to the gender and number of the accompanying noun:

	singular	plural
masculine	**um** [oong]	**uns** [oonsh]
feminine	**uma** [**oo**ma]	**umas** [**oo**mash]

um selo	uns selos
oong **say**loo	oonsh **say**loosh
a stamp	some stamps
uma rapariga	umas raparigas
ooma rapar**ee**ga	**oo**mash rapar**ee**gash
a girl	some girls

When the indefinite article is used in combination with **em** (in, on) it changes as follows:

masculine **em + um = num** [noong]
feminine **em + uma = numa** [n**oo**ma]

gostava de ir numa viagem ao Brasil
goosht**a**va deer n**oo**ma v-y**a**Jayng ow braz**ee**l
I'd like to go on a trip to Brazil

Adjectives and Adverbs

Adjectives must agree in gender and number with the noun they refer to. In the English-Portuguese section of this book, all adjectives are given in the masculine singular. Unlike English, Portuguese adjectives usually follow the noun.

The feminine singular of the adjective is formed by changing the masculine endings as follows:

masculine	feminine
-o	**-a**
-or	**-ora**
-ês	**-esa**

um cozinheiro estupendo	uma cozinheira estupenda
oong koozeen-y**ay**roo shtoop**ay**ndo	**oo**ma koozeen-y**ay**ra shtoop**ay**nda
a wonderful cook	a wonderful cook
um senhor encantador	**uma senhora encantadora**
oong sin-y**oh**r aynkantad**oh**r	**oo**ma sin-y**o**ra aynkantad**o**ra
a nice man	a nice woman

um rapaz inglês	**uma rapariga inglesa**
oong rap**a**z ingl**ay**sh	**oo**ma rapar**ee**ga ingl**ay**za
an English boy	an English girl

For other types of adjective, the feminine form is the same as the masculine:

um homem agradável	**uma mulher agradável**
oong **oh**mayng agrad**a**vil	**oo**ma mool-y**eh**r agrad**a**vil
a nice man	a nice woman

Note that the adjective **mau** (bad) is irregular: the feminine is **má**.

The plurals of adjectives are formed in the same way as the plurals of nouns, by adding an **-s**, an **-es** or changing **-l** to **-is**:

o preço alto	**os preços altos**
oo pr**ay**soo **a**ltoo	oosh pr**ay**sooz **a**ltoosh
the high price	the high prices
uma taxa alta	**as taxas altas**
ooma t**a**sha **a**lta	ash t**a**shaz **a**ltash
a high rate	the high rates
um homem agradável	**uns homens agradáveis**
oong **oh**mayng agrad**a**vil	oonz **oh**mayngz agrad**a**vay-ish
a nice man	some nice men

When the adjective ends in **-ês**, the **ê** is replaced by **e** in the plural:

um rapaz inglês	**uns rapazes ingleses**
oong rap**a**z ingl**ay**sh	oonsh rap**a**ziz ingl**ay**zish
an English boy	some English boys

Comparatives

The comparative is formed by placing **mais** (more) or **menos** (less) in front of the adjective or adverb and **que** (than) after it:

bonito	**mais bonito**
booneetoo	mīJ booneetoo
beautiful	more beautiful
quente	**menos quente**
kaynt	maynoosh kaynt
hot	less hot

este hotel é mais/menos caro que o outro
aysht ohtehl eh mīsh/maynoosh karoo ki oo ohtroo
this hotel is more/less expensive than the other one

tem um quarto mais barato?
tayng oong kwartoo mīJ baratoo
do you have a cheaper room?

pode falar mais devagar, por favor?
pod falar mīJ divagar poor favohr
could you speak more slowly please?

Superlatives

Superlatives are formed by placing one of the following before the adjective: **o/a mais** or **os/as mais** (depending on the noun's gender and number):

qual é o mais divertido?
kwaleh oo mīJ divirteedoo
which is the most entertaining?

o dia mais quente	**o carro mais rápido**
oo dee-a mīsh kaynt	oo karroo mīsh rapidoo
the hottest day	the fastest car

The following adjectives have irregular comparatives and superlatives:

bom	good	**melhor**	better	**o melhor**	the best
bong		mil-yor		oo mil-yor	
grande	big	**maior**	bigger	**o maior**	the biggest
grand		mī-or		oo mī-or	

mau	bad	**pior**	worse	**o pior**	the worst
mow		p-yor		oo p-yor	
pequeno	small	**menor**	smaller	**o menor**	the smallest
pik**ay**noo		min**o**r		oo min**o**r	

Note that **mais pequeno** (smaller) is also used.

'As ... as ...' is translated as follows:

Lisboa está tão bonita como sempre!
liJb**oh**-a shta towng boon**ee**ta k**oh**moo saympr
Lisbon is as beautiful as ever!

The superlative form ending in **-íssimo** indicates that something is 'very/extremely ...' without actually comparing it to something else:

lindo	**lindíssimo**
l**ee**ndoo	lind**ee**simoo
beautiful	very beautiful

Adverbs

There are two ways to form an adverb. If the adjective ends in **-o**, take the feminine and add **-mente** to form the corresponding adverb:

exacto	**exactamente**
iz**a**too	izatam**ay**nt
accurate	accurately

If the adjective ends in any other letter, add **-mente** to the basic masculine form:

feliz	**felizmente**
fil**ee**sh	filiJm**ay**nt
happy	happily

Possessive Adjectives

Possessive adjectives, like other Portuguese adjectives, agree with the noun in gender and number:

	singular masculine	singular feminine	plural masculine	plural feminine
my	**o meu** oo m**ay**-oo	**a minha** a m**ee**n-ya	**os meus** ooJ m**ay**-oosh	**as minhas** aJ m**ee**n-yash
your (sing, fam)	**o teu** oo t**ay**-oo	**a tua** a t**oo**-a	**os teus** oosh t**ay**-oosh	**as tuas** ash t**oo**-ash
his/her/its, your, their	**o seu** oo s**ay**-oo	**a sua** a s**oo**-a	**os seus** oosh s**ay**-oosh	**as suas** ash s**oo**-ash
our	**o nosso** oo n**o**soo	**a nossa** a n**o**sa	**os nossos** ooJ n**o**soosh	**as nossas** aJ n**o**sash

A more formal way of translating 'your' is:

	singular	plural
masculine	**do senhor** doo sin-y**oh**r	**dos senhores** doosh sin-y**oh**rish
feminine	**da senhora** da sin-y**o**ra	**das senhoras** dash sin-y**o**rash

See page 20 for when to use this.

a tua casa
a t**oo**-a k**a**za
your house

as suas pastilhas
ash soo-ash pasht**ee**l-yash
his/her/your/their tablets

a **sua mala**
a s**oo**-a m**a**la
his/her/your/their suitcase

os nossos amigos
oJ n**o**sooz am**ee**goosh
our friends

If when using **o seu**, **o sua** etc, it is unclear whether you mean 'his', 'her', 'your' or 'their', you can use the following after the noun instead:

dele	[dayl]	his
dela	[**deh**la]	her
deles	[**day**lish]	their (m)
delas	[**deh**lash]	their (f)
de vocês	[di vos**ay**sh]	your (pl)

o dinheiro dela	o dinheiro dele	o dinheiro de vocês
oo deen-y**ay**roo d**eh**la	oo deen-y**ay**roo dayl	oo deen-y**ay**roo di vos**ay**sh
her money	his money	your money

Possessive Pronouns

To translate 'mine', 'yours', 'theirs' etc, use one of the following forms. Like possessive adjectives, possessive pronouns must agree in gender and number with the object or objects referred to:

	singular		plural	
	masculine	feminine	masculine	feminine
mine	meu	minha	meus	minhas
	m**ay**-oo	m**ee**n-ya	m**ay**-oosh	m**ee**n-yash
yours (sing, fam)	teu	tua	teus	tuas
	t**ay**-oo	t**oo**-a	t**ay**-oosh	t**oo**-ash
his/hers, yours,theirs	seu	sua	seus	suas
	s**ay**-oo	s**oo**-a	s**ay**-oosh	s**oo**-ash
ours	nosso	nossa	nossos	nossas
	n**o**soo	n**o**sa	n**o**soosh	n**o**sash

A more formal way of translating 'yours' is:

	singular	plural
masculine	do senhor	dos senhores
	doo sin-y**oh**r	doosh sin-y**oh**rish
feminine	da senhora	das senhoras
	da sin-y**o**ra	dash sin-y**o**rash

See the section on subject pronouns for when to use this.

Generally, possessive pronouns are used with the definite article.

esta é a sua chave e esta é a minha
ehshteh a s**oo**-a sh**a**vee **eh**shteh a m**ee**n-ya
this is your key and this is mine

este carro não é o seu
aysht k**a**rroo nowng eh oo s**ay**-oo
this car is not yours

If when using **seu**, **sua** etc, it is unclear whether you mean 'his', 'hers', 'yours' or 'theirs', you can use the following after the noun instead:

dele	[dayl]	his
dela	[**deh**la]	hers
deles	[**day**lish]	theirs (m)
delas	[**deh**la]	theirs (f)
de vocês	[di vos**aysh**]	yours (pl)

não é dele, é dos amigos dele
nowng eh dayl eh dooz am**ee**gooJ dayl
it's not his, it's his friends'

Personal Pronouns

Subject Pronouns

eu	[**ay**-oo]	I
tu	[too]	you (sing, fam)
ele	[ayl]	he, it
ela	[**eh**la]	she, it
você	[vos**ay**]	you (sing, pol)
nós	[nosh]	we
eles	[aylsh]	they (m)
elas	[**eh**lash]	they (f)
vocês	[vos**aysh**]	you (pl)

Tu is used when speaking to one person and is the familiar form generally used when speaking to family, close friends and children.

Você and **vocês** are more formal and are used to address people you don't know well. They take the third person forms of verbs: **você** takes the same form as 'he/she/it'; **vocês** takes the same form as 'they'.

There is another way of saying 'you', which is used to address complete strangers or in formal situations. These forms all take the third person of the verb, i.e. the same as 'he/she/it' for the singular and 'they' for the plural:

	singular	plural
masculine	**o senhor** oo sin-y**oh**r	**os senhores** oosh sin-y**oh**rish
feminine	**a senhora** a sin-y**o**ra	**as senhoras** ash sin-y**o**rash

(Note that **Senhor** also means 'Mr' and **Senhora** means 'Mrs'.)

a senhora é a mãe da Rita?
a sin-y**o**ra eh a mayng da r**ee**ta
are you Rita's mother?

In Portuguese the subject pronoun is usually omitted:

não sabem
nowng s**a**bayng
they don't know

está cansado
sht**a** kans**a**doo
he is tired

But it may be retained for emphasis or to avoid confusion:

sou eu!
soh **ay**-oo
it's me!

somos nós!
s**oh**mooJ nosh
it's us!

eu pago as sandes e você paga as cervejas
ay-oo p**a**gwash sandsh ee vos**ay** p**a**gash sirv**ay**Jash
I'll pay for the sandwiches and you pay for the beers

ele é inglês e ela é americana
ayl**eh** ingl**ay**z ee **eh**leh amirik**a**na
he's English and she's American

Object Pronouns

object pronoun added to verb

me	[mi]	me
te	[ti]	you (sing, fam)
o	[oo]	him, it, you (sing, pol)
a	[a]	her, it, you (sing, pol)
você	[vos**ay**]	you (sing, pol)
nos	[noosh]	us
os	[oosh]	them (m), you (mpl)
as	[ash]	them (f), you (fpl)
vocês	[vos**ay**sh]	you (pl)

object pronoun used with prepositions

mim	[meeng]	me
ti	[tee]	you (sing, fam)
ele	[ayl]	he, it
ela	[**eh**la]	she, it
você/si	[vos**ay**/see]	you (sing, pol)
nós	[nosh]	we
eles	[aylsh]	them (m)
elas	[**eh**lash]	them (f)
vocês	[vos**ay**sh]	you (pl)

The object pronouns (as listed in the first table above) generally follow the verb:

pode ajudar-me?
pod aJood**a**rmi
can you help me?

comprei-as
kompr**ay**-ash
I bought them

But note the word order in the following:

não o vi
nowng oo vee
I didn't see him

The object pronouns (as listed in the right-hand column of the table above) are used after prepositions:

para você
p**a**ra vos**ay**
for you

com ele
kong ayl
with him

sem ela
sayng **eh**la
without her

depois de você
dip**oh**-ish di vos**ay**
after you

isso é para mim
eesoo eh p**a**ra meeng
that's for me

isso é para ti/si
eesoo eh p**a**ra tee/see
that's for you

After the preposition **com** (with), **mim**, **ti** and **si** change as follows:

comigo
koom**ee**goo
with me

contigo
kont**ee**goo
with you

consigo
kons**ee**goo
with you

If you are using an indirect object pronoun to mean 'to me', 'to you' etc (although 'to' might not always be said in English), you generally use the following:

me	[mi]	to me
te	[ti]	to you (sing, fam)
lhe	[l-yi]	to him, to her, to you (sing, pol)
o/a	[oo/a]	to it
nos	[noosh]	to us
lhes	[l-yish]	to them, to you (pl)

comprei-lhe flores
kompr**ay**l-yi fl**oh**rish
I bought flowers for him/her

pedi-lhe um favor
pid**ee**l-yi oong fav**oh**r
I asked him/her a favour

importa-se de lhe pedir que ...?
imp**o**rtasi di l-yi pid**ee**r ki
could you ask him/her to ...?

Reflexive Pronouns

These are used with reflexive verbs like **lavar-se** 'to wash (oneself)', i.e. where the subject and the object of the verb are one and the same person:

me	[mi]	myself
te	[ti]	yourself (fam)
se	[si]	himself, herself, itself, yourself (pol), themselves, yourselves, oneself
nos	[noosh]	ourselves

apresentar-se to introduce oneself

apresento-me: chamo-me Richard
aprisayntoomi: shamoomi Richard
may I introduce myself? my name's Richard

divertir-se to enjoy oneself

divertimo-nos muito na festa
divirteemoonooJ mweengtoo na fehshta
we enjoyed ourselves a lot at the party

Demonstratives

The English demonstrative adjective 'this' is translated by **este**. 'That' is translated either by **esse** or **aquele**. **Esse** refers to something nearby. **Aquele** refers to something further away.

Like other adjectives, demonstrative adjectives agree with the noun they qualify in gender and number but they are positioned in front of the noun. Their forms are:

masculine singular			feminine singular		
este	**esse**	**aquele**	**esta**	**essa**	**aquela**
aysht	ays	ak**ay**l	**eh**shta	**eh**sa	ak**eh**la

masculine plural			feminine plural		
estes	**esses**	**aqueles**	**estas**	**essas**	**aquelas**
ayshtish	**ay**sish	ak**ay**lish	**eh**shtash	**eh**sash	ak**eh**lash

este restaurante	esse camareiro	aquela praia
aysht rishtow**ran**t	ays kamar**ay**roo	ak**eh**la prī-a
this restaurant	that waiter	that beach (in the distance)

The demonstrative pronouns 'this one', 'that one', 'those', 'these' etc are the same as demonstrative adjectives in Portuguese:

queria estes/esses/aqueles
kir**ee**-a **ay**shtish/**ay**sish/ak**ay**lish
I'd like these/those/those (over there)

However, a neuter form also exists which is used when no specific noun is being referred to:

isto	isso	aquilo
eeshtoo	**ee**soo	ak**ee**loo
this	that	that (over there)

isso não é justo
eeso nowng eh J**oo**stoo
that's not fair

o que é isto?
oo ki eh **ee**shtoo
what is this?

Verbs

The basic form of the verb given in the English-Portuguese and Portuguese-English sections is the infinitive (e.g. to drive, to go etc). There are three verb types in Portuguese which can be recognized by their infinitive endings: **-ar**, **-er**, **-ir**. For example:

amar	[am**ar**]	to love
comer	[koom**ayr**]	to eat
partir	[part**eer**]	to leave

Present Tense

The present tense corresponds to 'I leave' in English. To form the present tense for the three main types of verb in

Portuguese, remove the **-ar**, **-er** or **-ir** and add the following endings:

amar to love

am-o	[**a**moo]	I love
am-as	[**a**mash]	you love (sing, fam)
am-a	[**a**ma]	he loves, she loves, you love (sing, pol)
am-amos	[am**a**moosh]	we love
am-am	[**a**mowng]	they love, you love (pl)

comer to eat

com-o	[**koh**moo]	I eat
com-es	[**koh**mish]	you eat (sing, fam)
com-e	[**koh**mi]	he eats, she eats, you eat (sing, pol)
com-emos	[kom**ay**moosh]	we eat
com-em	[**koh**mayng]	they eat, you eat (pl)

partir to leave

part-o	[**par**too]	I leave
part-es	[**par**tsh]	you leave (sing, fam)
part-e	[**part**]	he leaves, she leaves, it leaves, you leave (sing, pol)
part-imos	[par**tee**moosh]	we leave
part-em	[**par**tayng]	they leave, you leave (pl)

Some common verbs are irregular:

dar to give

dou	[doh]	I give
dás	[dash]	you give (sing, fam)
dá	[da]	he gives, she gives, it gives, you give (sing, pol)
damos	[**da**moosh]	we give
dão	[downg]	they give, you give (pl)

ir to go

vou	[voh]	I go
vais	[vīsh]	you go (sing, fam)
vai	[vī]	he/she/it goes, you go (sing, pol)
vamos	[**va**moosh]	we go
vão	[vowng]	they go, you go (pl)

pôr to put

ponho	[**poh**n-yoo]	I put
pões	[poyngsh]	you put (sing, fam)
põe	[poyng]	he/she/it puts, you put (sing, pol)
pomos	[**poh**moosh]	we put
põem	[**poh**-ayng]	they put, you put (pl)

ter to have

tenho	[**tay**n-yoo]	I have
tens	[tayngsh]	you have (sing, fam)
tem	[tayng]	he/she/it has, you have (sing, pol)
temos	[**tay**moosh]	we have
têm	[**tay**-ayng]	they have, you have (pl)

vir to come

venho	[**vay**n-yoo]	I come
vens	[vayngsh]	you come (sing, fam)
vem	[vayng]	he/she/it comes, you come (sing, pol)
vimos	[**vee**moosh]	we come
vêm	[**vay**-ayng]	they come, you come (pl)

The first person singular (the 'I' form) of the following verbs is irregular:

dizer	to say	**digo**	[**dee**goo]
fazer	to do, to make	**faço**	[**fa**soo]
saber	to know	**sei**	[say]
sair	to go out	**saio**	[**sī**-oo]
poder	to be able	**posso**	[**po**soo]

See page 33 for the present tense of the verbs **ser** and **estar**.

Past Tense:

Preterite Tense

The preterite is the tense most commonly used to express a completed action that has taken place in the past. To form the preterite tense for the three main types of verb in Portuguese, remove the **-ar**, **-er** or **-ir** and add the following endings:

am-ei	[am**ay**]	I loved
am-aste	[am**a**sht]	you loved (sing, fam)
am-ou	[am**oh**]	he loved, she loved, you loved (sing, pol)
am-ámos	[am**a**moosh]	we loved
am-aram	[am**a**rowng]	they loved, you loved (pl)
com-i	[kom**ee**]	I ate
com-este	[kom**ay**sht]	you ate (sing, fam)
com-eu	[kom**ay**-oo]	he ate, she ate, it ate, you ate (sing, pol)
com-emos	[kom**ay**moosh]	we ate
com-eram	[kom**ay**rowng]	they ate, you ate (pl)
part-i	[part**ee**]	I left
part-iste	[part**ee**sht]	you left (sing, fam)
part-iu	[part**ee**-oo]	he left, she left, it left, you left (sing, pol)
part-imos	[part**ee**moosh]	we left
part-iram	[part**ee**rowng]	they left, you left (pl)

The following verbs are irregular in the preterite:

dizer to say

disse	[dees]	I said
disseste	[dis**eh**sht]	you said (sing, fam)
disse	[dees]	he said, she said, you said (sing, pol)
dissemos	[dis**ay**moosh]	we said
disseram	[dis**eh**rowng]	they said, you said (pl)

fazer to do

fiz	[feesh]	I did
fizeste	[fiz**eh**sht]	you did (sing, fam)
fez	[faysh]	he did, she did, it did, you did (sing, pol)
fizemos	[fiz**ay**moosh]	we did
fizeram	[fiz**eh**rowng]	they did, you did (pl)

ter to have

tive	[teev]	I had
tiveste	[tiv**eh**sht]	you had (sing, fam)
teve	[tayv]	he had, she had, it had, you had (sing, pol)
tivemos	[tiv**ay**moosh]	we had
tiveram	[tiv**eh**rowng]	they had, you had (pl)

vir to come

vim	[veeng]	I came
vieste	[v-yehsht]	you (sing, fam)
veio	[v**ay**-oo]	he came, she came, it came, you came (sing, pol)
viemos	[v-y**ay**moosh]	we came
vieram	[v-y**eh**rowng]	they came, you came (pl)

The verbs **ser** (to be) and **ir** (to go) are irregular and have the same form in the preterite:

fui	[fwee]	I was; I went
foste	[fohsht]	you were (sing, fam); you went (sing, fam)
foi	[f**oh**-i]	he/she/it was, you were (sing, pol); he/she/it went, you went (sing, pol)
fomos	[f**oh**moosh]	we were; we went
foram	[f**oh**rowng]	they were, you were (pl, pol); they went, you went (pl)

quem te disse isso?
kayng ti dees **ee**soo
who told you that?

conhecemos o seu pai ontem
kon-yes**ay**mooz oo s**ay**-oo pī **oh**ntayng
we met your father yesterday

comprámos um carro no ano passado
kompr**a**mooz oong k**a**rroo noo **a**noo pas**a**doo
we bought a car last year

See page 33 for the preterite tense of the verbs **ser** and **estar**.

Imperfect Tense

This tense is used to express what was going on regularly over an indefinite period of time and is often translated by 'used to + verb'. It is formed as follows:

amar to love

am-ava	[am**a**va]	I used to love
am-avas	[am**a**vash]	you used to love (sing, fam)
am-ava	[am**a**va]	he/she used to love, you used to love (sing, pol)
am-ávamos	[am**a**vamoosh]	we used to love
am-avam	[am**a**vowng]	they used to love, you used to love (pl)

comer to eat

com-ia	[kom**ee**-a]	I used to eat, I was eating etc
com-ias	[kom**ee**-ash]	you used to eat (sing, fam)
com-ia	[kom**ee**-a]	he/she/it used to eat, used to eat (sing, pol)
com-íamos	[kom**ee**-amoosh]	we used to eat
com-iam	[kom**ee**-owng]	they used to eat, you used to eat (pl)

partir to leave

part-ia	[part**ee**-a]	I used to leave, I was leaving etc
part-ias	[part**ee**-ash]	you used to leave (sing, fam)
part-ia	[part**ee**-a]	he/she/it used to leave, you used to leave (sing, pol)
part-íamos	[part**ee**-amoosh]	we used to leave
part-iam	[part**ee**-owng]	they used to leave, you used to leave (pl)

todas as quartas-feiras saíamos para dar um passeio

tohdazash kwartash fayrash sa-ee-amoosh para dar oong passay-oo
every Wednesday we used to go for a walk, every Wednesday we went for a walk

sempre chegávamos cedo ao emprego
saympr shigavamoosh saydwow aympraygoo
we always arrived early at work

One useful irregular verb in the imperfect tense is:

ter to have

tinha	[teen-ya]	I used to have
tinhas	[teen-yash]	you used to have (sing, fam)
tinha	[teen-ya]	he/she/it used to have, you used to have (sing, pol)
tínhamos	[teen-yamoosh]	we used to have
tinham	[teen-yowng]	they used to have, you used to have (pl)

See page 33 for the imperfect tense of the verbs **ser** and **estar**.

Future Tense

To form the future tense in Portuguese (I will do, you will do etc), add the following endings to the infinitive. The same endings are used whether verbs end in **-ar**, **-er** or **-ir**:

amar to love

amar-ei	[amaray]	I will love
amar-ás	[amarash]	you will love (sing, fam)
amar-á	[amara]	he will love, she will love, you will love (sing, pol)
amar-emos	[amaraymoosh]	we will love
amar-ão	[amarowng]	they will love, you will love (pl)

voltarei mais tarde
voltaray mīsh tard
I'll come back later

The immediate future can also be translated by **ir** + infinitive:

vamos comprar uma garrafa de vinho tinto
vamoosh kompr**ar** **oo**ma garr**a**fa di v**ee**n-yoo t**ee**ntoo
we're going to buy a bottle of red wine

irei buscá-lo
ir**ay** booshk**a**loo
I'll fetch him, I'll go and fetch him

In Portuguese, as in English, the future can sometimes be expressed by the present tense:

o seu avião parte à uma
oo s**ay**-oo av-y**ow**ng p**a**rta **oo**ma
your plane takes off at one o'clock

However, Portuguese often uses the present tense where the future would be used in English:

dou-lhe oitocentos escudos
d**oh**l-yi oh-itos**ay**ntooz shk**oo**doosh
I'll give you eight hundred escudos

The following verbs are irregular in the future tense:

dizer to say

dir-ei	[dir**ay**]	I will say
dir-ás	[dir**ash**]	you will say (sing, fam)
dir-á	[dir**a**]	he will say, she will say, you will say (sing, pol)
dir-emos	[dir**ay**moosh]	we will say
dir-ão	[dir**ow**ng]	they will say, you will say (pl)

fazer to do

far-ei	[far**ay**]	I will do
far-ás	[far**ash**]	you will do (sing, fam)
far-á	[far**a**]	he will do, she will do, it will do, you will do (sing, pol)
far-emos	[far**ay**moosh]	we will do
far-ão	[far**ow**ng]	they will do, you will do (pl)

See page 34 for the future tense of the verbs **ser** and **estar**.

Use of the Past Participle

There are two auxiliary verbs in Portuguese: **ter** (more commonly used) and **haver**. These two combine with the past participle to make a compound form of the past tense.

To form the past participle, remove the infinitive endings and add the endings **-ado** or **-ido** as indicated below:

infinitive	past participle	
amar	**am-ado**	[am**a**doo]
comer	**com-ido**	[kom**ee**doo]
partir	**part-ido**	[part**ee**doo]

ela já tinha comprado o bilhete
ehla Ja **tee**n-ya kompr**a**doo oo bil-y**ay**t
she had already bought the ticket

Some further examples using the past participle:

este livro foi comprado em Lisboa
aysht l**ee**vroo f**oh**-i kompr**a**doo ayng liJb**oh**-a
this book was bought in Lisbon

temos comido bem
taymoosh kom**ee**doo bayng
we've been eating well

ela deve ter partido ontem
ehla dehv tayr part**ee**doo **oh**ntayng
she should have left yesterday

Some verbs have irregular past participles:

fazer to do, to make	**feito**	[f**ay**too]
abrir to open	**aberto**	[ab**eh**rtoo]
dizer to say	**dito**	[d**ee**too]
pôr to put	**posto**	[p**oh**shtoo]
ver to see	**visto**	[v**ee**shtoo]
vir to come	**vindo**	[v**ee**ndoo]
satisfazer to satisfy	**satisfeito**	[satishf**ay**too]

The Verb 'To Be'

There are two verbs 'to be' in Portuguese: **ser** and **estar**. They are conjugated as follows:

Present Tense

ser		
sou	[soh]	I am
és	[ehsh]	you are (sing, fam)
é	[eh]	he is, she is, it is, you are (sing, pol)
somos	[**soh**moosh]	we are
são	[sowng]	they are, you are (pl)

estar		
estou	[shtoh]	I am
estás	[shtash]	you are (sing, fam)
está	[shta]	he is, she is, it is, you are (sing, pol)
estamos	[sht**a**moosh]	we are
estão	[shtowng]	they are, you are (pl)

Preterite Tense (I was etc)

ser		estar	
fui	[fwee]	estive	[shteev]
foste	[fohsht]	estiveste	[shtiv**eh**sht]
foi	[**foh**-i]	esteve	[shtayv]
fomos	[**foh**moosh]	estivemos	[shtiv**ay**moosh]
foram	[**foh**rowng]	estiveram	[shtiv**eh**rowng]

Imperfect Tense (I used to be etc)

ser		estar	
era	[**eh**ra]	estava	[sht**a**va]
eras	[**eh**rash]	estavas	[sht**a**vash]
era	[**eh**ra]	estava	[sht**a**va]
éramos	[**eh**ramoosh]	estávamos	[sht**a**vamoosh]
eram	[**eh**rowng]	estavam	[sht**a**vowng]

Future Tense (I will be etc)

ser		estar	
serei	[siray]	estarei	[shtaray]
serás	[sirash]	estarás	[shtarash]
será	[sira]	estará	[shtara]
seremos	[siraymoosh]	estaremos	[shtaraymoosh]
serão	[sirowng]	estarão	[shtarowng]

Ser

Ser indicates an inherent quality, a permanent state or characteristic, i.e. something which is unlikely to change:

a neve é branca
a **neh**v eh br**a**nka
snow is white

Ser is also used with occupations, nationalities, the time and to indicate possession:

somos escoceses
s**oh**moosh shkoos**ay**zish
we are Scottish

este é o nosso carro
ayshteh oo n**o**soo k**a**rroo
this is our car

minha mãe é professora
m**ee**n-ya mayng eh proofes**oh**ra
my mum is a teacher

são cinco da tarde
sowng s**ee**nkoo da tard
it's five o'clock in the afternoon

Estar

Estar, on the other hand, is used to describe the temporary or passing qualities of something or someone:

estou zangado contigo
shtoh zang**a**doo kont**ee**goo
I'm angry with you

estou cansado
shtoh kans**a**doo
I'm tired

este café está frio
aysht kaf**eh** shta fr**ee**-oo
this coffee is cold

Notice the difference between the following two phrases:

Isabel é muito bonita
Iza**beh**l eh m**wee**ngtoo bon**ee**ta
Isabel is very pretty

Isabel está muito bonita (hoje)
Iza**beh**l shta m**wee**ngtoo bon**ee**ta (ohJ)
Isabel looks pretty (today)

Negatives

To express a negative in Portuguese, to say 'I don't want', 'it's not here' etc, place the word **não** in front of the verb:

percebo
pirs**ay**boo
I understand

não percebo
nowng pirs**ay**boo
I don't understand

gosto deste gelado
g**o**shtoo daysht Jil**a**doo
I like this ice cream

não gosto deste gelado
nowng g**o**shtoo daysht Jil**a**doo
I don't like this ice cream

aluguei-o aqui
aloog**ay**-oo ak**ee**
I rented it here

não o aluguei aqui
nowng oo aloog**ay** ak**ee**
I didn't rent it here

vão cantar
vowng kant**a**r
they're going to sing

não vão cantar
nowng vowng kant**a**r
they're not going to sing

Unlike English, Portuguese makes use of double negatives with words like 'nothing/anything' or 'nobody/anybody':

não há ninguém aqui
nowng a ning**ay**ng ak**ee**
there's nobody here

não comprámos nada
nowng kompr**a**moosh n**a**da
we didn't buy anything

não sabemos nada dela
nowng sab**ay**moosh n**a**da d**eh**la
we don't know anything about her

To say 'there's no ...', 'I've no ...' etc, make the accompanying verb negative:

não há vinho	**não tenho fósforos**
nowng a **vee**n-yoo	nowng **tay**n-yoo **fo**shfooroosh
there's no wine	I've no matches

To say 'not him', 'not her' etc, just use the personal pronoun followed by **não**:

nós, não	**ela, não**	**eu, não**
noJ nowng	**eh**la nowng	**ay**-oo nowng
not us	not her	not me

Imperative

The imperative form of the verb is used to give commands. To form the imperative, remove the **-ar**, **-er** or **-ir** from the infinitive and add these endings:

	tu	você	vocês
amar to love	**ama**	**am-e**	**am-em**
	ama	**a**mi	**a**mayng
comer to eat	**come**	**com-a**	**com-am**
	kohm	k**oh**ma	k**oh**mowng
partir to leave	**parte**	**part-a**	**part-am**
	part	p**a**rta	p**a**rtowng

coma devagar
k**oh**ma divag**ar**
eat slowly

When you are telling someone not to do something, use the forms above and place **não** in front of the verb:

não me interrompa, por favor	**não beba álcool!**
nowng mintirr**oh**mpa poor fav**oh**r	nowng b**ay**ba **a**lko-ol
don't interrupt me, please	don't drink alcohol!

não venha esta noite
nowng v**ay**n-ya **eh**shta n**oh**-it
don't come tonight

por favor, não fale tão rápido (to one person)
poor fav**oh**r nowng f**a**li towng r**a**pidoo
please, don't speak so fast

por favor, não falem tão rápido (to several people)
poor fav**oh**r nowng f**a**layng towng r**a**pidoo
please, don't speak so fast

Pronouns are added to the end of the imperative form:

acorde-me às oito, por favor
ak**o**rdimi az**oh**-itoo poor fav**oh**r
wake me up at eight o'clock, please

ajude-me, por favor
aJ**oo**dimi poor fav**oh**r
help me please

However, when the imperative is negative, pronouns are placed in front of it:

não as deixe aqui
nowng aJ daysh ak**ee**
don't leave them here

Questions

Often the word order remains the same in a question, but the intonation changes, the voice rising at the end of the question:

queres dançar?
k**eh**rish dans**a**r
do you want to dance?

fica longe?
f**ee**ka lohnJ
is it far?

Dates

Use the numbers on page 40 to express the date.

um de Setembro [oong di sit**ay**mbroo] the first of September
dois de Dezembro [d**oh**-iJ di diz**ay**mbroo] the second of December
vinte-e-um de Janeiro [v**ee**nti-oong di Jan**ay**roo] the twenty first of January

Days

Monday segunda-feira [sig**oo**nda f**ay**ra]
Tuesday terça-feira [t**ay**rsa f**ay**ra]
Wednesday quarta-feira [kw**a**rta f**ay**ra]
Thursday quinta-feira [k**ee**nta f**ay**ra]
Friday sexta-feira [s**ay**shta f**ay**ra]
Saturday sábado [s**a**badoo]
Sunday domingo [doom**ee**ngoo]

Months

January Janeiro [Jan**ay**roo]
February Fevereiro [fivr**ay**roo]
March Março [m**a**rsoo]
April Abril [abr**ee**l]
May Maio [m**ī**-oo]
June Junho [J**oo**n-yoo]
July Julho [J**oo**l-yoo]
August Agosto [ag**oh**shtoo]
September Setembro [sit**ay**mbroo]
October Outubro [oht**oo**broo]
November Novembro [noov**ay**mbroo]
December Dezembro [diz**ay**mbroo]

Time

what time is it? que horas são? [k-y**o**rash sowng]
one o'clock uma hora [**oo**ma **o**ra]
two o'clock duas horas [d**oo**-az **o**rash]
it's one o'clock é uma hora [eh **oo**ma **o**ra]
it's two o'clock são duas horas [sowng doo-az**o**rash]
it's three o'clock são três horas [trayz**o**rash]
five past one uma e cinco [**oo**mi s**ee**nkoo]
ten past two duas e dez [d**oo**-azi dehsh]
quarter past one uma e um quarto [**oo**mi-oong kw**a**rtoo]
quarter past two duas e um quarto [d**oo**-azi-oong]
half past ten dez e meia [dehz ee m**ay**-a]
twenty to ten dez menos vinte [dehJ m**ay**nooJ veent]
quarter to ten dez menos um quarto [dehJ m**ay**nooz oong kw**a**rtoo]
at eight o'clock às oito horas [az**oh**-itoo **o**rash]
at half past four às quatro e meia [ash kw**a**troo ee m**ay**-a]
2 a.m. duas da manhã [d**oo**-aJ da man-y**a**ng]
2 p.m. duas da tarde [tard]
6 a.m. seis da manhã [saysh da man-y**a**ng]
6 p.m. seis da tarde [tard]
noon meio-dia [m**ay**-oo d**ee**-a]
midnight meia-noite [m**ay**-a n**oh**-it]
an hour uma hora [**oo**ma **o**ra]
a minute um minuto [oong min**oo**too]
two minutes dois minutos [d**oh**-iJ min**oo**toosh]
a second um segundo [oong sig**oo**ndoo]
a quarter of an hour um quarto de hora [kw**a**rtoo d**o**ra]
half an hour meia hora [m**ay**-a **o**ra]
three quarters of an hour três quartos de hora [traysh kw**a**rtoosh d**o**ra]

Numbers

0 zero [**zeh**roo]
1 um [oong]
2 dois [**doh**-ish]
3 três [traysh]
4 quatro [**kwa**troo]
5 cinco [**seen**koo]
6 seis [saysh]
7 sete [seht]
8 oito [**oh**-itoo]
9 nove [nov]
10 dez [dehsh]
11 onze [ohnz]
12 doze [dohz]
13 treze [trayz]
14 catorze [ka**tohr**z]
15 quinze [keenz]
16 dezasseis [diza**say**sh]
17 dezassete [diza**seht**]
18 dezoito [diz**oh**-itoo]
19 dezanove [diza**no**v]
20 vinte [veent]
21 vinte e um [**vee**nti-oong]
22 vinte e dois [**vee**nti **doh**-ish]
23 vinte e três [**vee**nti traysh]
30 trinta [**tree**nta]
31 trinta e um [**tree**ntī-oong]
32 trinta e dois [**tree**ntī **doh**-ish]
40 quarenta [kwa**ray**nta]
50 cinquenta [sink**way**nta]
60 sessenta [ses**ay**nta]
70 setenta [set**ay**nta]
80 oitenta [oh-it**ay**nta]
90 noventa [noov**ay**nta]
100 cem [sayng]
101 cento e um [**say**ntwee oong]
120 cento e vinte [veent]
200 duzentos [dooz**ay**ntoosh], duzentas [dooz**ay**ntash]
300 trezentos [triz**ay**ntoosh], trezentas [triz**ay**ntash]
400 quatrocentos [kwatros**ay**ntoosh], quatrocentas [kwatros**ay**ntash]
500 quinhentos [keen-**y**ayntoosh], quinhentas [keen-y**ay**ntash]
600 seiscentos [sayshs**ay**ntoosh], seiscentas [sayshs**ay**ntash]
700 setecentos [setes**ay**ntoosh], setecentas [setes**ay**ntash]
800 oitocentos [oh-itoos**ay**ntoosh], oitocentas [oh-itoos**ay**ntash]
900 novecentos [noves**ay**ntoosh], novecentas [noves**ay**ntash]

1,000 mil [meel]
2,000 dois mil [**doh**-ish]
5,000 cinco mil [**see**nkoo]
10,000 dez mil [dehsh]
1,000,000 um milhão [mil-y**ow**ng]

um is used with masculine nouns:

um carro
oong k**a**rroo
one car

uma is used with feminine nouns:

uma bicicleta
ooma bisikl**eh**ta
one bike

With multiples of a hundred, the **-as** ending is used with feminine nouns:

trezentos homens
triz**ay**ntooz **oh**mayngsh
300 men

quinhentas mulheres
keen-y**ay**ntaJ mool-y**eh**rish
500 women

Ordinals

1st primeiro [prim**ay**roo]
2nd segundo [sig**oo**ndoo]
3rd terceiro [tirs**ay**roo]
4th quarto [kw**a**rtoo]
5th quinto [k**ee**ntoo]
6th sexto [s**ay**shtoo]
7th sétimo [s**eh**timoo]
8th oitavo [oh-it**a**voo]
9th nono [n**oh**noo]
10th décimo [d**eh**simoo]

Basic Phrases

yes
sim
seeng

no
não
nowng

OK
está bem
shta bayng

hello/hi
olá

good morning
bom dia
bong **dee**-a

good evening/good night
boa noite
b**oh**-a n**oh**-it

see you!
até logo!
at**eh** l**o**goo

goodbye
adeus
ad**ay**-oosh

please
se faz favor, por favor
si fash fav**oh**r, poor fav**oh**r

yes please
sim, por favor
seeng

thanks, thank you
(said by man/woman)
obrigado/obrigada
obrig**a**doo

no thanks, no thank you
não obrigado/obrigada
nowng

thank you very much
muito obrigado/obrigada
m**wee**ngtoo

don't mention it
não tem de quê
nowng tayng di kay

not at all
de nada
di

how do you do?
muito prazer
m**wee**ngtoo praz**ay**r

how are you?
como está?
k**oh**moo shta

fine, thanks
(said by man/woman) bem, obrigado/obrigada
bayng obrig**a**doo

pleased to meet you
(said to man/woman) muito prazer em conhecê-lo/conhecê-la
m**wee**ngtoo praz**ay**r ayng kon-yis**ay**loo

excuse me
(to get past) com licença
kong lis**ay**nsa
(to get attention) se faz favor
si fash fav**oh**r
(to say sorry) desculpe
dishk**oo**lp

(I'm) sorry
tenho muita pena
tayn-yoo mw**ee**ngta p**ay**na

sorry?/pardon (me)?
(didn't understand) como?
k**oh**moo

what did you say?
o que disse?
oo ki dees

I see/I understand
percebo
pirs**ay**boo

I don't understand
não percebo
nowng

do you speak English?
fala inglês?
ingl**ay**sh

I don't speak Portuguese
não falo português
nowng f**a**loo poortoog**ay**sh

can you speak more slowly?
pode falar mais devagar?
pod fal**ar** mīJ divag**ar**

could you repeat that?
podia repetir?
pood**ee**-a ripit**ee**r

can you write it down?
pode escrever isso?
pod shkriv**ay**r **ee**soo

I'd like ...
queria ...
kir**ee**-a

can I have ...?
pode dar-me ...?
pod d**a**rmi

do you have ...?
tem ...?
tayng

how much is it?
quanto é?
kwantw**eh**

cheers!
saúde!
sa-**oo**d

it is ...
é ...; está ...
eh; shta

where is ...?
onde é ...?; onde está ...?
ohnd**eh**; ohnd shta

is it far?
é longe?
eh lohnJ

Conversion Tables

1 centimetre = 0.39 inches
1 metre = 39.37 inches = 1.09 yards
1 kilometre = 0.62 miles = 5/8 mile

1 inch = 2.54 cm
1 foot = 30.48 cm
1 yard = 0.91 m
1 mile = 1.61 km

km	1	2	3	4	5	10	20	30	40	50	100
miles	0.6	1.2	1.9	2.5	3.1	6.2	12.4	18.6	24.8	31.0	62.1

miles	1	2	3	4	5	10	20	30	40	50	100
km	1.6	3.2	4.8	6.4	8.0	16.1	32.2	48.3	64.4	80.5	161

1 gram = 0.035 ounces   1 kilo = 1000 g = 2.2 pounds

g	100	250	500
oz	3.5	8.75	17.5

1 oz = 28.35 g
1 lb = 0.45 kg

kg	0.5	1	2	3	4	5	6	7	8	9	10
lb	1.1	2.2	4.4	6.6	8.8	11.0	13.2	15.4	17.6	19.8	22.0

kg	20	30	40	50	60	70	80	90	100
lb	44	66	88	110	132	154	176	198	220

lb	0.5	1	2	3	4	5	6	7	8	9	10	20
kg	0.2	0.5	0.9	1.4	1.8	2.3	2.7	3.2	3.6	4.1	4.5	9.0

1 litre = 1.75 UK pints / 2.13 US pints

1 UK pint = 0.57 litre
1 US pint = 0.47 litre

1 UK gallon = 4.55 litre
1 US gallon = 3.79 litre

centigrade / Celsius   °C = (°F - 32) x 5/9

°C	-5	0	5	10	15	18	20	25	30	36.8	38
°F	23	32	41	50	59	64	68	77	86	98.4	100.4

Fahrenheit   °F = (°C x 9/5) + 32

°F	23	32	40	50	60	65	70	80	85	98.4	101
°C	-5	0	4	10	16	18	21	27	29	36.8	38.3

English

→

Portuguese

A

a, an* um, uma [oong, **oo**ma]
about: about 20 mais ou menos vinte [mīz oh m**ay**noosh veent]
it's about 5 o'clock por v**o**lta das cinco [poor – s**ee**nkoo]
a film about Portugal um filme sobre Portugal [oong feelm sohbr poortoog**a**l]
above acima [as**ee**ma]
abroad no estrangeiro [noo shtranJ**ay**roo]
absolutely! (I agree) com certeza! [kong sirt**ay**za]
absorbent cotton o algodão em r**a**ma [algood**ow**ng ayng]
accelerator o acelerador [asilirad**oh**r]
accept aceitar [asayt**a**r]
accident o acidente [aseed**ay**nt]
there's been an accident houve um acidente [ohv oong]
accommodation o alojamento [alooJam**ay**ntoo]
see **room** and **hotel**
accurate exacto [ez**a**too]
ache a dor [dohr]
my back aches tenho dor nas costas [**tay**n-yoo – nash k**o**shtash]
across: across the road do outro lado da rua [doo **oh**troo l**a**doo da r**oo**-a]
adapter o adaptador [adaptad**oh**r]
address a morada [moor**a**da]
what's your address? qual é a sua morada? [kwal eh a s**oo**-a]

Most addresses in Portugal consist of a street name and number followed by a storey number, for example Rua de Alfonso Henriques 34-3°. This means that you need to go up to the third floor of no. 34 (US, fourth floor). An 'esq' or 'E' (standing for esquerda) after a floor number means you should go to the left; 'dir' or 'D' (for direita) indicates the apartment or office you're looking for is on the right.

For example:
Sr. Dr. Manuel Santos de Oliveira
Av. da Liberdade, 48, 2° Esq.
1100 - Lisboa
Portugal

address book o livro de moradas [**lee**vroo di moor**a**dash], o livro de endereços [ayndir**ay**soosh]
admission charge a entrada [ayntr**a**da]
adult (man/woman) o adulto [ad**oo**ltoo], a ad**u**lta
advance: in advance adiantado [ad-yant**a**doo]
aeroplane o avião [av-y**ow**ng]
Africa a **Á**frica
African (adj) africano [afrik**a**noo]

after depois [dip**oh**-ish]
after you você primeiro [vos**ay** prim**ay**roo]
after lunch depois do almoço [dwalm**oh**soo]
afternoon a tarde [tard]
in the afternoon à tarde
this afternoon esta tarde [**eh**shta]
aftershave o aftershave
aftersun cream a loção para depois do sol [loos**ow**ng – dip**oh**-ish doo]
afterwards depois
again outra vez [**oh**tra vaysh]
against contra
age a idade [eed**ad**]
ago: a week ago há uma semana [a **oo**ma sim**a**na]
an hour ago há uma hora [**o**ra]
agree: I agree concordo [konk**o**rdoo]
AIDS a SIDA [s**ee**da]
air o ar
by air de avião [dav-y**ow**ng]
air-conditioning o ar condicionado [kondis-yoon**a**doo]
airmail: by airmail por via aérea [poor v**ee**-a-**eh**r-ya]
airmail envelope o envelope de avião [aynvil**o**p dav-y**ow**ng]
airport o aeroporto [a-ayroop**oh**rtoo]
to the airport, please para o aeroporto, se faz favor [paroo – si fash fav**oh**r]
airport bus o autocarro do aeroporto [owtook**a**rroo doo]
aisle seat o lugar de corredor [loog**a**r di koorrid**oh**r]
alarm clock o despertador [dishpirtad**oh**r]
alcohol o álcool [**a**lko-ol]
alcoholic alcoólico [alko-**o**likoo]
all: all the boys todos os meninos [t**oh**dooz ooJ min**ee**noosh]
all the girls todas as meninas [t**oh**daz aJ min**ee**nash]
all of it todo [t**oh**doo]
all of them todos [t**oh**doosh]
that's all, thanks (said by man/woman) é tudo, obrigado/obrigada [eh t**oo**doo obrig**a**doo]
allergic: I'm allergic to ... (said by man/woman) sou alérgico/alérgica a ... [soh al**eh**rJikoo]
allowed: is it allowed? é permitido? [eh pirmit**ee**do]
all right está bem [shta bayng]
I'm all right estou bem [shtoh]
are you all right? (fam) estás bem? [shtash]
(pol) está bem? [shta]
almond a amêndoa [am**ay**ndoo-a]
almost quase [kwaz]
alone só [saw]
alphabet o alfabeto [alfab**e**too]

a	a	j	J**o**ta	s	ehs
b	bay	k	k**a**pa	t	tay
c	say	l	el	u	oo
d	day	m	em	v	vay
e	eh	n	en	w	vay d**oo**ploo
f	ehf	o	o	x	sheesh
g	Jay	p	pay	y	**ee**psilon
h	ag**a**	q	kay	z	zay
i	ee	r	err		

already já [Ja]
also também [tamb**ay**ng]
although embora [aymb**o**ra]
altogether totalmente [tootalm**ay**nt]
always sempre [s**ay**mpr]
am*: I am sou [soh]; estou [shtoh]
a.m.: at seven a.m. às sete da manhã [ash – man-y**a**ng]
amazing (surprising) espantoso [shpant**oh**zoo]
(very good) estupendo [shtoop**ay**ndoo]
ambulance a ambulância [amboolans-ya]
call an ambulance! chame uma ambulância! [sham **oo**ma]

For all emergency services dial 115.

America a América
American americano [amirik**a**noo]
I'm American (man/woman) sou americano/americana

among entre [ayngtr]
amount a quantia [kwant**ee**-ya]
amp: a 13-amp fuse um fusível de treze amperes [oong fooz**ee**vel di – amp**eh**rish]
and e [ee]
angry zangado
animal o animal
ankle o tornozelo [toornooz**ay**loo]
anniversary (wedding) o aniversário (de casamento) [anivirs**a**r-yoo (di kazam**ay**ntoo)]
annoy: this man's annoying me este homem está a aborrecer-me [aysht **oh**mayng shta aboorris**ay**rmi]
annoying aborrecido [aboorris**ee**doo], importuno [import**oo**noo]
another outro [**oh**troo]
can we have another room? pode dar-nos outro quarto? [pod d**a**r-nooz – kw**a**rtoo]
another beer, please outra cerveja, por favor [sirv**ay**Ja poor fav**oh**r]
antibiotics os antibióticos [antib-y**o**tikoosh]
antifreeze o anticongelante [–konJil**a**nt]
antihistamines os anti-histamínicos [–ishtam**ee**nikoosh]
antique: is it an antique? é uma antiguidade? [eh **oo**ma antigweed**a**d]
antique shop a casa de antiguidades [kaza

dantigweedadsh]
antiseptic o anti-séptico
any: have you got any bread/tomatoes? tem pão/tomates? [tayng]
do you have any? tem?
sorry, I don't have any desculpe, não tenho [dishkoolp nowng tayn-yoo]
anybody* alguém [algayng]
does anybody speak English? alguém fala inglês? [inglaysh]
there wasn't anybody there não estava lá ninguém [nowng shtava la ningayng]
anything* qualquer coisa [kwalkehr koh-iza]

dialogues

anything else? mais alguma coisa? [mīz algooma koh-iza]
nothing else, thanks (said by man/woman) mais nada, obrigado/obrigada [obrigadoo]

would you like anything to drink? gostaria de beber alguma coisa? [goostaree-a di bibayr]
I don't want anything, thanks (said by man/woman) não quero nada, obrigado/obrigada [nowng kehroo]

apart from além de [alayng di]
apartment o apartamento [apartamayntoo]
apartment block o bloco de apartamentos [blokoo dapartamayntoosh]
aperitif o aperitivo [apiriteevoo]
apology as desculpas [diskoolpash]
appendicitis a apendicite [apendi-seet]
appetizer a entrada [ayntrada]
apple a maçã [masang]
appointment a marcação [markasowng]

dialogue

good morning, how can I help you? bom dia, que deseja? [bong dee-a ki disayJa]
I'd like to make an appointment queria fazer uma marcação [kiree-a fazayr]
what time would you like? que hora prefere? [k-yora prefehri]
three o'clock três horas [trayz orash]
I'm afraid that's not possible, is four o'clock all right? infelizmente, não é possível, quatro horas está bem? [infiliJmayngt nowng eh pooseevil kwatroo orash shta bayng]
yes, that will be fine sim,

está bem [seeng]
the name was ...? o nome é ...? [oo nohm]

apricot o damasco [damashkoo]
April Abril [abreel]
Arab (adj) árabe [arabi]
are*: we are somos [sohmoosh]; estamos [shtamoosh]
you are (você) é [(vosay-)eh]; (você) está [shta]
they are são [sowng]; estão [shtowng]
area a região [riJ-yowng]
area code o código
arm o braço [brasoo]
arrange: will you arrange it for us? pode organizar isto para nós? [podi – eeshtoo – nosh]
arrival a chegada [shigada]
arrive chegar
when do we arrive? a que horas chegamos? [k-yorash shigamoosh]
has my fax arrived yet? meu fax já chegou? [may-oo – Ja shigoh]
we arrived today chegámos hoje [shigamoosh ohJ]
art a arte [art]
art gallery a galeria de arte [galiree-a dart]
artist (man/woman) o/a artista [arteeshta]
as: as big as tão grande quanto [towng grand kwantoo]
as soon as possible logo que possível [logoo ki pooseevil]
ashtray o cinzeiro [sinzayroo]
ask perguntar [pirgoontar], pedir [pideer]
I didn't ask for this não pedi isto [nowng pidee eeshtoo]
could you ask him to ...? importa-se de lhe pedir que ...? [importasi di l-yi – ki]
asleep: she's asleep ela está a dormir [ehla shta a doormeer]
aspirin a aspirina [ashpireena]
asthma a asma [aJma]
astonishing espantoso [shpantohzoo]
at: at the hotel no hotel [noo]
at the station na estação [nashtasowng]
at six o'clock às seis horas [ash sayz orash]
at Américo's na casa do Américo [dwamehrikoo]
athletics o atletismo [atleteeJmoo]
Atlantic Ocean o Oceano Atlântico [ohs-yanoo atlantikoo]
attractive atraente [atra-aynt]
aubergine a beringela [bireenJehla]
August Agosto [agohshtoo]
aunt a tia [tee-a]
Australia a Austrália [owshtral-ya]
Australian (adj) australiano [owshtral-yanoo]
I'm Australian (man/woman) sou australiano/australiana [soh]
automatic automático [owtoomatikoo]

automatic teller o caixa automático [kīsha owtoomatikoo]
autumn o Outono [ohtohnoo]
in the autumn no Outono [noo]
avenue a avenida [avineeda]
average (not good) mais ou menos [mīz oh maynoosh]
on average em média [ayng mehd-ya]
awake: is he awake? ele já acordou? [ayl Ja akoordoh]
away: go away! vá-se embora! [vasi aymbora]
is it far away? fica longe? [feeka lohnJ]
awful horrível [ohrreevil]
axle o eixo [ayshoo]

B

baby o bebé [bebeh]
baby food a comida de bebé [koomeeda di]
baby's bottle o biberão [bibirowng]
baby-sitter a baby-sitter
back (of body) as costas [koshtash]
(back part) a parte posterior [part pooshteriohr]
at the back atrás [atrash]
can I have my money back? posso reaver o meu dinheiro? [posoo r-yavayr oo may-oo deen-yayroo]
to come/go back voltar
backache a dor nas costas [dohr nash koshtash]
bacon o bacon
bad mau [mow], (f) má
a bad headache uma dor de cabeça forte [ooma dohr di kabaysa fort]
badly mal
bag o saco [sakoo]
(handbag) a mala de mão [di mowng]
(suitcase) a mala
baggage a bagagem [bagaJayng]
baggage check o depósito de bagagem [dipozitoo di baga-Jayng]
baggage claim a reclamação de bagagens [riklamasowng di baga-Jayngsh]
bakery a padaria [padaree-a]
balcony a varanda
a room with a balcony um quarto com varanda [oong kwartoo kong]
bald careca [karehka]
ball a bola
(small) a bolinha [boleen-ya]
ballet o ballet
ballpoint pen a caneta esferográfica [shfiroo-grafika]
banana a banana
band (musical) a banda
bandage a ligadura [ligadoora]
Bandaid® o adesivo [adezeevoo]
bank (money) o banco [bankoo]

All banks now charge a hefty commission on changing travellers' cheques; there are much lower commissions on foreign currency exchanges at **caixas** (savings banks or building societies) though this of course means carrying around large amounts of foreign cash.
You'll find a bank in all but the smallest towns. Standard opening hours are Monday to Friday from 8.30 a.m. to 3 p.m. In Lisbon and some of the Algarve resorts they may also open in the evening to change money, while some banks have installed automatic exchange machines for various currencies and denominations.
see **cheque**

bank account a conta bancária [bank**ar**-ya]
bar o bar

In most bars in Portugal, you do not have to pay when ordering: you wait until just before you leave. In a few places, you pay first at the cash desk then show your receipt (**a senha**) at the bar when ordering. Sometimes you may see the sign **pré-pagamento** when you have to pay in advance.
Larger cities and coastal resorts have cosmopolitan and sophisticated clubs and bars, although in rural areas local bars remain very much a male domain. Women travelling alone may find that they'll attract unwanted attention in such bars.

a bar of chocolate uma tablete de chocolate [tab**leh**t di shookoo**lat**]
barber's o barbeiro [barb**ay**roo]
basket o cesto [**say**shtoo]
(in shop) o cesto de compras [di k**oh**mprash]
bath o banho [b**a**n-yoo]
can I have a bath? posso tomar banho? [p**o**soo toom**ar**]
bathroom a casa de banho [k**a**za di]
with a private bathroom com casa de banho [kong]
bath towel a toalha de banho [tw**a**l-ya]
bathtub a banheira [ban-y**ay**ra]
battery a pilha [p**ee**l-ya]
(for car) a bateria [batir**ee**-a]
bay a baía [ba-**ee**-a]
be* ser [sayr]; estar [shtar]
beach a praia [prī-a]
on the beach na praia

The Portuguese tend to stick to a rather rigid swimming season, from early June until mid-September. Therefore you could have the beach to yourself on a baking hot day in May, while on an overcast weekend in August the beach will be packed. Open-air pools tend to close in September, regardless of the

weather.
Beware of the heavy undertow on many of Portugal's Atlantic beaches and don't swim if you see a red or yellow flag.

beach mat o colchão de praia [kolsh**ow**ng di prī-a]
beach umbrella o chapéu de sol [shap**eh**-oo]
beans os feijões [faiJ**oy**ngsh]
French beans os feijões-verdes [–vayrdsh]
broad beans as favas [f**a**vash]
beard a b**a**rba
beautiful bonito [boon**ee**too]
because porque [poork**ay**]
because of ... por causa do ... [poor k**ow**za doo]
bed a c**a**ma
I'm going to bed now vou p**a**ra a cama ag**o**ra [voh]
bed and breakfast alojamento e pequeno almoço [alooJam**ay**ntwee pik**ay**noo alm**oh**soo]
see **hotel**
bedroom o quarto [kw**a**rtoo]
beef a carne de v**a**ca [karn di]
beer a cerveja [sirv**ay**Ja]
two beers, please duas cervejas, por favor [d**oo**-ash sirv**ay**Jash poor fav**oh**r]

The most common Portuguese beer is **Sagres**, but there are a fair number of local varieties. Probably the best Portuguese beer is the blue-labelled **Super Bock**, which is rivalled only by **Sagres Europa**. For something unusual (and not recommended on a hot afternoon) try the green-labelled **Sagres Preta**, which is a dark beer, resembling British brown ale.
When drinking draft beer, order **uma imperial** if you want a regular glass; **uma caneca** will get you a half-litre. And when buying bottles, don't forget to take your empties back: they can represent as much as a third of the price.
Beer is sold in a **cervejaria** (literally: beer house), where you can go at all hours for a beer and a snack, and is also widely available in cafés and restaurants.

before antes [antsh]
begin começar [koomes**a**r]
when does it begin? quando é que começa? [kw**a**ndoo eh ki koom**eh**sa]
beginner (man/woman) o/a principiante [prinsip-y**a**nt]
beginning: at the beginning no início [noo in**ee**s-yoo]
behind atrás [atr**a**sh]
behind me atrás de mim [di meeng]
beige bege
Belgian (adj) b**e**lga
Belgium a Bélgica [b**eh**lJika]
believe acredit**a**r
below abaixo [ab**ī**shoo]
belt o cinto [s**ee**ntoo]
bend (in road) a curva [k**oo**rva]

berth (on ship) o beliche [bil**ee**sh]
beside: beside the ... junto da ... [J**oo**ntoo]
best o melhor [mil-y**o**r]
better melhor
are you feeling better? está melhor? [shta]
between entre [ayntr]
beyond para além de [paral**ay**ng di]
bicycle a bicicleta [bisikl**eh**ta]
big grande [grand]
too big grande demais [dimīsh]
it's not big enough não é suficientemente grande [nowng eh soofis-yayntim**ay**nt]
bike a bicicleta [bisikl**eh**ta]
(motorbike) a motocicleta [mootoosikl**eh**ta]
bikini o bikini
bill a conta
(US) a nota
could I have the bill, please? pode-me dar a conta, por favor? [p**o**d-mi – poor fav**oh**r]
bin o caixote de lixo [kīsh**o**t di l**ee**shoo]
bin liners os sacos de lixo [s**a**koosh]
bird o pássaro [p**a**saroo]
birthday o dia de anos [d**ee**-a d**a**noosh]
happy birthday! feliz aniversário! [fil**ee**z anivirs**a**r-yoo]
biscuit a bolacha [bool**a**sha]
bit: a little bit um pouco [oong p**oh**koo]
a big bit um pedaço grande [pid**a**soo grand]
a bit of ... um pedaço de ...
a bit expensive um pouco caro [p**oh**koo k**a**roo]
bite (by insect) a picada [pik**a**da]
(by dog) a mordedura [moorded**oo**ra]
bitter (taste etc) amargo [am**a**rgoo]
black preto [pr**ay**too]
blanket o cobertor [koobirt**oh**r]
bleach (for toilet) a lixívia [lish**ee**v-ya]
bless you! santinho! [sant**ee**n-yoo]
blind cego [s**eh**goo]
blinds as persianas [pirs-y**a**nash]
blister a bolha [b**o**l-ya]
blocked (road) cortado [koort**a**doo]
(pipe, sink) entupido [ayntoop**ee**doo]
blond (adj) louro [l**oh**roo]
blood o sangue [sang]
high blood pressure a tensão arterial alta [taynsowng artir-y**a**l]
blouse a blusa [bl**oo**za]
blow-dry secar com secador [kong sikad**oh**r]
I'd like a cut and blow-dry queria cortar e fazer brushing [kir**ee**-a – ee faz**ay**r]
blue azul [az**oo**l]
blue eyes os olhos azuis [**o**l-yoosh az**oo**-ish]
blusher o blusher
boarding house a pensão [payns**ow**ng]

boarding pass o cartão de embarque [kart**ow**ng daymb**ar**k]
boat o barco [b**ar**koo]
(for passengers) o ferry-boat
body o corpo [k**oh**rpoo]
boiled egg o ovo cozido [**oh**voo kooz**ee**doo]
boiler a caldeira [kald**ay**ra]
bone o osso [**oh**soo]
(in fish) a espinha [shp**ee**n-ya]
bonnet (of car) o capot [kap**oh**]
book o livro [l**ee**vroo]
(verb) reservar [rizirv**ar**]
can I book a seat? posso reservar um lugar? [p**o**soo – oong loog**ar**]

dialogue

I'd like to book a table for two queria reservar uma mesa para dois [kir**ee**-a – **oo**ma m**ay**za p**a**ra d**oh**-ish]
what time would you like it booked for? para que horas? [k-y**o**rash]
half past seven sete e meia [s**eh**-tee-m**ay**-a]
that's fine está bem [shta bayng]
and your name? e o seu nome? [yoo s**ay**-oo nohm]

bookshop a livraria [livrar**ee**-a]
bookstore a livraria [livrar**ee**-a]
boot (footwear) a bota
(of car) o porta-bagagens [p**o**rta-bag**a**Jayngsh]
border (of country) a fronteira [front**ay**ra]
bored: I'm bored (said by man/woman) estou chateado/chateada [shtoh shat-y**a**doo]
boring maçador [masad**oh**r]
born: I was born in Manchester nasci em Manchester [nash-s**ee** ayng]
I was born in 1960 nasci em mil novecentos e sessenta
borrow pedir emprestado [pid**ee**r aympriisht**a**doo]
may I borrow ...? posso pedir ... emprestado? [p**o**soo]
both ambos [**a**mboosh]
bother: sorry to bother you desculpe incomodá-lo [dishk**oo**lp eenkoo-mood**a**loo]
bottle a garrafa
a bottle of house red uma garrafa de vinho da casa tinto [**oo**ma – di v**ee**n-yoo da k**a**za t**ee**ntoo]
bottle-opener o abre-garrafas [abrigarr**a**fash]
bottom (of person) o traseiro [traz**ay**roo]
at the bottom of ... (hill) no sopé do ... [noo soop**eh** doo]
box a caixa [k**ī**sha]
box office a bilheteira [bil-yit**ay**ra]
boy o rapaz [rap**a**sh]
boyfriend o namorado [namoor**a**doo]
bra o soutien [soot-y**a**ng]
bracelet a pulseira [pools**ay**ra]
brake o travão [trav**ow**ng]

brandy o brandy
Brazil Brasil [brazeel]
Brazilian (adj) brasileiro [brazilayroo]
bread o pão [powng]
 white bread o pão branco [brankoo]
 brown bread o pão escuro [shkooroo]
 wholemeal bread o pão integral [eentigral]
break partir
 I've broken the ... quebrei o/a ... [kibray oo]
 I think I've broken my wrist acho que parti o pulso [ashoo ki – oo poolsoo]
break down avariar
 I've broken down meu carro avariou [may-oo karroo avari-oh]
breakdown (mechanical) a avaria [avaree-a]

If you break down you can get assistance from the **Automóvel Clube de Portugal**, which has reciprocal arrangements with foreign automobile clubs. If you're involved in a road accident, use the nearest roadside orange-coloured SOS telephone – press the button and wait for an answer.

breakdown service o pronto-socorro [prohntoo sookohrroo]
breakfast o pequeno almoço [pikaynoo almohsoo]
break-in: I've had a break-in minha casa foi roubada [meen-ya kaza foh-i rohbada]
breast o peito [paytoo]
breathe respirar [rishpirar]
breeze a brisa [breeza]
bridge (over river) a ponte [pohnt]
brief breve [brehv]
briefcase a pasta [pashta]
bright (light etc) brilhante [bril-yant]
 bright red vermelho vivo [veevoo]
brilliant (idea, person) brilhante [bril-yant]
bring trazer [trazayr]
 I'll bring it back later trago isto de volta mais tarde [tragoo eeshtoo di – mīsh tard]
Britain a Grã-Bretanha [grang britan-ya]
British britânico [britanikoo]
brochure o folheto [fool-yaytoo]
broken partido [parteedoo]
bronchitis bronquite [bronkeet]
brooch o alfinete [alfinayt]
broom a vassoura [vasohra]
brother o irmão [eermowng]
brother-in-law o cunhado [koon-yadoo]
brown castanho [kashtan-yoo]
bruise a contusão [kontoozowng]
brush (for hair, cleaning) a escova [shkova]
 (artist's) o pincel [peensehl]
bucket o balde [bowld]
buffet car a carruagem

restaurante [karrw**a**-Jayng rishtowr**a**nt]
buggy (for child) a cadeirinha de bebé [kadayr**ee**n-ya di beb**eh**]
building o edifício [idif**ee**s-yoo]
bulb (light bulb) a lâmpada
bullfight a tourada [tohr**a**da]
bullfighter o toureiro [tohr**ay**roo]

bullfighting
The Portuguese pride themselves on having a more humane attitude to bullfighting than their Spanish neighbours. In Portugal it is common to see matadors fighting on horseback, and the emphasis is more on skilled horsemanship than on macho daring. However, though the matadors do not kill the bulls in the ring in front of the audience, those animals deemed too weak to fight another day are killed immediately afterwards.

bullring a praça de touros [pr**a**sa di t**oh**roosh]
bull-running as garraiadas [garrī-**a**dash]
bumper o pára-choques [p**a**ra-sh**o**ksh]
bunk o beliche [bil**ee**sh]
bureau de change o câmbio [k**a**mb-yoo]
see **bank**
burglary o roubo [r**oh**boo]
burn a queimadura [kaymad**oo**ra]
(verb) queim**a**r
burnt: this is burnt isto está queimado [**ee**shtoo shta kaym**a**doo]
burst: a burst pipe um cano rebentado [oong k**a**noo ribaynt**a**doo]
bus o autocarro [owtook**a**rroo]
what number bus is it to ...? qual é o número do autocarro p**a**ra ...? [kwal-**eh** oo n**oo**miroo doo]
when is the next bus to ...? a que horas é o próximo autocarro para ...? [k-y**o**raz eh oo pr**o**simoo]
what time is the last bus? a que horas é o último autocarro? [**oo**ltimoo]

Buses shadow many of the main train routes as well as linking most of the country's smaller towns and villages. It's almost always quicker to go by bus though you'll pay slightly more than for the equivalent train ride. Comfortable express buses operate on longer routes, for which you'll usually have to reserve tickets in advance – certainly for the Lisbon-Algarve routes in summer. The local bus station is the place to pick up timetables and reserve seats on long-distance journeys, and local tourist offices can usually help with bus information. It's as well to be aware that bus services are considerably less frequent –

occasionally non-existent – at weekends, especially on rural routes; while at other times, you'll find that departures can be extremely early in the morning. This is because bus services are often designed to fit around school and market hours.

see **ticket**

dialogue

does this bus go to ...?
este autocarro vai p**a**ra ...? [aysht – vī]
no, you need a number ...
não, tem que apanhar o número ... [nowng tayng k-yapang-y**a**r oo n**oo**miroo]

business o negócios [nig**o**s-yoosh]
bus station a estação dos autocarros [shtas**ow**ng dooz owtook**a**rroosh]
bus stop a paragem do autocarro [par**a**Jayng doo owtook**a**rroo]
bust o peito [p**ay**too]
busy (restaurant etc) frequentado [frikwaynt**a**doo]
I'm busy tomorrow (said by man/woman) estou ocupado/ocup**a**da amanhã [shtoh okoop**a**doo – aman-y**a**ng]
but mas [mash]
butcher's o talho [t**a**l-yoo]
butter a manteiga [mant**ay**ga]
button o botão [boot**ow**ng]
buy compr**a**r
where can I buy ...? onde posso comprar ...? [ohnd p**o**soo]
by*: by bus de autocarro [dowtook**a**rroo]
by car de carro [di k**a**rroo]
written by ... escrito por ... [shkr**ee**too poor]
by the window à jan**e**la
by the sea à b**ei**ra-mar
by Thursday na qu**i**nta-f**ei**ra
bye adeus [ad**ay**-oosh]

C

cabbage a couve [kohv]
cabin (on ship) o camarote [kamar**o**t]
cable car o teleférico [telef**eh**rikoo]
café o café [kaf**eh**]
see **bar**
cagoule o impermeável de nylon [impirmi**a**-vil di]
cake o bolo [b**oh**loo]
cake shop a pastelaria [pashtila-r**ee**-a]
call chamar [sham**a**r]
(to phone) telefonar [telefoon**a**r]
what's it called? como se chama isto? [k**oh**moo si sh**a**ma **ee**shtoo]
he/she is called ... ele/ela chama-se ... [ayl/**eh**la sh**a**masi]

please call the doctor por favor, chame o médico [poor fav**oh**r sh**a**m-yoo m**eh**dikoo]
please give me a call at ... a.m. tomorrow chame-me, por favor, às ... horas amanhã [sh**a**mi-mi – ash ... **o**rash aman-y**a**ng]
please ask him to call me por favor, peça a ele que me telefone [p**e**sa-a ayl ki-mi telef**oh**n]
call back: I'll call back later volto mais tarde [v**o**ltoo mīsh tard]
(phone back) volto a telefonar mais tarde [v**o**ltwa telefoon**a**r]
call round: I'll call round tomorrow vou aí amanhã [voh a-**ee** aman-y**a**ng]
camcorder a câmara de vídeo [di v**ee**d-yoo]
camera a máquina fotográfica [m**a**kina footoogr**a**fika]
camera shop a loja de artigos fotográficos [l**o**Ja dart**ee**goosh fotogr**a**fikoosh]
camp acampar
can we camp here? podemos acampar aqui? [pood**ay**moosh – ak**ee**]
camping gas o gás para campismo [g**a**sh par kamp**ee**Jmoo]
campsite o parque de campismo [park di kamp**ee**Jmoo]

Portugal has over a hundred authorized campsites, most of them small, low-key and attractively located. Charges are per person and per tent, with showers and parking extra; even so, they are very reasonably priced. You can get a fairly complete list of campsites from any Portuguese tourist office, or a detailed booklet called **Roteiro Campista** (with prices, exact locations, facilities, etc) from Portuguese bookshops.
You'll need an international camping carnet to stay on most sites in Portugal. It serves as useful identification and covers you for third party insurance when camping.
Camping outside official grounds is legal, but has certain restrictions. You're not allowed to camp in urban zones, in zones where the water sources are protected, or less than 1km from campsites, beaches or other places frequented by the public.
However, the Algarve is an exception: this is the only region where camping rough is banned.

can a lata
a can of beer uma lata de cerveja [di sirv**ay**Ja]
can*: can you ...? você pode ...? [vos**ay** pod]
can I have ...? posso ter ...? [p**o**soo tayr]
I can't ... não posso ...

[nowng]
Canada o Canadá
Canadian canadiano [kanad-yanoo]
I'm Canadian (man/woman) sou canadiano/canadiana [soh]
canal o canal
cancel cancelar [kansilar]
candle a vela
candies os rebuçados [riboosadoosh]
canoe a canoa [kanoh-a]
canoeing a canoagem [kanwa-Jayng]
can-opener o abre-latas [abrilatash]
cap (hat) o boné [booneh]
(of bottle) a tampa
car o carro [karroo]
by car de carro
caravan a roulotte [roolot]
caravan site o parque de campismo [park di kampeeJmoo]
carburettor o carburador [karbooradohr]
card (birthday etc) o cartão [kartowng]
here's my (business) card aqui está o meu cartão (de visitas) [akee shta oo may-oo kartowng (di vizeetash)]
cardigan o casaco de malha [kazakoo di mal-ya]
cardphone o telefone de cartão [telefohn di kartowng]
careful cuidadoso [kwidadohzoo]
be careful! cuidado! [kwidadoo]
caretaker (man/woman) o/a guarda [gwarda]
car ferry o ferry-boat
car hire o aluguer de automóveis [aloogehr dowtoomovaysh]
see **rent**
carnival o carnaval
car park o parque de estacionamento [park di shtas-yonamayntoo]
carpet a carpete [karpeht]
carriage (of train) a carruagem [karrwa-Jayng]
carrier bag o saco plástico [sakoo plashtikoo]
carrot a cenoura [sinohra]
carry levar [livar]
carry-cot o porta-bebés [porta-bebehsh]
carton o pacote [pakot]
carwash a lavagem automática [lavaJayng owtoomatika]
case (suitcase) a mala
cash o dinheiro [deen-yayroo]
(verb) descontar [dishkongtar]
will you cash this for me? pode descontar isto para mim? [pod – eeshtoo – meeng]
see **bank**
cash desk a caixa [kīsha]
cash dispenser o caixa automático [owtoomatikoo]
cassette a cassete
cassette recorder o gravador de cassetes [gravadohr di]

castle o castelo [kashtehloo]
casualty department o serviço de urgências [sirveesoo doorJayns-yash]
cat o gato [gatoo]
catch pegar, apanhar [apan-yar]
where do we catch the bus to ...? onde podemos apanhar o autocarro para ...? [ohnd poodaymooz apan-yar oo owtookarroo]
cathedral a catedral [katidral]
Catholic (adj) católico [katolikoo]
cauliflower a couve-flor [kohv-flor]
cave a caverna
ceiling o tecto [tehtoo]
celery o alho francês [al-yoo fransaysh]
cellar (for wine) a cave [kav]
cellular phone o telefone celular [telefohn siloolar]
cemetery o cemitério [simitehr-yoo]
centigrade* centígrado [senteegradoo]
centimetre* o centímetro [senteemitroo]
central central [sen-tral]
central heating o aquecimento central [akesimayntoo]
centre o centro [sayntroo]
how do we get to the city centre? como é que vamos para o centro da cidade? [kohmoo eh ki vamoosh – oo sayntroo da sidad]
cereal os cereais [siri-īsh]
certainly certamente [sirtamaynt]
certainly not certamente que não [ki nowng]
chair a cadeira [kadayra]
champagne o champanhe [shampan-yi]
change (money) o troco [trohkoo]
(verb: money) trocar [trookar]
can I change this for ...? posso trocar isto por ...? [posoo – eeshtoo]
I don't have any change não tenho troco [nowng tayn-yoo]
can you give me change for a 10 escudos note? pode trocar-me uma nota de dez escudos? [pod trookarmi ooma – di dez-shkoodoosh]

dialogue

do we have to change (trains)? temos de mudar? [taymoosh di moodar]
yes, change at Coimbra/no, it's a direct train sim, troque em Coimbra/não, é um comboio directo [seeng tro-keeng kweembra/nowng eh oong kombohh-yo direhtoo]

changed: to get changed mudar de roupa [moodar di rohpa]

Ca

chapel a capela [kap**eh**la]
charge o preço [pr**ay**soo]
(verb) custar [koosht**ar**]
charge card o cartão de débito [kart**ow**ng di d**eh**beetoo]
see **credit card**
cheap barato [bar**a**too]
do you have anything cheaper? tem alguma coisa mais barata? [tayng alg**oo**ma k**oh**-iza mīsh]
check (US) o cheque [shehk]
(US: bill) a c**o**nta
see **bill**
check verific**ar**
could you check the ..., please? pode verificar o ..., se faz favor? [pod – oo ... si fash fav**ohr**]
checkbook o livro de cheques [l**ee**vroo di shehksh]
check card o cartão de garantia [kart**ow**ng di garant**ee**-a]
check-in o ch**e**ck-in
check in fazer o check-in [faz**ay**r oo]
where do we have to check in? onde temos que fazer o check-in? [**oh**nd t**ay**mooshk]
cheek (on face) a bochecha [boosh**ay**sha]
cheerio! adeuzinho! [aday-ooz**ee**n-yoo]
cheers! (toast) saúde! [sa-**oo**d]
cheese o queijo [k**ay**Joo]
chemist's a farmácia [farm**as**-ya]
see **pharmacy**
cheque o cheque [shehk]
do you take cheques? aceitam cheques? [as**ay**towng shehksh]

Travellers' cheques are accepted by all Portuguese banks and by exchange bureaux (**câmbios**) at airports and major train stations. However, commission rates can be extremely high, so you might prefer to use a credit card at a cashpoint machine/ATM, which incurs a small charge. Alternatively, most British banks can issue current account holders with a Eurocheque card and cheque book, with which you can pay for things in some shops and get cash from the majority of Portuguese banks; you'll pay a few pounds service charge a year but usually no commission on transactions.

cheque book o livro de cheques [l**ee**vroo di shehksh]
cheque card o cartão de garantia [kart**ow**ng di garant**ee**-a]
cherry a cereja [sir**ay**Ja]
chess o xadrez [shadr**ay**sh]
chest o peito [p**ay**too]
chewing gum a pastilha elástica [pasht**ee**l-ya il**a**shtika]
chicken o frango [fr**a**ngoo]
chickenpox a varicela [varis**eh**la]

child a criança [kry-**a**nsa]
children as crianças [kry-**a**nsash]

Portugal is child-friendly and families should find it as easy a place to roam as any other country. Cheap hotels and **pensões** will only rarely charge extra for children in their parents' room, and restaurants routinely offer small portions and extra plates. Museums and most sights don't usually charge for small children.

child minder a **a**ma
children's pool a piscina infantil [pish-s**ee**na infant**ee**l]
children's portion a dose para crianças [doz – kry-**a**nsash]
chin o queixo [k**ay**shoo]
china a porcelana [poorsil**a**na]
Chinese (adj) chinês [shin**ay**sh]
chips as batatas fritas [bat**a**tash fr**ee**tash]
chocolate o chocolate [shookool**a**t]
milk chocolate o chocolate com leite [kong layt]
plain chocolate o chocolate puro [p**oo**roo]
a hot chocolate um chocolate quente [oong – kaynt]
choose escolher [shkool-y**ay**r]
Christian name o nome próprio [nohm pr**o**pr-yoo]
Christmas o Nat**a**l
Christmas Eve a Véspera de Natal [v**eh**shpira di]
merry Christmas! feliz Natal! [fil**ee**J]
church a igreja [igr**ay**Ja]
cider a cidra [s**ee**dra]
cigar o charuto [shar**oo**too]
cigarette o cigarro [sig**a**rroo]

Portuguese public transport has a no smoking policy. However, mainly on the buses, you'll find that some passengers don't obey this rule – it is up to the driver to enforce it.

cigarette lighter o isqueiro [ishk**ay**roo]
cinema o cinema [sin**ay**ma]

Going to the movies in Portugal is extremely cheap, and films are often shown with the original (usually English-language) soundtrack with Portuguese subtitles. Listings can be found in the local newspaper or on boards placed in the central square of every small town.

circle o círculo [s**ee**rkooloo]
(in theatre) a plateia [plat**ay**-a]
city a cidade [sid**a**d]
city centre o centro da cidade [s**ay**ntroo]
clean (adj) limpo [l**ee**mpoo]
can you clean this for me? pode limpar isto para mim? [pod leemp**a**r **ee**shtoo – meeng]

Ch

cleaning solution (for contact lenses) a solução de limpeza [sooloos**ow**ng di leemp**ay**za]
cleansing lotion o creme de limpeza [kraym di]
clear claro [kl**a**roo]
clever inteligente [intiliJ**ay**nt]
cliff o rochedo [roosh**ay**doo]
climb escalar [shkal**a**r]
cling film a película aderente [pil**ee**koola adir**ay**nt]
clinic a clínica [kl**ee**nika]
cloakroom o vestiário [visht-y**a**r-yoo]
clock o relógio [ril**o**J-yoo]
close (verb) fechar [fish**a**r]

dialogue

what time do you close? a que horas fecham? [k-y**o**rash f**ay**showng]
we close at 8 p.m. on weekdays and 6 p.m. on Saturdays fechamos às oito da noite durante a semana e às seis da tarde aos sábados [fish**a**-mooz az-**oh**-itoo da n**oh**-it door**a**nta sim**a**na yash s**ay**sh da tard owsh s**a**badoosh]
do you close for lunch? fecham para almoço? [alm**oh**soo]
yes, between 1 and 3.30 p.m. sim, entre a uma e as três e meia da tarde [seeng **ay**ntri-a-**oo**ma ee-ash traysh ee m**ay**-a da tard]

closed fechado [fish**a**doo]
cloth (fabric) o tecido [tis**ee**doo]
(for cleaning etc) pano [p**a**noo]
clothes a roupa [r**oh**pa]

clothing
Some of the more remote inland regions of Portugal are still very conservative in outlook, with Catholicism and the family as the bedrocks of society. Whilst shorts are perfectly acceptable in cities and beach resorts, more modest attire is required when visiting a church or religious site. Nude sunbathing is illegal except in a few designated areas and going topless is rare, other than in the Algarve.

clothes line o estendal [shtend**a**l]
clothes peg a mola de roupa [di r**oh**pa]
cloud a nuvem [n**oo**vayng]
cloudy enevoado [inivw**a**doo]
clutch a embraiagem [aymbrī-**a**Jayng]
coach (bus) o autocarro [owtook**a**rroo]
(on train) a carruagem [karrw**a**-Jayng]
coach station a estação dos autocarros [shtas**ow**ng dooz owtook**a**rroosh]
coach trip a excursão [shkoors**ow**ng]
coast a costa [k**o**shta]
on the coast na costa

coat (long coat) o sobretudo [soobrit**oo**doo]
(jacket) o casaco [kaz**a**koo]
coathanger a cruzeta [kroozayta]
cockroach a barata
cocoa o cacau [kak**ow**]
coconut o coco [k**oh**koo]
cod o bacalhau fresco [bakal-y**ow** fr**ay**shkoo]
dried cod o bacalhau
code (for phoning) o indicativo [indikat**ee**voo]
what's the (dialling) code for Oporto? qual é o indicativo do Porto? [kwal eh oo – doo p**oh**rtoo]
coffee o café [kaf**eh**]
two coffees, please dois cafés, por favor [d**oh**-ish kaf**eh**sh poor fav**oh**r]

Useful terms are:
uma bica/um café small black, espresso-type coffee
um garoto/um pingo small coffee with milk
um galão large coffee with milk, often very weak, served in a tall glass
café descafeinado decaffeinated coffee

For white coffee that tastes of coffee rather than diluted warm milk, ask for **um café duplo com um pouco de leite** [oong kaf**eh** d**oo**ploo kong oong p**oh**koo di layt].

coin a moeda [mw**eh**da]
Coke® a coca-cola
cold frio [fr**ee**-oo]
I'm cold tenho frio [t**ay**n-yoo]
I have a cold estou constipado [shtoh konshtip**a**doo]
collapse: he's collapsed ele desmaiou [ayl diJmī-**oh**]
collar o colarinho [koolar**ee**n-yoo]
collect buscar [booshk**a**r]
I've come to collect ... vim buscar ... [veeng booshk**a**r]
collect call a chamada paga no destinatário [sham**a**da p**a**ga noo dishtinat**a**r-yoo]
college o colégio [kool**eh**J-yoo]
colour a cor [kohr]
do you have this in other colours? tem isto de outras cores? [tayng **ee**shto-di **oh**trash k**oh**rish]
colour film o filme colorido [feelm koolooree**doo**]
comb o pente [paynt]
come* vir [veer]

dialogue

where do you come from?
donde é? [dohnd**eh**]
I come from Edinburgh
sou de Edimburgo [soh dedeenb**oo**rgoo]

come back voltar
I'll come back tomorrow volto amanhã [v**o**ltoo aman-y**a**ng]

come in entrar [ayntr**a**r]
comfortable confortável [konfoort**a**vil]
compact disc o CD [say day]
company (business) a companhia [kompan-y**ee**-a]
compartment (on train) o compartimento [kompartim**ay**ntoo]
compass a bússola [b**oo**soola]
complain reclamar [riklam**a**r]
complaint a reclamação [riklamas**ow**ng]
I have a complaint tenho uma reclamação [t**ay**n-yoo]
completely completamente [komplitam**ay**nt]
computer o computador [kompootad**oh**r]
concert o concerto [kons**ay**rtoo]
concussion o traumatismo [trowmat**ee**Jmoo]
conditioner (for hair) o creme amaciador [kraym amas-yad**oh**r]
condom o preservativo [prizirvat**ee**voo]
conference a conferência [konfir**ay**ns-ya]
confirm confirmar [konfirm**a**r]
congratulations! parabéns! [parab**ay**ngsh]
connecting flight o voo de ligação [v**oh**-oo di ligas**ow**ng]
connection a ligação
conscious consciente [konsh-sy**ay**nt]
constipation a prisão de ventre [priz**ow**ng di vayntr]
consulate o consulado [konsool**a**doo]
contact contactar
contact lenses as lentes de contacto [layntsh di kont**a**too]
contraceptive o contraceptivo [kontrasipt**ee**voo]
convenient conveniente [konvin-y**ay**nt]
that's not convenient não é conveniente [nowng eh]
cook cozinhar [kozeen-y**a**r]
not cooked mal cozido [kooz**ee**doo]
cooker o fogão [foog**ow**ng]
cookie a bolacha [bool**a**sha]
cooking utensils os utensílios de cozinha [ootaynsee**e**l-yoosh di kooz**ee**n-ya]
cool fresco [fr**ay**shkoo]
cork a rolha [r**oh**l-ya]
(material) a cortiça [koort**ee**sa]
corkscrew o saca-rolhas [s**a**ka-r**oh**l-yash]
corner o canto [k**a**ntoo]
in the corner no canto [noo]
cornflakes os cornflakes
correct (right) certo [s**eh**rtoo]
corridor o corredor [koorrid**oh**r]
cosmetics os cosméticos [kooJm**eh**tikoosh]
cost custar [kooshtar]
how much does it cost? quanto custa? [kw**a**ntoo k**oo**shta]
cot a cama de bebé [k**a**ma di beb**eh**]
cotton a algodão [algood**ow**ng]

cotton wool o algodão em rama [ayng]
couch (sofa) o sofá [soofa]
couchette o beliche [bileesh]
cough a tosse [tos]
cough medicine o xarope [sharop]
could: could you ...? podia ...? [poodee-a]
could I have ...? queria ...? [kiree-a]
I couldn't ... (wasn't able to) não pude ... [nowng pood]
country (nation) o país [pa-eesh] (countryside) o campo [kampoo]
countryside o campo
couple (two people) o casal [kazal]
a couple of ... um par de ... [oong par di]
courgette a courgette
courier (man/woman) o/a guia [gee-a]
course (main course etc) o prato [pratoo]
of course é claro [eh klaroo]
of course not claro que não [ki nowng]
cousin (male/female) o primo [preemoo], a prima
cow a vaca
crab o caranguejo [karang-gayJoo]
cracker a bolacha de água e sal [boolasha dagwa ee]
craft shop a loja de artesanato [loJa dartizanatoo]
crash a colisão [kolisowng]
I've had a crash tive uma colisão [teev ooma]
crazy doido [doh-idoo]
cream as natas [natash] (lotion) o creme [kraym] (colour) creme
creche a creche
credit card o cartão de crédito [kartowng di krehdeetoo]
do you take credit cards? aceitam cartões de crédito? [asaytowng kartoyngsh]

Visa, American Express and Mastercard are the most useful credit cards in Portugal, though many smaller places and even some upmarket hotels do not accept them. In the banks of large towns, however, there are increasing numbers of cashpoint machines/ATMs for credit card cash advances (don't forget your PIN number). They charge interest on the withdrawal from day one, plus a currency conversion fee, as do the banks which give cash advances on the cards over the counter.

dialogue

can I pay by credit card? posso pagar com cartão de crédito? [posoo – kong]
which card do you want to use? que cartão deseja utilizar? [ki kartowng disayJa ootilizar]
Access/Visa
yes, sir sim, senhor [seeng

sin-y**or**]
what's the number? qual é o número? [kwal**eh** oo n**oo**miroo]
and the expiry date? e a data de validade? [ya d**a**ta de valid**ad**]

crisps as batatas fritas [bat**a**tash fr**ee**tash]
crockery a loiça [**loh**-isa]
crossing (by sea) a travessia [travis**ee**-a]
crossroads o cruzamento [kroozam**ay**ntoo]
crowd a multidão [mooltid**ow**ng]
crowded apinhado [apeen-y**a**doo]
crown (on tooth) a ponte [pohnt]
cruise o cruzeiro [krooz**ay**roo]
crutches as muletas [mool**ay**tash]
cry chorar [shoor**ar**]
cucumber o pepino [pip**ee**noo]
cup a chávena [sh**a**vena]
a cup of ..., please uma chávena de ..., se faz favor [si fash fav**oh**r]
cupboard o armário [arm**ar**-yoo]
cure curar [koor**ar**]
curly encaracolado [ayn-karakool**a**doo]
current a corrente [koorr**ay**nt]
curtains a cortinas [koort**ee**nash]
cushion a almofada [almoof**a**da]
custom o hábito [**a**beetoo]
customs a alfândega [alf**a**ndiga]
cut o corte [kort]
(verb) cort**ar**
I've cut myself cortei-me [koort**ay**mi]
cutlery os talheres [tal-y**eh**rish]
cycling o ciclismo [sikl**ee**Jmoo]
cyclist (man/woman) o/a ciclista [sikl**ee**shta]

D

dad o pap**á**
daily diariamente [d-yar-yam**ay**nt]
(adj) diário [d-y**ar**-yo]
damage avariar [avari-**ar**]
damaged avariado [avari-**a**do]
I'm sorry, I've damaged this desculpe, avariei isto [dishk**oo**lp avari-**ay ee**shtoo]
damn! raios me partam! [**ra**-yoosh mi p**ar**towng]
damp (adj) húmido [**oo**meedoo]
dance a dança [d**a**nsa]
(verb) danç**ar**
would you like to dance? queres dançar? [k**eh**rish]
dangerous perigoso [pirig**oh**zoo]
Danish (adj, language) dinamarquês [dinamark**ay**sh]
dark (adj) escuro [shk**oo**roo]
it's getting dark está a escurecer [sht**a**-a-shkooresa**yr**]
date*: **what's the date today?**

qual é a d**a**ta hoje? [kwal eh – ohJ]
let's make a date for next Monday vamos marc**a**r p**a**ra a próxima segunda-feira [**va**moosh – pr**o**sima sig**oo**nda f**ay**ra]
dates (fruit) as tâmaras [**ta**marash]
daughter a filha [**fee**l-ya]
daughter-in-law a n**o**ra
dawn a madrugada [madroog**a**da]
at dawn de madrugada [di]
day o dia [**dee**-a]
the day after o dia seguinte [sig**ee**nt]
the day after tomorrow depois de amanhã [dip**oh**-ish daman-y**a**ng]
the day before o dia anterior [antir-y**oh**r]
the day before yesterday anteontem [ant-y**oh**ntayng]
every day todos os dias [**toh**dooz-ooJ **dee**-ash]
all day o dia todo [**toh**doo]
in two days' time dentro de dois dias [**day**ntroo di d**oh**-iJ]
have a nice day bom dia [bong]
day trip a excursão de um dia [shkoors**ow**ng doong **dee**-a]
dead morto [m**oh**rtoo]
deaf surdo [s**oo**rdoo]
deal (business) o negócio [nig**o**s-yoo]
it's a deal é negócio fechado [eh – fish**a**doo]
death a morte [mort]
decaffeinated coffee o café descafeinado [kaf**eh** dishkafay-een**a**doo]
December Dezembro [dez**ay**mbroo]
decide decidir [disid**ee**r]
we haven't decided yet ainda não decidimos [a-**ee**nda nowng disid**ee**-moosh]
decision a decisão [disiz**ow**ng]
deck (on ship) o convés [konv**eh**sh]
deckchair a cadeira de lona [kad**ay**ra di l**oh**na]
deep fundo [f**oo**ndoo]
definitely de certeza [di sirt**ay**za]
definitely not de certeza que não [ki nowng]
degree (qualification) a licenciatura [lisayns-yat**oo**ra]
delay o atraso [atr**a**zoo]
deliberately de propósito [di proop**o**zitoo]
delicatessen a charcutaria [sharkootar**ee**-a]
delicious delicioso [dilis-y**oh**zo]
deliver entregar [ayntrig**a**r]
delivery (of mail) a distribuição [dishtribwees**ow**ng]
Denmark a Dinamarca [dinam**a**rka]
dental floss o fio dentário [**fee**-oo dent**a**r-yoo]
dentist (man/woman) o/a dentista [dent**ee**shta]

dialogue

it's this one here é este aqui [eh ayshtak**ee**]
this one? este?
no, that one não, aquele [nowng ak**ay**l]
here aqui
yes sim [seeng]

dentures a dentadura postiça [dentad**oo**ra poosht**ee**sa]
deodorant o desodorizante [dizoodooriz**a**nt]
department o departamento [dipartam**ay**ntoo]
department store os grandes armazéns [grandz armaz**ay**ngsh]
departure a saída [sa-**ee**da]
departure lounge a s**a**la de embarque [daymb**a**rk]
depend: it depends depende [dip**ay**nd]
it depends on ... depende de ... [di]
deposit (payment) o depósito [dip**o**zitoo]
description a descrição [dishkri-s**ow**ng]
dessert a sobremesa [sobrim**ay**za]
destination o destino [disht**ee**noo]
develop desenvolver [disaynvolv**ay**r]

dialogue

could you develop these films? pode revelar estas películas? [pod rivil**a**r **eh**shtash pil**ee**koolash]
yes, certainly sim, com certeza [seeng kong sirt**ay**za]
when will they be ready? quando ficam prontas? [kw**a**ndoo f**ee**kowng pr**oh**ntash]
tomorrow afternoon amanhã à tarde [aman-y**a**ng a tard]
how much is the four-hour service? quanto custa o serviço de quatro horas? [kw**a**ntoo k**oo**shtoo sirv**ee**so di kw**a**troo-w**o**rash]

diabetic (man/woman) o diabético [d-yab**eh**tikoo], a diab**é**tica
diabetic foods os alimentos p**a**ra diabéticos [alim**ay**ntoosh d-yab**eh**tikoosh]
dial marc**a**r
dialling code o indicativo [indikat**ee**voo]

To phone abroad from Portugal, dial 00, the country code (given below), followed by the area code (minus the initial zero) and the number:

Australia 61	Canada 1
Ireland 353	New Zealand 64
UK 44	USA 1

Portuguese Area Codes

Braga 053	Porto 02
Coimbra 039	Setúbal 065
Évora 066	Tavira 081
Faro 089	Viana do Castelo 058
Guarda 071	Vila Real 150
Lagos 082	Viseu 032
Lisboa 01	

diamond o diamante [d-yam**a**nt]
diaper a fr**a**lda
diarrhoea a diarreia [dy-arr**ay**-a]
do you have something for diarrhoea? tem algum antilaxante? [tayng alg**oo**ng anti-lash**a**nt]
diary (for business) a agenda [aJ**ay**nda]
(for personal experiences) o diário [oo di**a**r-yoo]
dictionary o dicionário [dis-yoon**a**r-yoo]
didn't* see **not**
die morrer [moorr**ayr**]
diesel o gasóleo [gaz**o**l-yoo]
diet a dieta [d-y**eh**ta]
I'm on a diet estou de dieta [shtoh di]
I have to follow a special diet tenho que seguir uma dieta especial [**tay**n-yoo ki sig**ee**r **oo**ma – shpis-y**al**]
difference a diferença [difir**ay**nsa]
what's the difference? qual é a diferença? [kwal eh]
different diferente [difir**ay**nt]
this one is different este é diferente [aysht eh]
a different table outra mesa [**oh**tra m**ay**za]
difficult difícil [dif**ee**sil]
difficulty a dificuldade [difikoold**a**d]
dinghy o bote de borracha [bot di boorr**a**sha]
dining room a s**a**la de jantar [di Jant**a**r]
dinner (evening meal) o jant**a**r
to have dinner jantar
direct (adj) directo [dir**eh**too]
is there a direct train? há um comboio directo? [a oong komb**oh**-yo]
direction a direcção [direhs**ow**ng]
which direction is it? em que direcção fica? [ayng ki – f**ee**ka]
is it in this direction? fica nesta direcção? [n**eh**shta]
directory enquiries as informações [infoormas**oy**ngsh]

For directory enquiries within Portugal, dial 118; for international enquiries, dial 166.

dirt a sujidade [sooJid**a**d]
dirty sujo [s**oo**Joo]
disabled deficiente [difis-y**ay**nt]
is there access for the disabled? há acesso p**a**ra deficientes? [a as**eh**soo – difis-y**ay**ntsh]
disappear desaparecer

[dizaparis**ay**r]

it's disappeared desapareceu [dizaparis**ay**-oo]

disappointed decepcionado [disips-yoon**a**doo]

disappointing decepcionante [disips-yon**a**nt]

disaster a tragédia [traJ**eh**d-ya]

disco o disco [d**ee**shkoo]

discount o desconto [dishk**oh**ntoo]

is there a discount? pode fazer-me um desconto? [pod faz**ay**rm-oong]

disease a doença [dw**ay**nsa]

disgusting nojento [nooJ**ay**ntoo]

dish (meal) o prato [pr**a**too]

(bowl) a tigela [tiJ**eh**la]

dishcloth o pano de loiça [p**a**noo di l**oh**-isa]

disinfectant o desinfectante [dizinfit**a**nt]

disk (for computer) a disquete [dishk**eh**t]

disposable diapers/nappies as fraldas descartáveis [fr**a**ldaJ dishkart**a**vaysh]

distance a distância [disht**a**ns-ya]

in the distance ao longe [ow lohnJ]

distilled water a água destilada [**a**gwa dishtil**a**da]

district o bairro [b**ī**rroo]

disturb perturbar [pirtoob**a**r]

diversion (detour) o desvio [diJv**ee**-oo]

diving board a prancha de saltos [pr**a**nsha di s**a**ltoosh]

divorced divorciado [divoors-y**a**doo]

dizzy: I feel dizzy sinto tonturas [s**ee**ntoo tont**oo**rash]

do* fazer [faz**ay**r]

what shall we do? que vamos fazer? [ki-v**a**moosh]

how do you do it? como se faz? [k**oh**moo si fash]

will you do it for me? importa-se de mo fazer? [imp**o**rtasi di moo]

dialogues

how do you do? muito prazer [mw**ee**ngtoo praz**ay**r]
nice to meet you muito prazer
what do you do? (work) o que é que faz? [oo ki **eh**-ki faJ]
I'm a teacher, and you? (said by man/woman) sou profess**o**r/profess**o**ra, e você? [soh – ee vos**ay**]
I'm a student sou estud**a**nte

what are you doing this evening? que vai fazer hoje à noite? [ki vī – **oh**J-ya n**oh**-it]
we're going out for a drink, do you want to join us? vamos tomar uma bebida, quer vir conosco? [v**a**moosh toom**a**r **oo**ma bib**ee**da kehr veer kon**oh**shkoo]

do you want cream? quer natas? [n**a**tash]
I do, but she doesn't quero, mas ela não [k**eh**roo maz-**eh**la nowng]

doctor (man/woman) o médico [m**eh**dikoo], a médica
we need a doctor precisamos de um médico [prisiz**a**moosh doong]
please call a doctor por favor, chame um médico [poor fav**oh**r sham oong]

In the case of serious illness, you can get the address of an English-speaking doctor from a British or American consular office or, with luck, from the local police or tourist office, or a major hotel.
As an EU country, Portugal has reciprocal health agreements with other member states for free health care. EU citizens will need form E111, available from main post offices. Reassuring as the EU health agreements may sound, however, some form of travel insurance is still worthwhile – and essential for North Americans and Australasians, who must pay for any medical treatment in Portugal.
In many parts of Portugal public health care lags behind much of northern Europe and you may well prefer to get private treatment. With insurance you have to pay on the spot, but will be able to claim back the cost later, along with the charges for any drugs prescribed by pharmacies. Be sure to keep all your receipts.
In an emergency dial 115.

dialogue

where does it hurt? onde dói? [ohnd doy]
right here bem aqui [bayng ak**ee**]
does that hurt now? dói agora?
yes sim [seeng]
take this to the pharmacy leve isto à farmácia [lehv **ee**sht-wa farm**a**s-ya]

document o documento [dookoom**ay**ntoo]
dog o cão [kowng]
doll a boneca [boon**eh**ka]
domestic flight voo doméstico [v**oh**oo doom**eh**shtikoo]
donkey o burro [b**oo**rroo]
don't!* não! [nowng]
don't do that! não faça isto! [f**a**sa **ee**shtoo]
door a porta
doorman o porteiro [poort**ay**roo]
double duplo [d**oo**ploo]
double bed a cama de casal [di kaz**a**l]
double room o quarto de casal [kw**a**rtoo]

doughnut a fartura [fart**oo**ra]
down embaixo [aymbīshoo]
down here aqui embaixo [ak**ee**]
put it down over there deite-o lá [d**ay**t-yoo la]
it's down there on the right é lá embaixo, à direita [eh – a dir**ay**ta]
it's further down the road é nesta rua mais abaixo [n**e**shta r**oo**-a mīz abīshoo]
downmarket (restaurant etc) barato [bar**a**too]
downstairs embaixo [aymbīshoo]
dozen a dúzia [d**oo**z-ya]
half a dozen a meia dúzia [m**ay**-a]
drain (in sink, in road) o cano de esgoto [k**a**noo diJg**oh**too]
draught beer imperial [eempir-y**a**l]
draughty: it's draughty faz corrente de ar [fash koorr**ay**nt dar]
drawer a gaveta [gav**ay**ta]
drawing o desenho [dis**ay**n-yoo]
dreadful horrível [ohrr**ee**vil]
dream o sonho [s**oh**n-yoo]
dress o vestido [vishteedoo]
dressed: to get dressed vestir-se [vishteersi]
dressing (for cut) o penso [p**ay**nsoo]
salad dressing o tempero [taymp**ay**roo]
dressing gown o roupão [rohp**ow**ng]
drink a bebida [bib**ee**da]
(verb) beber [bib**ay**r]
a cold drink uma bebida fresca [**oo**ma – fr**ay**shka]
fancy a quick drink? vamos tomar uma bebida? [v**a**moosh toom**a**r **oo**ma bib**ee**da]
can I get you a drink? o que bebe? [oo ki behb]
what would you like (to drink)? o que gostaria de beber? [gooshtar**ee**-ya di]
I don't drink não bebo [nowng b**ay**boo]
I'll just have a drink of water só um copo de água [saw oong k**o**poo d**a**gwa]
drinking water a água potável [**a**gwa poot**a**vil]
is this drinking water? esta água é potável? [shta – eh]

Water is drinkable from the tap anywhere in the country, and from some fresh water sources, too. Be wary, however, of pools and streams in the south of the country.

drive conduzir [kondooz**ee**r]
we drove here viemos de carro [v-y**ay**moosh di k**a**rroo]
I'll drive you home levo-o a casa de carro [l**eh**voo a k**a**za di k**a**rroo]

driving

Car rental rates in Portugal are among the lowest in Europe, but bear in mind that Portugal has one of the highest accident rates, mainly because the narrow and winding roads fail to deter impatient drivers from attempting to overtake at high speeds. When driving, always keep your wits about you, keep your speed down and look out for cars overtaking in the opposite direction but on your side of the road. Machismo is common, and male drivers sometimes find it an affront if they are overtaken by a woman. In such situations, try not to get aggravated; if necessary pull over and let the driver overtake.

Traffic drives on the right; speed limits are 60km/hr in towns and villages; 90km/hr on normal roads; 120km/hr on motorways. At road junctions, unless there's a sign to the contrary, vehicles coming from the right have priority. If you're stopped by the police, they'll want to see your documents – carry them in the car at all times.

The legal alcohol limit when driving is .05 %, but do not drink and drive.

see **motorway**

driver (of car: man/woman) o condutor [kondoot**ohr**], a condut**o**ra
(of bus: man/woman) o/a motorista [mootoor**ee**shta]

driving licence a c**a**rta de condução [di kondoos**ow**ng]

drop: just a drop, please (of drink) só um pouco, se faz favor [saw oong p**oh**koo si fash fav**ohr**]

drug o medicamento [medikam**ay**ntoo]

drugs (narcotics) a dr**o**ga

drunk (adj) bêbado [b**ay**badoo]

drunken driving a condução enquanto embriagado [kondoos**ow**ng aynkw**a**ntoo aymbr-yag**a**doo]

dry (adj) seco [s**ay**koo]

dry-cleaner a tinturaria [teentoorar**ee**-a]

duck o pato [p**a**too]

due: he was due to arrive yesterday ele devia chegar ontem [ayl div**ee**-a shig**a**r **oh**ntayng]
when is the train due? a que horas é o comboio? [k-y**o**raz eh oo komb**oh**-yo]

dull (pain) moinho [moo-**ee**n-yoo]

dummy (baby's) a chupeta [shoop**ay**ta]

during durante [door**a**nt]

dust o pó [paw]

dustbin o caixote de lixo [kīsh**o**t di l**ee**shoo]

dusty empoeirado [aympoo-ayr**a**doo]

Dutch holandês [oland**ay**sh]

duty-free (goods) duty-free

duty-free shop a free-shop

Apart from standard brands of spirits, there are no great savings to be made at airport duty-free shops. For national specialities – including wine, port, and brandy – you're better off buying from local grocery and liquor stores.

duvet o edredão [idrid**ow**ng]

E

each (every) c**a**da
how much are they each? quanto é cada um? [kwantw**eh** – oong]
ear a orelha [or**ay**l-ya]
earache: I have earache tenho dor de ouvidos [**tay**n-yoo dohr dohv**ee**doosh]
early cedo [**say**doo]
early in the morning de manhã cedo [di man-y**a**ng]
I called by earlier passei aqui mais cedo [pas**ay** akee mīsh]
earrings os brincos [br**ee**nkoosh]
east o leste [lehsht]
in the east no leste
Easter Semana S**a**nta [sim**a**na], Páscoa [**pa**shkwa]
easy fácil [**fa**sil]
eat comer [koom**ay**r]
we've already eaten, thanks (said by man/woman) já comemos, obrigado/obrig**a**da [Ja koom**ay**moosh obrig**a**doo]

eating habits
Lunch is usually served from noon to 3 p.m. and dinner from 7.30 p.m. onwards, but you shouldn't count on being able to eat much after 10 p.m. outside the cities and tourist resorts.
Eating alone in a Portuguese restaurant is considered perfectly normal, even for women, particularly at lunchtime when many Portuguese eat a full three-course meal. Evening meals are more often family affairs; it is not uncommon to see a restaurant full of children playing, even at midnight.

eau de toilette a eau de toilette
EC CE [say eh]
economy class classe económica [klas-ekoon**oh**mika]
Edinburgh Edimburgo [edeenb**oo**rgoo]
eels as enguias [ing**ee**-ash]
egg o ovo [**oh**voo]
eggplant a beringela [bireenJ**eh**la]
either: either ... or ... ou ... ou ... [oh]
either of them qualquer um deles [kwalkayr**oo**m d**ay**lish]
elastic o elástico [il**a**shtikoo]
elastic band o elástico
elbow o cotovelo [kootoov**ay**loo]
electric eléctrico [el**eh**trikoo]

electrical appliances os aparelhos eléctricos [aparayl-yoosh]
electric fire o aquecedor eléctrico [akesidohr]
electrician o electricista [eletriseeshta]
electricity a electricidade [eletrisidad]
see **voltage**
elevator (in building) o elevador [elevadohr]
else: something else outra coisa [ohtra koh-iza]
somewhere else noutro sítio [nohtroo seet-yoo]

dialogue

would you like anything else? deseja mais alguma coisa? [disayJa mīz algooma koh-iza]
no, nothing else, thanks (said by man/woman) não, mais nada, obrigado/obrigada [nowng mīsh – obrigadoo]

e-mail o correio eletrônico [koorray-oo elehtronikoo]
embassy a embaixada [aymbīshada]
emergency a emergência [emirJayns-ya]
this is an emergency! isto é uma emergência! [eeshtoo eh ooma]
emergency exit a saída de emergência [sa-eeda di emayrJayns-ya]
empty vazio [vazee-oo]
end o fim [feeng]
at the end of the street no fim da rua [noo feeng da roo-a]
when does it end? quando acaba? [kwandoo]
engaged (toilet, telephone) ocupado [okoopadoo]
(to be married) noivo [noh-ivoo]
engine (car) o motor [mootohr]
England a Inglaterra [inglatehrra]
English (adj, language) inglês [inglaysh]
I'm English (man/woman) sou inglês/inglesa [soh]
do you speak English? fala inglês?
enjoy: to enjoy oneself divertir-se [divirteersi]

dialogue

how did you like the film? gostou do filme? [goostoh doo feelm]
I enjoyed it very much; did you enjoy it? gostei imenso, você gostou? [gooshtay imaynsoo vosay gooshtoh]

enjoyable divertido [divirteedoo]
enlargement (of photo) a ampliação [ampl-yasowng]
enormous enorme [enorm]

enough suficiente [soofis-**yay**nt]
there's not enough ... não há suficiente ... [nowng a]
it's not big enough não é suficientemente grande [eh soofis-yayntim**ayn**t]
that's enough, thanks (said by man/woman) está bem, obrigado/obrig**a**da [shta bayng obrig**a**doo]
entrance a entrada [ayntr**a**da]
envelope o envelope [aynvil**o**p]
epileptic (man/woman) o epiléptico [epil**eh**ptikoo], a epil**é**ptica
equipment o equipamento [ekipam**ay**ntoo]
error un erro [**ay**rroo]
especially especialmente [shpis-yalm**ay**nt]
essential essencial [esayns-y**a**l]
it is essential that ... é essencial que ... [eh – ki]
EU UE [oo eh]
Euro o euro [**ay**-ooroo]
Eurocheque o Eurocheque [ay-ooroosh**eh**k]
see cheque
Eurocheque card o cartão Eurocheque [kart**ow**ng]
Europe a Europa [ay-oor**o**pa]
European (adj) europeu [ay-ooroop**ay**-oo], (f) europeia [ay-ooroop**ay**-a]
even: even the British até os britânicos [at**eh**-oosh brit**a**nikoosh]
even men até mesmo os homens [at**eh** m**ay**Jmo osh **oh**mayngsh]
even if ... mesmo se ... [si]
evening a noite [**noh**-it]
this evening esta noite [**eh**shta]
in the evening à noite
evening meal o jantar [oo Jant**ar**]
eventually no fim [noo feeng]
ever já [Ja]

dialogue

> have you ever been to Lamego? já esteve alguma vez em Lamego? [Ja shtayv alg**oo**ma vaysh ayng lam**ay**goo]
> yes, I was there two years ago sim, estive lá há dois anos [seeng shteev la a d**oh**-iz **a**noosh]

every c**a**da
every day todos os dias [**toh**dooz-ooz d**ee**-ash]
everyone toda a gente [**toh**da a Jaynt]
everything tudo [**too**doo]
everywhere em toda a parte [ayng t**oh**da part]
exactly! exactamente! [ezatam**ay**nt]
exam o exame [ez**a**m]
example o exemplo [ez**ay**mploo]
for example por exemplo [poor]
excellent excelente [ish-sil**ay**nt]
excellent! excelente!

except excepto [ish-s**eh**too]
excess baggage o excesso de bagagem [ish-s**eh**soo di bag**a**Jayng]
exchange rate a cotação cambial [kootas**ow**ng kamby**a**l]
exciting emocionante [emoos-yoon**a**nt]
excuse me (to get past) com licença [kong lis**ay**nsa]
(to get attention) se faz favor [si fash fav**oh**r]
(to say sorry) desculpe [dishk**oo**lp]
exhaust (pipe) o tubo de escape [t**oo**boo dishk**a**p]
exhausted (tired) exausto [ez**ow**shtoo]
exhibition a exposição [shpoozis**ow**ng]
exit a saída [sa-**ee**da]
where's the nearest exit? onde é a saída mais próxima? [ohnd**eh** – mīsh pr**o**sima]
expect esperar [shpir**a**r]
expensive caro [k**a**roo]
experienced experiente [shpir-y**ay**nt]
explain explicar [shplik**a**r]
can you explain that? pode explicar-me isso? [pod shplik**a**rm **ee**soo]
express (mail) o correio expresso [koorr**ay**-oo shpr**eh**soo]
(train) o Rápido [r**a**pidoo]
extension (telephone) a extensão [shtens**ow**ng]
extension 221, please extensão duzentos e vinte e um, por favor [dooz**ay**ntooz ee v**ee**nti-oong poor fav**oh**r]
extension lead a extensão [shtens**ow**ng]
extra: can we have an extra one? pode dar-nos mais um/uma? [pod d**a**r-noosh mīsh oong/**oo**ma]
do you charge extra for that? paga-se extra por isto? [p**a**gasi **ay**shtra poor **ee**shtoo]
extraordinary extraordinário [shtra-ohrdin**a**r-yoo]
extremely extremamente [shtremam**ay**nt]
eye o olho [**oh**l-yoo]
will you keep an eye on my suitcase for me? pode dar uma olhada na minha mala, por favor? [pod dar-oomool-y**a**da na m**ee**n-ya m**a**la poor av**oh**r]
eyebrow pencil o lápis para as sobrancelhas [lapsh p**a**rash sobrans**ay**l-yash]
eye drops as gotas para os olhos [g**oh**tash p**a**rooz **o**l-yoosh]
eyeglasses (US) os óculos [**o**kooloosh]
eyeliner o lápis para os olhos [lapsh p**a**rooz **o**l-yoosh]
eye make-up remover o desmaquilhador de olhos [dishmakil-yad**oh**r d**o**l-yoosh]
eye shadow a sombra para os olhos

F

face a cara

factory a fábrica [fabrika]

Fahrenheit* Fahrenheit

faint (verb) desmaiar [diJmī-ar]

she's fainted ela desmaiou [ehla diJmī-oh]

I feel faint sinto que vou desmaiar [seentoo ki voh]

fair (funfair, tradefair) a feira [fayra]

(adj) justo [Jooshtoo]

fairly bastante [bashtant]

fake falso [falsoo]

fall cair [ka-eer]

she's had a fall ela deu uma queda [ehla day-oo ooma kehda]

fall (US) o Outono [ohtohnoo]

in the fall no Outono [noo]

false falso [falsoo]

family a família [fameel-ya]

famous famoso [famohzoo]

fan (electrical) a ventoinha [vayntween-ya]

(handheld) o leque [lehk]

(sports: man/woman) o adepto [adehptoo], a adepta

fan belt a correia da ventoinha [koorray-a da vayntween-ya]

fantastic fantástico [fantashtikoo]

far longe [lohnJ]

dialogue

is it far from here? é longe daqui? [eh – dakee]

no, not very far não, não é muito longe [nowng – mweengtoo]

well how far? bem, qual é a distância? [bayng kwal eh a dishtans-ya]

it's about 20 kilometres são mais ou menos vinte quilómetros [sowng mīz oh maynoosh veengt kilomitroosh]

fare o bilhete [bil-yayt]

farm a quinta [keenta]

fashionable na moda

fast rápido [rapidoo]

fat (person) gordo [gohrdoo]

(on meat) a gordura [goordoora]

father o pai [pī]

father-in-law o sogro [sohgroo]

faucet a torneira [toornayra]

fault o defeito [difaytoo]

sorry, it was my fault desculpe, foi culpa minha [foh-i koolpa meen-ya]

it's not my fault a culpa não é minha [nowng eh meen-ya]

faulty avariado [avariadoo]

favourite favorito [favooreetoo]

fax o fax

to send a fax mandar um fax

February Fevereiro [fivrayroo]

feel sentir [saynteer]

I feel hot estou com calor [shtoh kong kalohr]

I feel unwell não me sinto

bem [nowng mi **see**ntoo bayng]
I feel like going for a walk estou com vontade de dar um passeio [shtoh kong vont**a**d di dar oong pas**ay**-oo]
how are you feeling? como se sente? [**koh**moo si saynt]
I'm feeling better sinto-me melhor [**see**ntoomi mil-y**or**]
felt-tip (pen) a caneta de feltro [kan**ay**ta di f**ay**ltroo]
fence a vedação [vidas**ow**ng]
fender o pára-choques [p**a**ra-sh**o**ksh]
ferry o ferry-boat
festival o festival [fishtiv**a**l]
fetch buscar [booshk**ar**]
I'll fetch him vou buscá-lo [voh booshk**a**-loo]
will you come and fetch me later? pode vir buscar-me mais tarde? [pod veer booshk**ar**mi mīsh tard]
feverish febril [febr**ee**l]
few: a few alguns [alg**oo**nsh]
I'll give you a few dou-lhe alguns [d**oh**l-yalg**oo**nsh]
a few days poucos dias [p**oh**koosh d**ee**-ash]
fiancé o noivo [n**oh**-ivoo]
fiancée a noiva
field o campo [k**a**mpoo]
fight a briga [br**ee**ga]
figs os figos [f**ee**goosh]
fill in preencher [pri-aynsh**ayr**]
do I have to fill this in? tenho de preencher isto? [t**ay**n-yoo di – **ee**shtoo]
fill up encher [aynsh**ayr**]
fill it up, please encha o depósito, por favor [**ay**nsha oo dep**o**zitoo poor fav**ohr**]
filling (in cake, sandwich) recheio [rish**ay**-oo]
(in tooth) o chumbo [sh**oo**mboo]
film o filme [feelm]

dialogue

do you have this kind of film? tem este tipo de filme? [tayng aysht t**ee**po]
yes, how many exposures? sim, quantas fotografias? [seeng kwant**a**sh footoografe**e**-ash]
36 trinta-e-seis [treentī-s**ay**sh]

film processing a revelação de filmes [rivilas**ow**ng di f**ee**lmsh]
filter coffee o café de filtro [kaf**eh** di f**ee**ltroo]
filter papers os filtros de café [feeltr**oo**sh]
filthy nojento [nooJ**ay**ntoo]
find encontrar [aynkontr**ar**]
I can't find it não consigo encontrar [nowng kons**ee**goo]
I've found it encontrei-o [aynkongtr**ay**-oo]
find out descobrir [dishkoobr**eer**]
could you find out for me? pode descobrir para mim? [pod — meeng]
fine (weather) bom [bong]

(punishment) a multa [**moo**lta]

dialogues

how are you? como está? [**koh**moo shta]
I'm fine, thanks (said by man/woman) bem, obrigado/obrigada [bayng obrig**a**doo]

is that OK? assim está bem? [as**ee**ng shta bayng]
that's fine, thanks está bem, obrigado/obrigada [shta]

finger o dedo [**day**doo]
finish terminar
I haven't finished yet ainda não terminei [a-**ee**nda nowng termin**ay**]
when does it finish? quando é que termina? [kw**a**ndoo eh ki term**ee**na]
fire o fogo [**foh**goo]
(blaze) o incêndio [ins**ay**nd-yoo]
fire! fogo!
can we light a fire here? podemos fazer uma fogueira aqui? [pood**ay**moosh faz**ay**r **oo**ma foog**ay**ra ak**ee**]
it's on fire está a arder [shta a ard**ay**r]
fire alarm o alarme de incêndios [al**a**rm dins**ay**nd-yoosh]
fire brigade os bombeiros [bomb**ay**roosh]

For all emergency services dial 115.

fire escape a saída de emergência [sa-**ee**da demirJ**ay**ns-ya]
fire extinguisher o extintor [shtint**oh**r]
first primeiro [prim**ay**roo]
I was first (said by man/woman) eu era o primeiro/a primeira [**ay**-oo **eh**ra]
at first ao princípio [ow prins**ee**p-yoo]
the first time a primeira vez [vaysh]
first on the left primeira à esquerda [**a**-shk**ay**rda]
first aid os primeiros socorros [prim**ay**roosh sook**o**rroosh]
first aid kit a caixa de primeiros socorros [kīsha di]
first class (travel etc) primeira classe [klas]
first floor o primeiro andar
(US) o rés de chão [rehJ doo]
first name o nome próprio [nohm pr**o**pr-yoo]
fish o peixe [paysh]
(verb) pescar [pishk**a**r]
fishing village a aldeia de pescadores [ald**ay**-a di pishkad**oh**rish]
fishmonger's a peixaria [payshar**ee**-a]
fit (attack) ataque [at**a**k]

fit: it doesn't fit me não me serve [nowng mi sehrv]
fitting room a cabina de provas [kab**ee**na di pr**o**vash]
fix (repair) repar**a**r
can you fix this? (repair) pode reparar isto? [pod – **ee**shtoo]
fizzy gasoso [gaz**oh**zoo]
flag a bandeira [band**ay**ra]
flannel a toalha de c**a**ra [tw**a**l-ya di]
flash (for camera) o flash
flat (apartment) o apartamento [apartam**ay**ntoo]
(adj) plano [pl**a**noo]
I've got a flat tyre tenho um pneu furado [t**ay**n-yoo oong pn**ay**-oo foor**a**doo]
flavour o sabor [sab**oh**r]
flea a pulga [p**oo**lga]
flight o voo [v**oh**-oo]
flight number o número de voo [n**oo**miroo di]
flippers as barbatanas [barbat**a**-nash]
flood a inundação [inoondas**ow**ng]
floor (of room) o chão [showng]
(storey) o and**a**r
on the floor no chão
florist a florista [floor**ee**shta]
flour a farinha [far**ee**n-ya]
flower a flor [flohr]
flu a gripe [greep]
fluent: he speaks fluent Portuguese ele f**a**la português fluentemente [el – poortoog**ay**sh flwentim**ay**nt]
fly a mosca [m**oh**shka]
(verb: person) ir de avião [eer dav-y**ow**ng]
fog o nevoeiro [nivw**ay**roo]
foggy: it's foggy está enevoado [shta inivw**a**doo]
folk dancing a dança folclórica [d**a**nsa foolkl**o**rika]
folk music a música folclórica [m**oo**zika]

folksinging
Fado is Portugal's most famous music. It is lyrical and sentimental and thought to have its origins in African slave songs. There are several **Casas de Fados** in Lisbon and in other cities. You can also hear fado songs in an **Adega Típica**.

follow seguir [sig**ee**r]
follow me siga-me [s**ee**gami]
food a comida [koom**ee**da]
food poisoning a intoxicação aliment**a**r [intoksikas**ow**ng]
food shop/store a mercearia [mirs-yar**ee**-a]
foot* (of person, measurement) o pé [peh]
on foot a pé
football (game) o futebol [footb**o**l]
(ball) a b**o**la de futebol
football match o desafio de futebol [dizaf**ee**-oo di]
for: do you have something for ...? (headache/diarrhoea etc) tem alguma coisa p**a**ra ...? [tayng alg**oo**ma k**oh**-iza]

dialogues

who's the bacalhau for? para quem é o bacalhau? [kayng eh-oo bakal-yow]
that's for me é para mim [eh – meeng]
and this one? e este? [ee-aysht]
that's for her é para ela [ehla]

where do I get the bus for Castelo de São Jorge? onde posso apanhar o autocarro para o Castelo de São Jorge? [ohnd posoo apan-yar oo owtookarroo paroo kashtehloo di sowng JorJ]
the bus for o Castelo de São Jorge leaves from Praça do Comércio o autocarro para o Castelo de São Jorge sai da Praça do Comércio [sī da prasa doo koomehrsyo]

how long have you been here for? há quanto tempo está aqui? [a kwantoo taympoo shta akee]
I've been here for two days, how about you? estou aqui há dois dias, e você? [shtoh akee a doh-iJ dee-ash ee vosay]
I've been here for a week estou aqui há uma semana [shtoh akee a ooma simana]

forehead a testa [tehshta]
foreign estrangeiro [shtranJayroo]
foreigner (man/woman) o estrangeiro [shtranJayroo], a estrangeira
forest a floresta [floorehshta]
forget esquecer [shkisayr]
I forget, I've forgotten esqueci-me [shkiseemi]
fork o garfo [garfoo]
(in road) a bifurcação [bifoorkasowng]
form (document) o impresso [imprehsoo]
formal (dress) de cerimónia [di sirimon-ya]
fortnight a quinzena [keenzayna]
fortunately felizmente [filiJmaynt]
forward: could you forward my mail? pode passar a enviar-me o correio? [pod – aynv-yarmi oo koorray-oo]
forwarding address a nova morada [moorada]
foundation cream o creme de base [kraym di baz]
fountain a fonte [fohnt]
foyer (of hotel, theatre) o foyer [fwī-ay]
fracture a fractura [fratoora]
France a França [fransa]
free livre [leevr]

(no charge) gratuito [gratoo-eetoo]
is it free (of charge)? é gratuito? [eh]
freeway a autoestrada [owtooshtrada]
see **motorway**
freezer o congelador [konJiladohr]
French (adj, language) francês [fransaysh]
French fries as batatas fritas [batatash freetash]
frequent frequente [frikwaynt]
how frequent is the bus to Évora? com que frequência há autocarros para Évora? [kong ki frikwaynsya a owtookarroosh – ehvoora]
fresh fresco [frayshkoo]
fresh orange o sumo natural de laranja [soomoo natooral di laranJa]
Friday sexta-feira [sayshta fayra]
fridge o frigorífico [frigoo-reefikoo]
fried frito [freetoo]
fried egg o ovo estrelado [ohvoo shtriladoo]
friend (male/female) o amigo [ameegoo], a amiga
friendly simpático [simpatikoo]
from de [di]
when does the next train from Braga arrive? quando chega o próximo comboio de Braga? [kwandoo shayg-oo prosimoo kombohh-yo di]
from Monday to Friday de segunda a sexta-feira [di sigoonda-a sayshta fayra]
from next Thursday a partir da próxima quinta-feira [a parteer da prosima keenta fayra]

dialogue

where are you from? de onde é? [dohnd-eh]
I'm from Slough sou de Slough [soh di]

front a frente [fraynt]
in front em frente [ayng]
in front of the hotel em frente ao hotel [ow]
at the front na frente [na]
frost a geada [J-yada]
frozen gelado [Jiladoo]
frozen food a comida congelada [koomeeda konJilada]
fruit a fruta [froota]
fruit juice o sumo de fruta [soomoo di froota]
fry fritar
frying pan a frigideira [friJidayra]
full cheio [shay-oo]
it's full of ... está cheio de ... [shta – di]
I'm full (said by man/woman) estou satisfeito/satisfeita [shtoh satisfaytoo]
full board a pensão completa [paynsowng komplehta]

fun: it was fun foi divertido [**foh**-i divir**tee**doo]
funeral o funeral [fooner**al**]
funny (strange) estranho [shtr**an**-yoo]
(amusing) engraçado [ayngras**a**doo]
furniture a mobília [moob**ee**l-ya]
further mais longe [mīJ lohnJ]
it's further down the road é mais abaixo na rua [ab**ī**shoo na r**oo**-a]

dialogue

how much further is it to Santarém? quantos quilómetros faltam para Santarém? [kw**a**ntoosh kil**o**mitroosh f**a**ltowng – santar**ayng**]
about 5 kilometres mais ou menos cinco quilómetros [mīz oh m**ay**noosh s**ee**nkoo]

fuse o fusível [fooz**ee**vil]
the lights have fused as luzes fundiram-se [aJ l**oo**zish foond**ee**rowngsi]
fuse box a caixa de fusíveis [kīsha di fooz**ee**vaysh]
fuse wire o fio de fusível [f**ee**-oo di fooz**ee**vil]
future o futuro [foot**oo**roo]
in future no futuro [noo]

G

gallon* o galão [gal**ow**ng]
game (cards, match etc) o jogo [J**oh**goo]
(meat) a caça [k**a**sa]
garage (for fuel) a bomba de gasolina [di gazool**ee**na]
(for repairs, parking) a garagem [gar**a**Jayng]
garden o jardim [Jard**ee**ng]
garlic o alho [**a**l-yoo]
gas o gás [gash]
gas cylinder (camping gas) a bilha de gás [b**ee**l-ya di gash]
gasoline (US) a gasolina [gazool**ee**na]
see **petrol**
gas permeable lenses as lentes semi-rígidas [layntsh simi-r**ee**Jidash]
gas station a bomba de gasolina [b**oh**mba di gazool**ee**na]
gate o portão [poort**ow**ng]
(at airport) o portão de embarque [daymb**a**rk]
gay o homossexual [ohmooseksw**a**l]
gay bar o gay bar
gearbox a caixa de velocidades [kīsha di viloosid**a**dsh]
gear lever a avalanca das mudanças [dash mood**a**nsash]
gears a mudança [mood**a**nsa]
general (adj) geral [Jer**a**l]
gents (toilet) a casa de banho

dos homens [kaza di ban-yoo dooz ohmayngsh]

genuine (antique etc) genuíno [Jinweenoo]

German (adj, language) alemão [alimowng]

German measles a rubéola [roobeh-ola]

Germany a Alemanha [aliman-ya]

get (fetch) ir buscar [eer]

will you get me another one, please? pode trazer-me outro, por favor? [pod trazayrmohtroo poor favohr]

how do I get to ...? como vou para ...? [kohmoo voh]

do you know where I can get this? sabe onde posso comprar isto? [sabohnd posoo – eeshtoo]

dialogue

can I get you a drink? posso oferecer-lhe uma bebida? [posoo ofrisayrl-yooma bibeeda]

no, I'll get this one, what would you like? não, eu ofereço esta, o que gostaria? [nowng ay-oo ofraysoo ehshta oo ki gooshtaree-a]

a glass of red wine um copo de vinho tinto [oong kopoo di veen-yoo teento]

get back (return) voltar

get in (arrive) chegar [shigar]

get off sair [sa-eer]

where do I get off? onde é que saio? [ohndeh ki sī-yoo]

get on (to train etc) apanhar [apan-yar]

get out (of car etc) sair [sa-eer]

get up (in the morning) levantar-se [livantarsi]

gift a lembrança [laymbransa]

If you are invited to dinner in a Portuguese home, don't take a bottle of wine, which is considered very much a staple of the meal. A bunch of flowers, chocolates or a small gift will be much more appreciated.

gift shop a loja de lembranças [loJa di laymbransash]

gin o gin [Jeeng]

a gin and tonic, please um gin-tónico por favor [oong Jeeng tonikoo poor favohr]

girl a rapariga [rapareega]

girlfriend a namorada

give* dar

can you give me some change? pode dar-me troco? [pod darmi trohkoo]

I gave it to him dei-lhe [dayl-yi]

will you give this to ...? pode dar isto a ...? [eeshtoo]

dialogue

how much do you want for this? quanto quer por isto? [kwantoo kehr poor eeshtoo]
20 escudos vinte escudos [veent-shkoodoosh]
I'll give you 15 escudos dou-lhe quinze escudos [dohl-yi keenz]

give back devolver [divolvayr]
glad contente [kontaynt]
glass (material) o vidro [veedroo]
(for drinking) o copo [kopoo]
a glass of wine um copo de vinho [oong – di veen-yoo]
glasses os óculos [okooloosh]
gloves as luvas [loovash]
glue a cola
go* ir [eer]
we'd like to go to the Museu de Arte Antiga queremos ir ao Museu de Arte Antiga [kiraymoosh eer ow moosay-oo dartanteega]
where are you going? onde vai? [ohnd vī]
where does this bus go? para onde vai este autocarro? [aysht owtookarroo]
let's go! vamos! [vamoosh]
she's gone (left) ele foi-se embora [ayl foh-isaymbora]
where has he gone? onde ele foi? [ohndayl foh-i]
I went there last week fui lá na semana passada [fwee la na simana]
hamburger to go o hamburger para levar
go away ir embora [eer aymbora]
go away! vá-se embora! [vas-aymbora]
go back (return) voltar
go down (the stairs etc) descer [dishsayr]
go in entrar [ayntrar]
go out* (in the evening) sair [sa-eer]
do you want to go out tonight? quer sair esta noite? [kehr – ehshta noh-it]
go through atravessar
go up (the stairs etc) subir [soobeer]
goat a cabra
goat's cheese o queijo de cabra [kayJoo di]
God Deus [day-oosh]
goggles os óculos protectores [okooloosh prootetohrish]
gold o ouro [ohroo]
golf o golfe [golf]
golf course o campo de golfe [kampoo di]
good bom [bong]
good! bem! [bayng]
it's no good não presta [nowng prehshta]
goodbye adeus [aday-oosh]
good evening boa noite [boh-a noh-it]
Good Friday Sexta-Feira Santa [sayshta fayra]

Good Friday is a public holiday in Portugal. All over the country there are religious processions; almost everything will be closed and transport services greatly reduced.

good morning bom dia [**bong** dee-a]
good night boa noite [**boh**-a **noh**-it]
goose o ganso [**gan**soo]
got: we've got to leave temos que ir [**tay**moosh ki-**eer**]
have you got any ...? tem ...? [tayng]
government o governo [goov**ayr**noo]
gradually gradualmente [gradwalm**ay**nt]
grammar a gramática
gram(me) o grama
granddaughter a neta [**neh**ta]
grandfather o avô [av**oh**]
grandmother a avó [av**aw**]
grandson o neto [**neh**too]
grapefruit a toranja [toor**an**Ja]
grapefruit juice o sumo de toranja [**soo**moo di toor**an**Ja]
grapes as uvas [**oo**vash]
grass a relva [**reh**lva]
grateful agradecido [agradis**ee**doo]
gravy o molho [**moh**l-yo]
great (excellent) óptimo [**o**timoo]
that's great! isso é optimo! [**ee**soo eh]
a great success um grande sucesso [oong gr**a**nd soos**eh**soo]
Great Britain a Grã-Bretanha [gran brit**an**-ya]
Greece a Grécia [gr**eh**s-ya]
greedy (for food) glutão [gloot**ow**ng]
Greek (adj, language) grego [gr**ay**goo]
green verde [vayrd]
green card (car insurance) a carta verde
greengrocer's o lugar [loog**ar**]

greeting people
The Portuguese are fairly formal in their greetings; even the young will greet each other with **bom dia** (good day) or **boa tarde** (good afternoon). Older people still address each other as **Senhor**, **Senhora** or with other titles such as **Dona** or **Doutor**. The popularity of Brazilian soap operas has led to many Brazilian expressions being assimilated into colloquial Portuguese; you may hear younger people saying **ciao** (which the Brazilians adopted from Italian) on parting, for example. You will also commonly hear the Brazilian greeting **tudo bem?** (literally: is everything OK?) rather than the more traditional Portuguese **como está?** (how are you?).

grey cinzento [sinz**ay**ntoo]
grill o grelhador [gril-yad**ohr**]
grilled grelhado [gril-y**a**doo]

grocer's o merceeiro [mirs-yayroo]
ground o chão [showng]
on the ground no chão [noo]
ground floor o rés de chão [rehJ doo]
group o grupo [groopoo]
guarantee a garantia [garantee-a]
is it guaranteed? tem garantia? [tayng]
guest (man/woman) o convidado [konvidadoo], a convidada
guesthouse a pensão [paynsowng]

The main budget travel standby is a room in a guesthouse or **pensão**: these are officially graded from one to three stars. Most serve meals, usually in a bargain-priced, all-inclusive package, but they rarely insist that you take them. Guesthouses that don't serve meals are sometimes called **residenciais**, though in price and all other respects they are virtually identical. Similar to pensões, and generally at the cheaper end of the scale, are **hospedarias** or **casas de hóspedes** – boarding houses. Always ask to see the room before you take it, and don't be afraid to ask if there's a cheaper one – especially if you're travelling alone, when you'll frequently be asked to pay more or less the full price of a double. **Tem um quarto mais barato?** (do you have a less expensive room?) is a useful phrase. A budget alternative is to go for rooms (**quartos** or **dormidas**) in private houses. Most commonly available in the seaside resorts, these are sometimes advertised, or more often hawked at bus and train stations. Rates should be a little below that of a guesthouse, except on the Algarve where you can pay more. It's always worth haggling over prices, especially if you're prepared to commit yourself to a longish stay.

guide (person) a guia [gee-a]
guidebook o livro-guia [leevroo–]
guided tour a excursão com guia [shkoorsowng kong]
guitar a viola
gum (in mouth) a gengiva [JenJeeva]
gun a pistola [pishtola]
gym o ginásio [Jinaz-yoo]

H

hair o cabelo [kabayloo]
hairbrush a escova de cabelo [shkohva di]
haircut o corte de cabelo [kort]
hairdresser's (unisex, women's) o cabeleireiro [kabilayrayroo]
(men's) o barbeiro [barbayroo]

It is usual to make an appointment (**marcação**) at the hairdresser's. Hairdressers expect to be tipped about 10 per cent of the bill.

hairdryer o secador de cabelo [sikad**oh**r di kab**ay**loo]
hair gel o gel para o cabelo [Jehl p**a**roo]
hairgrips a m**o**la para o cabelo
hair spray a l**a**ca
half* a metade [mit**a**d]
half an hour meia hora [m**ay**-a **o**ra]
half a litre meio litro [m**ay**-oo l**ee**troo]
about half that mais ou menos metade disto [mīz oh m**ay**noosh mit**a**d-d**ee**shtoo]
half board a meia pensão [m**ay**-a payns**ow**ng]
half-bottle a meia garr**a**fa
half fare o meio bilhete [m**ay**-oo bil-y**ay**t]
half price metade do preço [mit**a**d doo pr**ay**soo]
ham o fiambre [f-y**a**mbr]
hamburger o hamburger [amb**oo**rger]
hammer o martelo [mart**eh**loo]
hand a mão [mowng]
handbag a m**a**la de mão [di]
handbrake o travão de mão [trav**ow**ng]
handkerchief o lenço [l**ay**nsoo]
handle (on door) o fecho [f**ay**shoo]
(on suitcase etc) a pega [p**eh**ga]
hand luggage a bagagem de mão [bag**a**Jayng]
hang-gliding a asa-delta [aza-d**eh**lta]
hangover a ressaca [ris**a**ka]
I've got a hangover estou de ressaca [shtoh di]
happen acontecer [akontis**ay**r]
what's happening? o que se p**a**ssa? [oo ki si]
what has happened? o que aconteceu? [oo ki-akoontis**ay**-oo]
happy contente [kont**ay**nt]
I'm not happy about this não estou contente com isso [nowng shtoh – kong **ee**soo]
harbour o porto [p**oh**rtoo]
hard duro [d**oo**roo]
(difficult) difícil [dif**ee**sil]
hard-boiled egg o ovo cozido [**oh**voo kooz**ee**doo]
hard lenses as lentes rígidas [layntsh r**ee**Jidash]
hardly mal
hardly ever quase nunca [kwaz n**oo**nka]
hardware shop a loja de ferragens [l**o**Ja di firr**a**Jayngsh]
hat o chapéu [shap**eh**-oo]
hate detestar [ditisht**a**r]
have* ter [tayr]
can I have a ...? pode dar-me ...? [pod d**a**rmi]
do you have ...? tem ...? [tayng]
what'll you have? o que vai tomar? [oo ki vī toom**a**r]
I have to leave now tenho de

ir agora [tayn-yoo deer]
do I have to ...? tenho de ...? [di]
can we have some ...? posso ter ...? [posoo tayr]
hayfever a febre dos fenos [fehbr doosh faynoosh]
hazelnuts as avelãs [avelangsh]
he* ele [el]
head a cabeça [kabaysa]
headache a dor de cabeça [di]
headlights o farol
headphones os auscultadores [owshkooltadohrish]
health see **doctor**
health food shop a loja de produtos naturais [loJa di proodootoosh natoorīsh]
healthy saudável [sowdavil]
hear ouvir [ohveer]

dialogue

can you hear me?
consegue ouvir-me?
[konsehg ohveer-mi]
I can't hear you, could you repeat that? não o consigo ouvir, podia repetir? [nowng oo konseegoo – poodee-a ripiteer]

hearing aid o aparelho para a surdez [aparayl-yoo – soordaysh]
heart o coração [koorasowng]
heart attack o enfarte [aynfart]
heat o calor [kalohr]
heater o aquecedor [akesidohr]
heating o aquecimento [akesimayntoo]
heavy pesado [pizadoo]
heel (of foot) o calcanhar [kalkan-yar]
(of shoe) o salto
could you put new heels on these? podia pôr uns saltos novos? [poodee-a pohr oongsh saltoosh novoosh]
heelbar o sapateiro rápido [sapatayroo rapidoo]
height (of person) a altura [altoora]
(mountain) a altitude [altitood]
helicopter o helicóptero [elikoptiroo]
hello olá
(answer on phone) está [shta]
helmet (for motorcycle) o capacete [kapasayt]
help a ajuda [aJooda]
(verb) ajudar
help! socorro! [sookohrroo]
can you help me? pode ajudar-me? [pod – mi]
thank you very much for your help (said by man/woman) obrigado/obrigada pela sua ajuda [obrigadoo – pila soo-a]
helpful prestável [preshtavil]
hepatitis a hepatite [epateet]
her*: I haven't seen her não a vi [nowng a vee]
to her para ela [ehla]
with her com ela [kong]
for her para ela
that's her é ela [eh]
that's her towel esta é a toalha dela [ehshta-eh – dehla]

herbal tea o chá de ervas [sha dehrvash]
herbs as ervas
here aqui [akee]
here is/are ... aqui está/estão ... [shta/shtowng]
here you are aqui tem [tayng]
hers* dela [dehla]
that's hers isso é dela [eesoo eh]
hey! eh!
hi! (hello) olá! [oola]
hide esconder [shkondayr]
high alto [altoo]
highchair a cadeira de bébé [kadayra di bebeh]
highway a autoestrada [owtooshtrada]
see motorway
hill o monte [mohnt]
him*: I haven't seen him não o vi [nowng oo vee]
to him para ele [ayl]
with him com ele [kong]
for him para ele
that's him é ele [eh]
hip a anca
hire alugar [aloogar]
for hire para alugar
where can I hire a bike? onde posso alugar uma bicicleta? [ohnd posoo]
see rent
his*: it's his car é o carro dele [eh-oo karroo dayl]
that's his isto é dele [eeshtweh]
hit bater [batayr]
hitch-hike andar à boleia [boolay-a]
hobby o passatempo [–taympoo]
hold segurar [sigoorar]
hole o buraco [boorakoo]
holiday as férias [fehr-yash]
on holiday de férias [shtoh di]
Holland Holanda [olanda]
home a casa [kaza]
at home (in my house etc) em casa [ayng]
(in my country) no meu país [noo may-oo pa-eesh]
we go home tomorrow vamos embora amanhã [vamoosh aymbora aman-yang]
honest honesto [onehshtoo]
honey o mel [mehl]
honeymoon a lua-de-mel [loo-a di]
hood (US: of car) o capot [kapoh]
hope esperar [shpirar]
I hope so espero que sim [shpehroo ki seeng]
I hope not espero que não [nowng]
hopefully: hopefully ... espero que ...
horn (of car) a buzina [boozeena]
horrible horrível [ohrreevil]
horse o cavalo [kavaloo]
horse riding andar a cavalo
hospital o hospital [oshpital]
hospitality a hospitalidade [oshpitalidad]
thank you for your hospitality (said by man/woman)

obrigado/obrigada pela sua hospitalidade [obrigadoo – pila soo-a]

hot quente [kaynt]
(spicy) picante [pikant]
I'm hot tenho calor [tayn-yoo kalohr]
it's hot today está imenso calor hoje [shta imaynsoo – ohJ]

hotel o hotel [ohtehl]

A one-star hotel usually costs about the same as a three-star **pensão** (guesthouse); sometimes establishments classified as one-star hotels are not very different from guesthouses. Indeed, it's not uncommon to find a two- or three-star pensão offering much better quality rooms than a one-star hotel. Prices for two- and three-star hotels, though, are noticeably higher, and there's a further and more dramatic shift in rates as you move into the four- and five-star hotel league. **Estalagens** and **albergarias** are other types of hotel in the upper price ranges.
For a different type of accommodation, you could try one of the 32 government-run **pousadas** which are often converted from old monasteries or castles and located in dramatic countryside settings. They're rated in three categories, and, as with other hotels, charge different prices in low, middle and high season.

hotel room o quarto de hotel [kwartoo dohtehl]

hour a hora [ora]

house a casa [kaza]

house wine o vinho da casa [veen-yoo]

how como [kohmoo]
how many? quantos? [kwantoosh]
how do you do? muito prazer [mweengtoo prazayr]

dialogues

how are you? como está? [shta]
fine, thanks, and you? (said by man/woman) bem, obrigado/obrigada, e você? [bayng obrigadoo – ee vosay]

how much is it? quanto é? [kwantweh]
it's 500 escudos são quinhentos escudos [sowng kin-yayntooz-shkoodoosh]
I'll take it vou levar [voh]

humid húmido [oomeedoo]

hunger a fome [fohm]

hungry: are you hungry? tens fome? [taynsh]

hurry apressar-se [aprisarsi]
I'm in a hurry estou com pressa [shtoh kong prehsa]
there's no hurry não há pressa [nowng a]

hurry up! despacha-te! [dishp**a**shat]
hurt doer [dwayr]
it really hurts dói-me [d**oy**mi]
husband o meu marido [m**ay**-oo mar**ee**doo]
hydrofoil o hydroplano [idroopl**a**noo]
hypermarket hipermercado [eepermerk**a**doo]

I

I* eu [**ay**-oo]
ice gelo [J**ay**loo]
with ice com gelo [kong]
no ice, thanks (said by man/woman) sem gelo, obrigado/obrigada [sayng – obrig**a**doo]
ice cream o gelado [Jil**a**doo]
ice-cream cone o cone de gelado [kohn di]
iced coffee o café glacé [kaf**eh** glas**ay**]
ice lolly o gelado [Jil**a**doo]
ice rink o rinque de patinagem [r**ee**nk di patin**a**Jayng]
ice skates os patins de gelo [pat**ee**nJ di J**ay**loo]
idea a ideia [id**ay**-a]
idiot o idiota [id-y**o**ta]
if se [si]
ignition a ignição [ignis**ow**ng]
ill doente [dwaynt]
I feel ill sinto-me doente [s**ee**ntoomi]
illness a doença [dw**ay**nsa]
imitation (leather etc) a imitação [imitas**ow**ng]
immediately imediatamente [imed-yatam**ay**nt]
important importante [impoort**a**nt]
it's very important é muito importante [eh mw**ee**ngtoo]
it's not important não é importante [nowng]
impossible impossível [impoos**ee**vil]
impressive impressionante [impris-yoon**a**nt]
improve melhorar [mil-yor**a**r]
I want to improve my Portuguese quero melhorar o meu português [k**eh**roo – oo m**ay**-oo poortoog**ay**sh]
in*: it's in the centre fica no centro [f**ee**ka noo s**ay**ntroo]
in my car no meu carro [noo m**ay**-oo k**a**rroo]
in Beja em Beja [ayng b**eh**Ja]
in two days from now daqui a dois dias [dak**ee** a d**o**-iJ d**ee**-ash]
in five minutes em cinco minutos [ayng s**ee**nkoo min**oo**toosh]
in May em Maio [m**ī**-oo]
in English em inglês [ingl**ay**sh]
in Portuguese em português [poortoog**ay**sh]
is he in? ele está? [el shta]
inch* a polegada [poolig**a**da]
include incluir [inklw**ee**r]
does that include meals? isso inclui as refeições? [**ee**soo

inkl**oo**-i refays**oy**ngsh]
is that included? isso está incluído no preço? [shta inklw**ee**doo noo pr**ay**soo]
inconvenient pouco conveniente [p**oh**koo konvin-y**ay**nt]
incredible incrível [inkr**ee**vil]
Indian (adj) indiano [ind-y**a**noo]
indicator o indicador [indikad**oh**r]
indigestion a indigestão [indiJisht**ow**ng]
indoor pool a piscina coberta [pish-s**ee**na koob**eh**rta]
indoors dentro de casa [d**ay**ntroo di k**a**za], em recinto fechado [ayng ris**ee**ntoo fish**a**doo]
inexpensive barato [bar**a**too]
infection a infecção [infehs**ow**ng]
infectious infeccioso [infehs-y**oh**zoo]
inflammation a inflamação [inflamas**ow**ng]
informal informal [infoorm**a**l]
information a informação [infoormas**ow**ng]
do you have any information about ...? tem alguma informação sobre ...? [tayng alg**oo**ma – sohbr]
information desk o balcão de informações [balk**ow**ng dinfoormas**oy**ngsh]
injection a injecção [inJehs**ow**ng]
injured ferido [fir**ee**doo]
she's been injured ela ficou ferida [**eh**la fik**oh** fir**ee**da]
in-laws os sogros [oosh s**o**groosh]
inner tube (for tyre) a câmara de ar [k**a**ma-ra dar]
innocent inocente [inoos**ay**nt]
insect o insecto [ins**eh**too]
insect bite a picada de insecto [dins**eh**too]
do you have anything for insect bites? tem alguma coisa para picada de insectos? [tayng alg**oo**ma k**oh**-iza – ins**eh**toosh]
insect repellent o repele-insectos [rip**eh**l ins**eh**toosh]
inside dentro [d**ay**ntroo]
inside the hotel dentro do hotel [dwoht**eh**l]
let's sit inside vamos sentar-nos lá dentro [v**a**moosh sent**a**r-noosh]
insist insistir [insisht**ee**r]
I insist insisto [ins**ee**shtoo]
insomnia a insónia [ins**o**n-ya]
instant coffee o café instantâneo [kaf**eh** inshtant**a**n-yoo]
instead em vez [ayng vaysh]
give me that one instead dê-me antes aquele [daym antsh ak**ay**l]
instead of ... em vez de ... [di]
insulin a insulina [insool**ee**na]
insurance o seguro [sig**oo**roo]
intelligent inteligente [intiliJ**ay**nt]

interested: I'm interested in ... (said by a man/woman) estou muito interessado/ interessada em ... [shtoh mweengtoo intrisadoo – ayng]
interesting interessante [intrisant]
that's very interesting isso é muito interessante [eesoo eh mweengtoo]
international internacional [intayrnas-yoonal]
Internet Internet [intirneht]
interpret interpretar [interpritar]
interpreter (man/woman) o/a intérprete [intehrprit]
intersection o cruzamento [kroozamayntoo]
interval (at theatre) o intervalo [intervaloo]
into para
I'm not into ... não me interesso por ... [nowng mintrehsoo poor]
introduce apresentar [aprizentar]
may I introduce ...? posso apresentar ... [posoo]
invitation o convite [konveet]
invite convidar [konvidar]
Ireland a Irlanda [eerlanda]
Irish irlandês [eerlandaysh]
I'm Irish (man/woman) sou irlandês/sou irlandesa [soh – eerlandayza]
iron (for ironing) o ferro de engomar [fehrroo dayngoomar]
can you iron these for me? pode engomar-me isto? [pod ayngoomarm eeshtoo]
is* é [eh]; está [shta]
island a ilha [eel-ya]
it* o [oo], (f) a
it is ... é ... [eh]; está ... [shta]
is it ...? é ...?; está ...?
where is it? onde é? [ohndeh]; onde está?
it's him é ele [ayl]
it was ... era ... [ehra]; estava ... [shtava]
Italian (adj, language) italiano [ital-yanoo]
Italy Itália [ital-ya]
itch: it itches faz comichão [fash koomishowng]

J

jack (for car) o macaco [makakoo]
jacket o casaco [kazakoo]
jam a compota
jammed: it's jammed está encravado [shta aynkravadoo]
January Janeiro [Janayroo]
jar o jarro
jaw a maxila [makseela]
jazz o jazz
jealous ciumento [s-yoomayntoo]
jeans os jeans
jellyfish a alforreca [alfoorrehka]
jersey a camisola [kamizola]
jetty o pontão [pontowng]
jeweller's a ourivesaria [ohrivezaree-a]
jewellery a joalharia [Jwal-

yaree-a]
Jewish judaico [Joodīkoo]
job o emprego [aympraygoo]
jogging o jogging
to go jogging praticar jogging
joke a piada [p-yada]
journey a viagem [v-yaJayng]
have a good journey! boa viagem! [boh-a]
jug o jarro [Jarroo]
a jug of water um jarro de água [oong – dagwa]
juice o sumo [soomoo]
July Julho [Jool-yoo]
jump pular [poolar]
jumper a camisola [kamizola]
jump leads os cabos para ligar a bateria [kaboosh – batiree-a]
junction o cruzamento [kroozamayntoo]
June Junho [Joon-yoo]

June is festival month in Portugal. June 10th is a national holiday (the national day of Portugal and a celebration of the poet Camões). Each town and village also celebrates its own saint's day (many of which are in June) with street parties, music and dancing; all shops and many restaurants close on these holidays. Lisbon's saint's day honours Santo Antonio on June 13th. Pots of marjoram are displayed on every windowsill and the Alfama region of the city is turned into one large all-night street party, with people setting up impromptu sardine barbecues outside their houses and handing wine and food out to passers-by. São João in Porto is celebrated on June 23rd, again with dancing and drinking in the streets, but with the added tradition of the city's youth running around hitting everyone in sight with squeaky plastic hammers. Note also that any holiday which falls on a Tuesday or Thursday is likely to be preceded or followed by a bridging day to make a long weekend, so facilities could be closed for a full four days.

just (only) só [saw]
just two só dois/duas
just for me só para mim [meeng]
just here aqui mesmo [akee mayJmoo]
not just now agora não [nowng]
we've just arrived acabámos de chegar [akabamooJ di shigar]

K

keep guardar [gwardar]
keep the change guarde o troco [gward oo trohkoo]
can I keep it? posso ficar com ele/ela? [posoo fikar kong ayl/ehla]
you can keep it pode ficar com ele/ela [pod]

ketchup o ketchup
kettle a chaleira [shal**ay**ra]
key a chave [shav]
the key for room 201, please a chave do quarto duzentos e um, faz favor [doo kw**a**rtoo dooz**ay**ntooz-yoong fash fav**oh**r]
keyring o chaveiro [shav**ay**roo]
kidneys (in body, food) os rins [reengsh]
kill mat**a**r
kilo* o quilo [k**ee**loo]
kilometre* o quilómetro [kil**o**mitroo]
how many kilometres is it to ...? quantos quilómetros são até ...? [kw**a**ntoosh kil**o**mitroosh sowng at**eh**]
kind (generous) am**á**vel
that's very kind é muito amável [eh mw**ee**ngtoo]

dialogue

which kind do you want? que tipo deseja? [ki t**ee**poo dis**ay**Ja]
I want this/that kind desejo este/aquele tipo [aysht/ak**ay**l]

king o rei [ray]
kiosk o quiosque [k-yoshk]
kiss o beijo [b**ay**Joo]
(verb) beijar [bayJ**a**r]
kitchen a cozinha [kooz**ee**n-ya]
kitchenette a cozinha pequena [pik**ay**na]
Kleenex® os lenços de papel [l**ay**nsoosh di pap**eh**l]
knee o joelho [Jw**ay**l-yoo]
knickers as cuecas de mulher [ash kw**eh**kaJ di mool-y**eh**r]
knife a faca [f**a**ka]
knock bater [bat**ay**r]
knock down atropelar [atropil**a**r]
he's been knocked down ele foi atropelado [el f**oh**-i atropil**a**doo]
knock over (object) derrubar [dirroob**a**r]
(pedestrian) atropelar [atropil**a**r]
know* (somebody, a place) conhecer [koon-yis**ai**r]
(something) sab**e**r
I don't know não sei [nowng say]
I didn't know that não sabia isso [nowng sab**ee**-a **ee**soo]
do you know where I can find ...? sabe onde posso encontrar ...? [s**a**bohnd p**o**swaynkontr**a**r]

L

label (on clothes) a etiqueta [etik**ay**ta]
(on bottles etc) o rótulo [r**o**tooloo]
ladies' room, ladies' (toilets) o quarto de banho das senhoras [kw**a**rtoo di b**a**n-yoo dash sin-y**o**rash]
ladies' wear a roupa de senhoras [r**oh**pa di]

lady a senhora [sin-**yo**ra]
lager a cerveja [sir**vay**-Ja]
see **beer**
lake o lago [**la**goo]
lamb (meat) o borrego [boor**ray**goo]
lamp o candeeiro [kand-**yay**roo]
lane (motorway) a faixa [**fī**sha]
(small road) a viela [v-**yeh**la]
language a língua [**lee**ngwa]
language course o curso de línguas [**koo**rsoo di **lee**ngwash]
large grande [grand]
last o último [**oo**ltimoo]
last week semana passada [sim**a**na]
last Friday sexta-feira passada [**say**shta-**fay**ra]
last night ontem à noite [**oh**ntayng a n**oh**-it]
what time is the last train to Fátima? a que horas parte o último comboio p**a**ra Fátima? [ky**o**rash part-yoo-**oo**ltimoo komb**oh**-yo]
late tarde [tard]
sorry I'm late desculpe o atraso [dishk**oo**lp oo atr**a**zoo]
the train was late o comboio estava atrasado [oo komb**oh**-yo sht**a**va atraz**a**doo]
we must go – we'll be late temos que ir – vamos atrasar-nos [**tay**moosh ki-**eer** – v**a**mooz-atraz**a**r noosh]
it's getting late está a ficar tarde [sht**a**-a fik**a**r]
later, later on mais tarde [mīsh]
I'll come back later volto mais tarde [v**o**ltoo]
see you later até logo [a-t**eh**]
latest o último [**oo**ltimoo]
by Wednesday at the latest quarta-feira o mais tard**a**r [kw**a**rta-f**ay**ra oo mīsh]
laugh rir [reer]
launderette a lavandaria automática [lavandar**ee**-a owtoom**a**tika]
laundromat a lavandaria automática [lavandar**ee**-a owtoom**a**tika]
laundry (clothes) a roupa p**a**ra lav**a**r [r**oh**pa]
(place) a lavandaria [lavandar**ee**-a]
lavatory os lavabos [lav**a**boosh]
law a lei [lay]
lawn o relvado [relv**a**doo]
lawyer (man/woman) o advogado [advoog**a**doo], a advog**a**da
laxative o laxativo [lashat**ee**voo]
lazy preguiçoso [prigis**oh**zoo]
lead (electrical) o fio [**fee**-oo]
(verb) conduzir [kondooz**ee**r]
where does this lead to? onde vai ter esta estrada? [ohnd vī tayr **eh**shta shtr**a**da]
leaf a folha [f**oh**l-ya]
leaflet o panfleto [panfl**ay**too]
leak a fuga [**foo**ga]
(verb) ter uma fuga [tayr **oo**ma]
the roof leaks há uma fuga de água no telhado [a – d**a**gwa noo til-y**a**doo]
learn aprender [apraynd**ay**r]

English → Portuguese

Le

least: not in the least de nenhum modo [di nin-y**oo**ng m**o**doo]
at least pelo menos [p**i**loo m**ay**noosh]
leather o cabedal [kabid**a**l]
leave (depart) partir [part**ee**r]
(behind) deixar [daysh**a**r]
I am leaving tomorrow parto amanhã [p**a**rtoo aman-y**a**ng]
he left yesterday ele partiu ontem [ayl part**ee**-oo **oh**ntayng]
may I leave this here? posso deixar isto aqui? [p**o**soo – **ee**shtwak**ee**]
I left my coat in the bar deixei meu casaco no bar [daysh**ay** m**ay**-oo kaz**a**koo noo]
when does the bus for Lagos leave? quando parte o autocarro para Lagos? [kw**a**ndoo p**a**rtoo owtook**a**rroo – l**a**goosh]
leeks o alho francês [**a**l-yoo frans**ay**sh]
left esquerdo [shk**ay**rdoo]
on the left, to the left à esquerda [a shk**ay**rda]
turn left vire à esquerda [v**ee**ra]
there's none left não há mais [nowng a mīsh]
left-handed canhoto [kan-y**oh**too]
left luggage (office) o depósito de bagagem [dip**o**zitoo di bag**a**Jayng]
leg a perna [p**eh**rna]
lemon o limão [lim**ow**ng]
lemonade a limonada [limoon**a**da]
lemon tea o chá de limão [sha di lim**ow**ng]
lend emprestar [aympprisht**a**r]
will you lend me your ...? empresta-me o seu ...? [aympr**eh**shtamoo s**ay**-oo]
lens (of camera) a objectiva [obJet**ee**va]
lesbian a lésbica [l**eh**Jbika]
less* menos [m**ay**nosh]
less than menos do que [doo ki]
less expensive mais barato [mīJ bar**a**too]
lesson a lição [lis**ow**ng]
let (allow) deixar [daysh**a**r]
will you let me know? diz-me depois? [d**ee**Jmi dip**oh**-ish]
I'll let you know depois digo-lhe [d**ee**gool-yi]
let's go for something to eat vamos sair para comer alguma coisa [v**a**moosh sa-**ee**r – koom**ay**r algooma k**oh**-iza]
let off: will you let me off at ...? é capaz de parar em ...? [eh kap**a**J di – ayng]
letter a carta
do you have any letters for me? tem alguma carta para mim? [tayng alg**oo**ma – meeng]
letterbox o marco de correio [m**a**rkoo di koor**ay**-oo]

Ordinary letterboxes follow the British pillar-box design and are also painted red; the blue letterboxes are for express mail (**correio azul**).

lettuce a alface [alf**a**s]
lever a alav**a**nca
library a biblioteca [bibl-yoot**eh**ka]
licence a licença [lis**ay**nsa]
lid a t**a**mpa
lie (verb: tell untruth) mentir [maynt**ee**r]
lie down deitar-se [dayt**a**rsi]
life a vida [v**ee**da]
lifebelt o cinto de salvação [s**ee**ntoo di salvas**ow**ng]
lifeguard o banheiro [ban-y**ay**roo]
life jacket o colete de salvação [kool**ay**t di salvas**ow**ng]
lift (in building) o elevador [elevad**oh**r]
could you give me a lift? pode dar-me uma boleia? [pod d**a**rm**oo**ma bool**ay**-a]
would you like a lift? quer uma boleia? [kehr]
light a luz [loosh]
(not heavy) leve [lehv]
do you have a light? (for cigarette) tem lume? [tayng loom]
light green verde claro [vayrd kl**a**roo]
light bulb a l**â**mpada
I need a new light bulb preciso duma lâmpada [pris**ee**zoo d**oo**ma]
lighter (cigarette) o isqueiro [shk**ay**roo]

lightning a trovoada [troovw**a**da]
like gostar [goosht**a**r]
I like it gosto [g**o**shtoo]
I like going for walks gosto de passear a pé [di pas-y**a**r a peh]
I like you gosto de si [di see]
I don't like it não gosto [nowng]
do you like ...? você gosta de ...? [vos**ay** g**o**shta di]
I'd like a beer queria uma cerveja [kir**ee**-a **oo**ma sirv**ay**Ja]
I'd like to go swimming queria ir nad**a**r [eer]
would you like a drink? gostaria duma bebida? [gooshtar**ee**-a d**oo**ma bib**ee**da]
would you like to go for a walk? quer ir dar uma v**o**lta? [kehr]
what's it like? como é? [k**oh**moo eh]
I want one like this quero um como este [k**eh**roo oong kohmw**ay**sht]
lime a lima [l**ee**ma]
lime cordial o sumo de lima [s**oo**moo di]
line a linha [l**ee**n-ya]
could you give me an outside line? dá-me uma linha? [dam**oo**ma]
lips os lábios [l**a**b-yoosh]
lip salve o baton p**a**ra o cieiro [bat**o**ng – oo s-y**ay**roo]
lipstick o baton [bat**o**ng]
liqueur o licor [lik**oh**r]

Lisbon Lisboa [liJ**boh**-a]
listen escutar [shkoo**tar**]
litre* o litro [**lee**troo]
a litre of white wine um litro de vinho branco [di **veen**-yoo br**a**nkoo]
little pequeno [pik**ay**noo]
just a little, thanks só um pouco, por favor [saw oong p**oh**koo poor fav**oh**r]
a little milk pouco leite [layt]
a little bit more um pouquinho mais [oong pohk**ee**n-yoo mīsh]
live (verb) viver [viv**ay**r]
we live together vivemos juntos [viv**ay**mooJ J**oo**ntoosh]

dialogue

where do you live? onde é que vive? [ohnd**eh** ki veev]
I live in London vivo em Londres [**vee**vwayng l**oh**ndrish]

lively animado [anim**a**doo]
liver (in body, food) o fígado [**fee**gadoo]
loaf o pão [powng]
lobby (in hotel) o hall
lobster a lagosta [lag**oh**shta]
local local [look**al**]
can you recommend a local wine? pode recomendar um vinho da região? [pod rikoomaynd**ar** oong v**ee**n-yoo da riJ-y**ow**ng]
can you recommend a local restaurant? pode recomendar um restaurante local? [rishtawr**ant**]
lock a fechadura [fishad**oo**ra]
(verb) fechar à chave [fish**ar** a shav]
it's locked está fechado à chave [shta fish**a**dwa shav]
lock out: I've locked myself out (of room) fechei o quarto com a chave lá dentro [fish**ay** oo kw**ar**too kong – d**ay**ntroo]
locker (for luggage etc) o cacifo [kas**ee**foo]
lollipop o chupa-chupa [sh**oo**pa–]
London Londres [l**oh**ndrish]
long comprido [kompr**ee**doo]
how long will it take to fix it? quanto tempo vai demorar para consertar? [kw**a**ntoo t**ay**mpoo vī dimoor**ar** – konsirt**ar**]
how long does it take? quanto tempo demora? [dim**o**ra]
a long time muito tempo [mw**ee**ngtoo]
one day/two days longer mais um dia/dois dias [mīz oong d**ee**-a/d**o**-iJ d**ee**-ash]
long-distance call a chamada de longa distância [sham**a**da di – disht**a**ns-ya]
look: I'm just looking, thanks (said by man/woman) estou só a ver, obrigado/obrigada [shtoh saw a vayr obrig**a**doo]
you don't look well parece não estar bem [par**eh**s nowng

shtar bayng]
look out! cuidado! [kwid**a**doo]
can I have a look? posso ver? [p**o**soo vayr]
look after tomar conta (de) [toom**a**r k**oh**nta]
look at olhar (para) [ol-y**a**r]
look for procurar [prookoor**a**r]
I'm looking for ... procuro ... [prook**oo**roo]
loose (handle etc) solto [s**oh**ltoo]
lorry o camião [kam-y**ow**ng]
lose perder [pird**ay**r]
I've lost my way perdi-me [pird**ee**m]
I'm lost, I want to get to ... (said by man/woman) estou perdido/perdida, quero ir para ... [shtoh pird**ee**doo – k**eh**roo eer]
I've lost my bag perdi o meu saco [pird**ee** oo m**ay**-oo s**a**koo]
lost property (office) a secção de perdidos e achados [sehks**ow**ng di pird**ee**dooz ee-ash**a**doosh]
lot: a lot, lots muito [mw**ee**ngtoo]
not a lot não muito [nowng]
a lot of people muita gente [mw**ee**ngta Jayngt]
a lot bigger muito maior [mī-**o**r]
I like it a lot gosto imenso [g**o**shtoo im**ay**nsoo]
lotion a loção [loos**ow**ng]
loud alto [**a**ltoo]
lounge (in house, hotel) a sala
(in airport) a sala de espera [dishp**eh**ra]
love o amor [am**oh**r]
(verb) amar
I love Portugal adoro Portugal [ad**o**roo poortoog**a**l]
lovely (meal, food) delicioso [dilis-y**oh**zoo]
(view) encantador [aynkantad**oh**r]
(weather) excelente [ish-sil**ay**nt]
(present) adorável
low baixo [b**ī**shoo]
luck a sorte [sort]
good luck! boa sorte! [b**oh**-a]
luggage a bagagem [bag**a**Jayng]
luggage trolley o carrinho de bagagem [karr**ee**n-yoo di]
lump (on body) o inchaço [insh**a**soo]
lunch o almoço [alm**oh**soo]
lungs os pulmões [poolm**oy**ngsh]
luxurious (hotel, furnishings) luxuoso [loosh-w**oh**zoo]
luxury o luxo [l**oo**shoo]

M

machine a máquina [m**a**kina]
mad (insane) doido [d**oh**-idoo]
(angry) zangado [zang**a**doo]
Madeira (place) a Madeira [mad**ay**ra]
(wine) o (vinho da) Madeira [v**ee**n-yoo]

Madeira is from Portugal's Atlantic island province. Widely available, it comes in four main varieties: **Sercial** (a dry aperitif), **Verdelho** (a medium-dry aperitif), **Bual** (a medium-sweet wine) and **Malvasia** (Malmsey, a sweet, heavy dessert wine). Each improves with age and special vintages are very expensive.

magazine a revista [ri**vee**shta]
maid (in hotel) a criada [kr-**ya**da]
maiden name o nome de solteira [nohm di sool**tay**ra]
mail o correio [koo**rray**-oo]
(verb) pôr no correio [pohr noo]
is there any mail for me? há algum correio p**a**ra mim? [a alg**oo**m – meeng]
see **post office**
mailbox o marco de correio [m**ar**koo di koo**ray**-oo], a caixa do correio [k**ī**sha doo]
see **letterbox**
main principal [prinsip**al**]
main course o prato principal [pr**a**too prinsip**al**]
main post office a central de correios [sentr**al** di koorr**ay**-oosh]
main road (in town) a rua principal [r**oo**-a prinsip**al**]
(in country) a estrada principal [shtr**a**da]
mains switch o disjuntor principal [diJoont**ohr**]
make* (brand name) a m**a**rca
(verb) fazer [faz**ay**r]
I make it 500 escudos calculo que sejam quinhentos escudos [kalk**oo**loo ki s**ay**Jowng kin-**yay**ntooz-shk**oo**doosh]
what is it made of? de que é feito? [di k-yeh f**ay**too]
make-up a maquilhagem [makil-y**a**Jayng]
man o homem [**oh**mayng]
manager o gerente [Jer**ay**nt]
can I see the manager? pode chamar o gerente? [pod sham**ar**]
manageress a gerente
manual manual [manw**al**]
many muitos [m**wee**ngtoosh]
not many não muitos [nowng]
map o m**a**pa

You can pick up a wide range of free brochures and maps from the Portuguese National Tourist Office before you go. Once in Portugal, local tourist offices (**turismo**) often have useful local maps and leaflets that you won't find in the national offices. However, if you're doing any real exploration, or driving, it's worth investing in a good road map.

March Março [m**ar**soo]
margarine a margarina [margar**ee**na]
market o mercado [mirk**a**doo]
marmalade a comp**o**ta de laranja [di lar**a**nJa]

married: I'm married (said by a man/woman) sou casado/casada [soh kaz**a**doo]
are you married? você é casado/casada? [vos**ay** eh]
mascara o rímel [**ree**mil]
match (football etc) o jogo [J**oh**goo]
matches os fósforos [**fo**shfooroosh]
material (fabric) o tecido [tis**ee**doo]
matter: it doesn't matter não faz mal [n**ow**ng faJ m**a**l]
what's the matter? o que se passa? [oo ki si]
mattress o colchão [koolsh**ow**ng]
May Maio [m**ī**-oo]
may: may I have another one? (different one) pode dar-me outro/outra? [pod d**a**rmi **oh**troo]
may I come in? posso entrar? [p**o**swayntr**a**r]
may I see it? posso vê-lo/vê-la? [p**o**soo v**ay**loo/v**ay**la]
may I sit here? posso sentar-me aqui? [p**o**soo saynt**a**rm ak**ee**]
maybe talvez [talv**ay**sh]
mayonnaise a maionese [mī-on**eh**z]
me* mim [meeng]
that's for me isto é para mim [**ee**shtw**eh** p**a**ra meeng]
send it to me envie-o/a para mim [aynv**ee**-yoo]
me too eu também [**ay**-oo tamb**ay**ng]
meal a refeição [rifays**ow**ng]

dialogue

did you enjoy your meal? gostou da comida? [goosht**oh** da koom**ee**da]
it was excellent, thank you (said by man/woman) estava excelente, obrigado/obrigada [sht**a**va ish-sel**ay**nt obrig**a**doo]

mean: what do you mean? o que quer dizer? [oo ki kehr diz**ay**r]

dialogue

what does this word mean? o que significa esta palavra? [oo ki signif**ee**ka **eh**shta]
it means ... in English significa ... em inglês [ayng ingl**ay**sh]

measles o sarampo [sar**a**mpoo]
meat a carne [karn]
mechanic o mecânico [mek**a**nikoo]
medicine o remédio [rim**eh**d-yoo]
Mediterranean o Mediterrâneo [miditirr**a**n-yoo]
medium médio [m**eh**d-yoo]
medium-dry meio seco [m**ay**-oo s**ay**koo]
medium-rare médio [m**eh**d-yoo]

medium-sized de tamanho médio [di taman-yoo]
meet encontrar [aynkontrar]
nice to meet you muito prazer [mweengtoo prazayr]
where shall I meet you? onde nos encontramos? [ohnd noozaynkontramoosh]
meeting a reunião [r-yoon-yowng]
meeting place o local de encontro [lookal daynkohntroo]
melon o melão [milowng]
men os homens [ohmayngsh]
mend consertar [konsirtar]
could you mend this for me? pode consertar-me isto? [pod konsirtarm eeshtoo]
menswear a roupa de homens [rohpa dohmayngsh]
mention mencionar [mayns-yoonar]
don't mention it não tem de quê [nowng tayng di kay]
menu a ementa [emaynta]
may I see the menu, please? posso ver a ementa, faz favor [posoo vayr īmaynta fash favohr]
see **menu reader** page 248
message o recado [rikadoo]
are there any messages for me? há algum recado para mim? [a algoong – meeng]
I want to leave a message for ... gostava de deixar um recado para ... [gooshtava di dayshar oong]
metal o metal [mital]
metre* o metro [mehtroo]
microwave (oven) microondas [mikroo-ohndash]
midday o meio-dia [may-oo dee-a]
at midday ao meio-dia [ow]
middle: in the middle no meio [noo may-oo]
in the middle of the night no meio da noite [noh-it]
the middle one o/a do meio [oo/a doo]
midnight a meia-noite [may-a noh-it]
at midnight à meia-noite
might: I might go pode ser que eu vá [pod sayr ki-ay-oo]
I might not go pode ser que eu não vá [nowng]
I might want to stay another day sou capaz de querer ficar mais um dia [soh kapaJ di kirayr fikar mīsh oong dee-a]
migraine a enxaqueca [aynshakayka]
mild (taste) suave [swav]
(weather) ameno [amaynoo]
mile* a milha [meel-ya]
milk o leite [layt]
milkshake o batido [bateedoo]
millimetre* o milímetro [mileemitroo]
minced meat a carne picada [karn pikada]
mind: never mind não faz mal [nowng faJ mal]
I've changed my mind mudei de ideias [mooday diday-yash]

dialogue

do you mind if I open the window? importa-se se abrir a janela? [importasi s-yabreer a Janehla]
no, I don't mind não, não me importo [nowng mimportoo]

mine*: it's mine é meu [eh may-oo]
mineral water a água mineral [agwa]
mints as pastilhas de mentol [pashteel-yaJ di]
minute o minuto [minootoo]
in a minute dentro de um momento [dayntroo doong moomayntoo]
just a minute um momento [oong]
mirror o espelho [shpayl-yoo]
Miss a Senhora [sin-yora]
Miss! se faz favor! [si fash favohr]
miss: I missed the bus perdi o autocarro [pirdee oo-owtookarro]
missing falta
there's a suitcase missing falta uma mala [ooma]
mist a névoa [nehvwa]
mistake o erro [ayrroo]
I think there's a mistake julgo que há um erro [Joolgoo k-ya oong]
sorry, I've made a mistake desculpe, enganei-me [dishkoolp aynganaym]
misunderstanding o mal-entendido [malayntayndeedoo]
mix-up: sorry, there's been a mix-up desculpe, houve uma confusão [ohvooma konfoozowng]
mobile phone o telemóvel [telemovil]
modern moderno [moodehrnoo]
modern art gallery a galeria de arte moderna [galiree-a dart moodehrna]
moisturizer o creme hidratante [kraymeedratant]
moment: I won't be a moment não demoro nada [nowng dimoroo]
monastery o mosteiro [mooshtayroo]
Monday segunda-feira [segoonda fayra]
money o dinheiro [deen-yayroo]
month o mês [maysh]
monument o monumento [moonoomayntoo]
moon a lua [loo-a]
Moor o mouro [moh-ooroo]
Moorish mourisco [moreeshkoo]
moped a motorizada [mootoorizada]
more* mais [mīsh]
can I have some more water, please? mais água, por favor [mīz agwa poor favohr]
more expensive mais caro

[maīsh k**a**roo]
more interesting mais interessante [mīzintris**a**nt]
more than 50 mais de cinquenta [mīz di sinkw**ay**nta]
more than that mais do que isso [mīz doo ki **ee**soo]
a lot more muito mais [m**wee**ngtoo mīsh]

dialogue

would you like some more? deseja um pouco mais? [dis**ay**Ja oong p**oh**koo mīsh]
no, no more for me, thanks (said by man/woman) não, não mais para mim, obrigado/obrigada [nowng – meeng obrig**a**doo]
how about you? e você? [ee vos**ay**]
I don't want any more, thanks (said by man/woman) não quero mais, obrigado/obrigada [nowng k**eh**roo mīsh]

morning a manhã [man-y**a**ng]
this morning esta manhã [**eh**shta]
in the morning de manhã [di]
Morocco o Marrocos [marr**o**koosh]
mosquito o mosquito [mooshk**ee**too]

Mosquitoes can be intolerable at certain times of year and in certain areas but there seems to be no pattern to this, though the north is often cited as being particularly bad. December and January are usually mosquito-free. Mosquito-repellent lotion and coils are widely sold in towns and resorts.

mosquito repellent o repele-mosquitos [rip**eh**l mooshk**ee**toosh]
most: I like this one most of all gosto mais deste [g**o**shtoo mīJ daysht]
most of the time a maior parte do tempo [a mī-**or** part doo t**ay**mpoo]
most tourists a maioria dos turistas [mī-oor**ee**-a doosh toor**ee**shtash]
mostly principalmente [prinsipalm**ay**nt]
mother a mãe [mayng]
motorbike a motocicleta [mootoosikl**eh**ta]
motorboat o barco a motor [b**a**rkwa moot**oh**r]
motorway a autoestrada [owtooshtr**a**da]

The motorway network is gradually expanding from a central spine that links Lisbon with Porto and the Algarve. The motorways are all toll roads, which adds to the cost of a journey

Mo

but has one distinct advantage for foreign visitors: because of the relatively high tolls, local drivers have been priced off the motorways, making them the least congested in Europe.
see **driving**

mountain a montanha [mont**a**n-ya]
in the mountains nas montanhas [naJ mont**a**n-yash]
mountaineering o alpinismo [alpin**ee**Jmoo]
mouse o rato [**ra**too]
moustache o bigode [big**od**]
mouth a boca [b**oh**ka]
mouth ulcer a **a**fta
move (one's car, house etc) mudar [mood**ar**]
he's moved to another room mudou-se para outra s**a**la [mood**oh**si p**a**ra **oh**tra]
could you move your car? podia mudar o s**eu** c**a**rro? [pood**ee**-a]
could you move up a little? pode chegar um pouquinho p**a**ra lá? [pod shig**ar** oong pohk**ee**n-yoo]
where has it moved to? p**a**ra onde se mudou? [**oh**ndsi mood**oh**]
movie o filme [feelm]
movie theater o cinema [sin**ay**ma]
Mr o Senhor [sin-y**ohr**]
Mrs a Senhora [sin-y**o**ra]
much muito [mw**ee**ngtoo]
much better/worse muito melhor/pior [mil-y**or**/pi-**or**]
much hotter muito mais quente [mīsh kaynt]
not (very) much não muito [nowng]
I don't want very much não quero muito [k**eh**roo]
mud a l**a**ma
mug (for drinking) a caneca [kan**eh**ka]
I've been mugged (said by man/woman) fui assaltado/ assalt**a**da [fwee asalt**a**doo]
mum a mamã [mam**a**ng]
mumps a papeira [pap**ay**ra]
museum o museu [mooz**ay**-oo]

Museums, churches and monuments are open from around 10 a.m. to 12.30 p.m. and from 2 to 6 p.m., though the larger ones stay open through lunchtime. Almost all museums are closed on Mondays; also almost everything is closed on national public holidays and local holidays.

mushrooms os cogumelos [kogoom**eh**loosh]
music a música [m**oo**zika]
musician (man) o músico [m**oo**zikoo]
Muslim (adj) muçulmano [moosoolm**a**noo]
mussels os mexilhões [mishil-y**oy**ngsh]
must: I must ... tenho de ... [t**ay**n-yoo di]

I mustn't drink alcohol não devo beber álcool [nowng **day**voo bib**ayr** **al**ko-ol]
mustard a mostarda [mooshtarda]
my* o meu [**may**-oo], a minha [**meen**-ya], os meus [**may**-oosh], as minhas [**meen**-yash]
myself: I'll do it myself (said by man/woman) eu mesmo/mesma faço isso [**ay**-oo **may**Jmoo – **f**asoo **ee**soo]
by myself (said by man/woman) sozinho [soz**ee**n-yoo]/sozinha

N

nail (finger) a unha [**oo**n-ya]
(metal) o prego [pr**eh**goo]
nailbrush a escova de unhas [shk**oh**va d**oo**n-yash]
nail varnish o verniz de unhas [virn**ee**J d**oo**n-yash]
name o nome [nohm]
my name's John o meu nome é John [oo **may**-oo nohm eh]
what's your name? como se chama? [**koh**moo si sh**a**ma]
what is the name of this street? qual é o nome desta rua? [kawl**eh** oo nohm d**eh**shta r**oo**-a]

Most Portuguese have several names: one or two Christian names and at least two surnames (the mother's last surname and the father's last surname). Portuguese names are often extremely long, especially those for distinguished families. This is because 'good' family names are retained when people get married. It is usual for the woman to add her husband's surname after her own family name. So if Maria Amaro Pires marries João Costa, she may become Maria Amaro Pires Costa.

napkin o guardanapo [gwardan**a**poo]
nappy a fralda
narrow (street) estreito [shtr**ay**too]
nasty (person) mau [mow], (f) má
(weather, accident) grave [grav]
national nacional [nas-yoon**a**l]
nationality a nacionalidade [nas-yoonalid**a**d]
natural natural [natoor**a**l]
nausea as náuseas [n**ow**z-yash]
navy (blue) azul-marinho [az**oo**l mar**ee**n-yoo]
near perto [p**eh**rtoo]
is it near the city centre? é perto do centro da cidade? [eh – doo s**ay**ntroo da sid**a**d]
do you go near the Paço Real? passa perto do Passo Real? [p**eh**rtoo doo p**a**soo ri-**a**l]
where is the nearest ...? onde fica o/a ... mais próximo/próxima ...? [ohnd f**ee**ka oo/a ... mīsh pr**o**simoo]
nearby perto daqui [p**eh**rtoo

dakee]
nearly quase [kwaz]
necessary necessário [nisisar-yoo]
neck o pescoço [pishkohsoo]
necklace o colar [koolar]
necktie a gravata
need: I need ... preciso de ... [priseezoo di]
do I need to pay? preciso de pagar?
needle a agulha [agool-ya]
negative (film) o negativo [nigateevoo]
neither: neither (one) of them nenhum deles [nin-yoong daylish]
neither ... nor ... nem ... nem ... [nayng]
nephew o sobrinho [soobreen-yoo]
net (in sport) a rede [rayd]
Netherlands a Holanda [olanda]
network map o mapa
never nunca [noonka]

dialogue

have you ever been to Fátima? já esteve em Fátima? [Jashtayvayng]
no, never, I've never been there não, nunca estive lá [nowng noonkshteev la]

new novo [nohvoo]
news (radio, TV etc) as notícias [nootees-yash]
newsagent's a tabacaria [tabakaree-a]
newspaper o jornal [Joornal]
newspaper kiosk o quiosque de jornais [k-yoshk di Joornīsh]
New Year Ano Novo [anoo nohvoo]

The Portuguese celebrate New Year's Eve (**Véspera de Ano Novo**) in parties at home, with friends or at restaurants. January 6th, **Dia de Reis**, is not as important in Portugal as in Spain, but there is a special cake baked for this day which contains a broad bean and a present; the person who gets the broad bean is supposed to pay for the cake next year. Dia de Reis is celebrated more in country areas, where traditionally people go from door to door, singing and improvising songs about the owner of the house and are invited in for something to eat.

Happy New Year! Feliz Ano Novo! [fileez anoo nohvoo]
New Year's Eve a véspera do dia de Ano Novo [vehshpira doo dee-a danoo]
New Zealand Nova Zelândia [nova ziland-ya]
New Zealander: I'm a New Zealander (man/woman) sou neo-zelandês/neo-zelandesa [soh neh-o zilandaysh/neh-o zilandayza]

next próximo [prosimoo]
the next corner/street on the left a próxima esquina/rua à esquerda [shkeena/roo-a a shkayrda]
at the next stop na próxima paragem [paraJayng]
next week na próxima semana [simana]
next to próximo de [di]
nice (food, person) agradável (looks, view etc) bonito [booneetoo]
niece a sobrinha [soobreen-ya]
night a noite [noh-it]
at night à noite
good night boa noite [boh-a]

dialogue

do you have a single room for one night? tem um quarto individual para uma noite? [tayn-yoong kwartwindividwal para ooma]
yes, madam sim, senhora [seeng sin-yora]
how much is it per night? quanto é por noite? [kwantweh poor]
it's 600 escudos for one night são seiscentos escudos por uma noite [sowng saysayntooshkoodoosh poor ooma]
thank you, I'll take it (said by man/woman) obrigado/obrigada, fico com ele [obrigadoo – feekoo kong ayl]

nightclub a boite [bwat]
nightdress a camisa de dormir [kameeza di doormeer]
night porter o porteiro da noite [poortayroo da noh-it]
no* não [nowng]
I've no change não tenho troco [tayn-yoo trohkoo]
there's no ... left não há mais ... [a mīsh]
no way! de maneira nenhuma! [di manayra nin-yooma]
oh no! (upset) oh não! [nowng]
nobody* ninguém [ningayng]
there's nobody there não há ninguém lá [nowng a – la]
noise o barulho [barool-yoo]
noisy: it's too noisy é barulhento demais [eh barool-yayntoo dimīsh]
non-alcoholic não alcoólico [nowng alkwolikoo]
none* nenhum [nin-yoong]
nonsmoking carriage a carruagem para não fumadores [karrwaJayng – nowng foomadohrish]
noon o meio-dia [may-oo dee-a]
no-one* ninguém [ningayng]
nor: nor do I nem eu [nayng ay-oo]
normal normal
north o norte [nort]
in the north no norte [noo]
to the north ao norte [ow]
north of Braga ao norte de Braga [di]

northeast o nordeste [noordehsht]
northern setentrional [setayntr-yoonal]
Northern Ireland a Irlanda do Norte [eerlanda doo nort]
northwest o noroeste [norwehsht]
Norway a Noruega [noorwehga]
Norwegian (adj) norueguês [noorwegaysh]
nose o nariz [nareesh]
nosebleed a hemorragia nasal [emoorraJee-ya nazal]
not* não [nowng]
no, I'm not hungry não, não tenho fome [tayn-yoo fohm]
I don't want anything, thank you (said by man/woman) não quero nada, obrigado/obrigada [kehroo – obrigadoo]
it's not necessary não é necessário [eh nesesar-yoo]
I didn't know that não sabia [sabee-a]
not that one – this one esse não – este [ays – aysht]
note (banknote) a nota
notebook o bloco de apontamentos [blokoo dapontamayntoosh]
notepaper (for letters) o papel de carta [papehl di]
nothing* nada
nothing for me, thanks (said by man/woman) nada para mim, obrigado/obrigada [meeng obrigadoo]
nothing else mais nada [mīJ]
novel o romance [roomans]
November Novembro [noovaymbroo]
now agora
number o número [noomiroo]
I've got the wrong number enganei-me no número [aynganaym noo]
what is your phone number? qual é o número do seu telefone? [kwaleh oo – doo say-oo telefohn]
number plate a chapa da matrícula [shapa da matreekoola]
nurse (man/woman) o enfermeiro [aynfirmayroo], a enfermeira
nut (for bolt) a porca
nuts a noz [nosh]

O

occupied (toilet, telephone) ocupado [okoopadoo]
o'clock* horas [orash]
October Outubro [ohtoobroo]
odd (strange) estranho [shtran-yoo]
of* de [di]
off (lights) desligado [diJligadoo]
it's just off Praça do Comércio mesmo ao lado da Praça do Comércio [meJmoo ow ladoo da prasa doo koomehrs-yoo]
we're off tomorrow partimos

amanhã [parteemoozaman-yang]
offensive (language, behaviour) ofensivo [ofaynseevoo]
office (place of work) o escritório [shkritor-yoo]
officer (said to policeman) Senhor Guarda [sin-yohr gwarda]
often muitas vezes [mweengtaJ vayzish]
not often não muitas vezes [nowng]
how often are the buses? com que frequência há autocarros? [kong ki frikwaynsya a owtookarroosh]
oil (for car, for cooking) o óleo [ol-yoo]
ointment a pomada [poomada]
OK está bem [shta bayng]
are you OK? você está bem? [vosay shta bayng]
is that OK with you? está bem para si? [see]
is it OK to ...? pode-se ...? [podsi]
that's OK thanks (said by man/woman) está bem obrigado/obrigada [obrigadoo]
I'm OK, thanks (I've got enough) não quero, obrigado/obrigada [nowng kehro]
(I feel OK) sinto-me bem [seentoom]
is this train OK for ...? este comboio vai para ... [aysht kombohyoo vī]
I'm sorry, OK? desculpe-me, está bem? [dishkoolpimi]
old velho [vehl-yoo]

dialogue

how old are you? que idade tem? [keedad tayng]
I'm 25 tenho vinte-e-cinco anos [tayn-yoo veentiseenkoo]
and you? e você? [ee vosay]

old-fashioned antiquado [antikwadoo]
old town (old part of town) a cidade antiga [sidad anteega]
in the old town na cidade antiga
olive oil o azeite [azayt]
olives a azeitona [azaytohna]
black/green olives as azeitonas pretas/verdes [azaytohnash praytash/vayrdsh]
omelette a omeleta [omilayta]
on* sobre [sohbr]
on the street/beach na praia/rua
is it on this road? é nesta rua? [eh nehshta]
on the plane no avião [nwav-yowng]
on Saturday no sábado [noo]
on television na televisão
I haven't got it on me não o tenho comigo [nowng oo tayn-yoo koomeegoo]
this one's on me (drink) esta bebida sou eu que pago [ehshta bibeeda soh ay-oo kih

pagoo]
the light wasn't on a luz não estava acesa [looJ nowng shtava asayza]
what's on tonight? qual é o programa para esta noite? [kwaleh oo proograma parehshta noh-it]
once (one time) uma vez [ooma vaysh]
at once (immediately) imediatamente [imid-yatamaynt]
one* um [oong], uma [ooma]
the white one o/a branco/branca [oo/a brankoo]
one-way ticket o bilhete simples [bil-yayt seemplish]
onion a cebola [sibohla]
only só [saw], somente [somaynt]
only one só um/uma [oong/ooma]
it's only 6 o'clock ainda são só seis horas [a-eenda sowng saw sayz orash]
I've only just got here acabei de chegar [akabay di shigar]
on/off switch o interruptor de ligar/desligar [intirrooptohr di ligar/diJligar]
open* (adj) aberto [abehrtoo]
(verb) abrir [abreer]
when do you open? quando abre? [kwandwabr]
I can't get it open não consigo abrir [nowng konseegwabreer]
in the open air ao ar livre [ow ar leevr]
opening times as horas de abertura [orash dabirtoora]
open ticket o bilhete em aberto [bil-yaytayng abehrtoo]
opera a ópera [opira]
operation (medical) a operação [opirasowng]
operator (telephone: man/woman) o/a telefonista [telefooneeshta]

For European numbers dial 099 and for the rest of the world dial 098.

opposite: the opposite direction na direcção oposta [direhsowng oposhta]
the bar opposite o bar do outro lado [doo ohtroo ladoo]
opposite my hotel em frente ao meu hotel [ayng fraynt ow]
optician o oculista [okooleeshta]
or ou [oh]
orange (fruit) a laranja [laranJa]
(colour) cor de laranja [kohr di]
orange juice (fresh) o sumo de laranja [soomoo]
(fizzy) a laranjada com gás [laranJada kongash]
(diluted) o refresco de laranja [rifrayshkoo di]
orchestra a orquestra [orkehshtra]
order: can we order now? (in restaurant) podemos pedir agora? [poodaymoosh pideer]
I've already ordered, thanks

(said by man/woman) já pedi, obrigado/obrigada [Ja pidee obrigadoo]
I didn't order this não pedi isto [nowng – eeshtoo]
out of order avariado [avar-yadoo]
ordinary vulgar [voolgar]
other outro [ohtroo]
the other one o outro [oo]
the other day outro dia [dee-a]
I'm waiting for the others estou a esperar outras pessoas [stoh a shpirar ohtrash pisoh-ash]
do you have any others? tem mais algum/alguma? [tayng mīsh algoong/algooma]
otherwise doutro modo [dohtroo modoo]
our* nosso [nosoo], nossa [nosa], nossos [nosoosh], nossas [nosash]
ours* nosso, nossa, nossos, nossas
out: he's out saiu [sa-ee-oo]
three kilometres out of town a três quilómetros da cidade [traysh kilomitrooJ da sidad]
outdoors fora de casa [di kaza]
outside do lado de fora [doo ladoo di]
can we sit outside? podemos sentar-nos lá fora? [poodaymoosh sayntarnoosh]
oven o forno [fohrnoo]
over: over here aqui [akee]
over there ali [alee]
over five hundred mais de quinhentos/quinhentas [mīsh di]
it's over terminado [tirminadoo]
overcharge: you've overcharged me você vendeu-me mais caro [vosay venday-oomi mīsh karoo]
overcoat o sobretudo [soobritoodoo]
overlooking: I'd like a room overlooking the courtyard queria um quarto que dê para o pátio [kiree-a oong kwartoo ki day paroo pat-yoo]
overnight (travel) de noite [di noh-it]
overtake ultrapassar [ooltrapasar]
owe: how much do I owe you? quanto lhe devo? [kwantoo l-yi dayvoo]
own: my own ... o meu próprio ... [oo may-oo propr-yoo]
are you on your own? (to man/woman) está sozinho/sozinha? [shta sawzeen-yoo]
I'm on my own (said by man/woman) estou sozinho/sozinha [shtoh]
owner (man/woman) o dono [dohnoo], a dona
oysters as ostras [ohshtrash]

P

pack fazer as malas [fazayr aJ malash]
a pack of ... um pacote de ... [oong pakot di]
package (parcel) a encomenda [aynkoomaynda]
package holiday a excursão organizada [shkoorsowng organizada]
packed lunch o almoço embalado [almohsw-aymbaladoo]
packet: a packet of cigarettes o maço de cigarros [masoo di sigarroosh]
padlock o cadeado [kad-yadoo]
page (of book) a página [paJina]
could you page Mr ...? pode chamar o Sr ...? [pod shamar oo sin-yohr]
pain a dor [dohr]
I have a pain here tenho uma dor aqui [tayn-yoo ooma dohr akee]
painful doloroso [dooloorohzoo]
painkillers os analgésicos [analJehzikoosh]
paint a tinta [teenta]
painting a pintura [pintoora]
pair: a pair of ... um par de ... [oong di]
Pakistani (adj) paquistanês [pakishtanaysh]
palace o palácio [palas-yoo]
pale pálido [palidoo]
pale blue azul claro [azool klaroo]
pan a panela [panehla]
panties as cuecas [kwehkash]
pants (underwear) as cuecas [kwehkash]
(US) as calças [kalsash]
pantyhose os collants [koolansh]
paper o papel [papehl]
(newspaper) o jornal [Joornal]
a sheet of paper uma folha de papel [ooma fohlya di]
paper handkerchiefs os lenços de papel [laynsoosh]
paragliding o parapentismo [parapaynteeJmoo]
parcel a encomenda [aynkoomaynda]
pardon (me)? (didn't understand/hear) desculpe? [dishkoolp], como? [kohmoo]
parents os pais [pīsh]
parents-in-law os sogros [sohgroosh]
park o jardim público [Jardeeng pooblikoo]
(verb) estacionar [shtas-yoonar]
can I park here? posso estacionar aqui? [posoo – akee]

Parking is extremely difficult in city and town centres: only the top hotels have their own car parks and you can expect to spend ages looking for a space, often ending up on the outskirts of town and having to walk to the centre.

parking lot o parque de estacionamento [park di shtas-yoonam**ayn**too]
part a parte [part]
partner (boyfriend/girlfriend) o companheiro [kompan-**yay**roo], a companh**ei**ra
party (group) o grupo [gr**oo**poo] (celebration) a festa [**feh**shta]
pass (in mountains) o desfiladeiro [dishfilad**ay**roo]
passenger (man/woman) o passageiro [pasaJ**ay**roo], a passag**ei**ra
passport o passaporte [pasap**o**rt]

It is advisable to carry an ID card with you at all times, but as a tourist you are unlikely to be fined if caught without one.

past*: in the past no passado [noo pas**a**doo]
just past the information office logo a seguir ao escritório de informações [l**o**goo a sig**ee**r owshkrit**o**r-yoo dinfoormas**oy**ngsh]
path o caminho [kam**ee**n-yoo]
pattern o desenho [diz**ay**n-yoo]
pavement o passeio [pas**ay**-oo]
on the pavement no passeio [noo]
pavement café o café de esplanada [kaf**eh** dishplan**a**da]
pay pag**a**r
can I pay, please? por favor, queria pagar [poor fav**oh**r kir**ee**-a]
it's already paid for já está pago [Ja shta p**a**goo]

dialogue

who's paying? quem vai pagar? [kayng vī]
I'll pay eu pago [**ay**-oo p**a**goo]
no, you paid last time, I'll pay não, você pagou da última vez, eu pago [nowng vos**ay** pag**oh** da-**oo**ltima v**ay**sh]

pay phone o telefone público [telef**oh**n p**oo**blikoo]
peaceful tranquilo [trankw**ee**loo]
peach o pêssego [p**ay**sigoo]
peanuts os amendoins [amayndw**ee**nsh]
pear a pêra [p**ay**ra]
peas as ervilhas [irv**ee**l-yash]
peculiar (taste, custom) estranho [shtr**a**n-yoo]
pedestrian crossing o passagem de peões [pasaJ**ay**ng di p-yoyngsh], a pasadeira de peões [pasad**ay**ra]

You should be particularly careful when crossing the road, because pedestrian crossings are often ignored by drivers.

pedestrian precinct a zona para peões [**zoh**na p**a**ra p-yoyngsh]
peg (for washing) a m**o**la
(for tent) a cavilha [kav**ee**l-ya]
pen a caneta [kan**ay**ta]
pencil o lápis [lapsh]
penfriend (man/woman) o/a correspondente [koorrishpond**ay**nt]
penicillin a penicilina [penisil**ee**na]
penknife o canivete [kaniv**eh**t]
pensioner (man/woman) o reformado [rifoorm**a**doo], a reform**a**da
people a gente [Jaynt]
the other people in the hotel as outras pessoas no hotel [az**oh**trash pis**oh**-ash nwoht**eh**l]
too many people gente demais [dimīsh]
pepper (spice) a pimenta [pim**ay**nta]
(vegetable) o pimento [pim**ay**ntoo]
peppermint (sweet) a hortelã-pimenta [ortil**a**ng pim**ay**nta]
per: per night por noite [poor n**oh**-it]
how much per day? quanto é por dia? [kwantw**eh** poor d**ee**-a]
per cent por cento [s**ay**ntoo]
perfect perfeito [pirf**ay**too]
perfume o perfume [pirf**oo**m]
perhaps talvez [talv**ay**sh]
perhaps not talvez não [nowng]
period (of time, menstruation) o período [pir**ee**-oodoo]
perm a permanente [pirman**ay**nt]
permit a licença [lis**ay**nsa]
person a pessoa [pis**oh**-a]
personal stereo o Walkman®
petrol a gasolina [gazool**ee**na]

Four-star petrol (**super**) is relatively expensive: about 25 per cent more than in Britain, and nearly twice the US equivalent. Unleaded petrol (**sem chumbo**) is now widely available, and most rental cars run on it.

petrol can a l**a**ta de gasolina [di gazool**ee**na]
petrol station a bomba de gasolina [b**oh**mba di]
pharmacy a farmácia [farm**a**s-ya]

For minor health complaints you should go to a **farmácia**; in larger towns there's usually one where English is spoken. Pharmacists are highly trained and can dispense many drugs that would be available only with a prescription in Britain or North America.

phone o telefone [telef**oh**n]
(verb) telefon**a**r [telefoon**a**r]

International calls can be made direct from almost any phone booth, but in most of them you'll need a good stock of coins and a great deal of patience as the international lines are often blocked and you need to insert a large amount to make the connection. In busy tourist areas, it's easier to use **credifones**, which you can use with phonecards available from post offices – note that there are two different types of phonecard, each only valid in the corresponding credifone.

You'll find payphones in bars and cafés (and, increasingly, in Turismo offices and newsagents), usually indicated by the sign of a red horse on a white circle over a green background and the legend **Correio de Portugal – Telefone**. Otherwise, you could go to the main post office, which is very likely to have phone cabins – just tell the clerk the number you want to phone, and pay for your call afterwards. Except in Lisbon and Porto, most telephone offices are closed in the evening, but there is no cheap-rate period anyway for international calls. Reverse charge (collect) calls can be made from any phone, dialling 099 for a European connection and 098 for the rest of the world.

phone book a lista telefónica [**lee**shta telef**oh**nika]

phone box a cabina telefónica [kab**ee**na]

phonecard o cartão de telefone [kart**ow**ng di telef**oh**n]

phone number o número de telefone [n**oo**miroo]

photo a fotografia [footoograf**ee**-a]

excuse me, could you take a photo of us? faz favor, pode tirar-nos uma fotografia? [fash fav**oh**r pod tir**a**rnooz **oo**ma]

phrasebook o livro de expressões [**lee**vroo dishpris**oy**ngsh]

piano o piano [p-y**a**noo]

pickpocket (man/woman) o/a carteirista [kartayr**ee**shta]

pick up: will you be there to pick me up? estarás lá para apanhar-me? [shtar**a**J – apan-y**a**rmi]

picnic o piquenique [pikin**ee**k]

picture (drawing, painting) a pintura [peent**oo**ra]

(photograph) a fotografia [footoograf**ee**-a]

pie a tarte [tart]

piece o pedaço [pid**a**soo]

a piece of ... um bocado de ... [oong book**a**doo di]

pilchards as sardinhas [sard**ee**n-yash]

pill a pílula [**pee**loola]

I'm on the pill estou a tomar a pílula [shtoh a toom**a**r]

pillow a almofada [almoof**a**da]

pillow case a fronha da almofada [fr**oh**n-ya]

pin o alfinete [alfin**ay**t]

pineapple o ananás [anan**a**sh]

pineapple juice o sumo de ananás [s**oo**moo danan**a**sh]

Ph

pink cor de rosa [kohr di **ro**za]
pipe (for smoking) o cachimbo [kash**ee**mboo]
(for water) o cano [**ka**noo]
pipe cleaner o desentupidor de cachimbo [dizayntoopid**oh**r di kash**ee**mboo]
pity: it's a pity é uma pena [eh **oo**ma p**ay**na]
pizza a pizza
place o lugar [loog**a**r]
at your place na sua casa [s**oo**-a k**a**za]
at his place na casa dele [dayl]
plain (not patterned) liso [l**ee**zoo]
plane o avião [av-y**ow**ng]
by plane de avião [dav-y**ow**ng]
plant a planta
plaster cast o gesso [J**ay**soo]
plasters o adesivo [adiz**ee**voo]
plastic o plástico [pl**a**shtikoo]
plastic bag o saco de plástico [s**a**koo di]
plate o prato [pr**a**too]
platform o cais [kīsh]
which platform is it for Fátima? qual é o cais para Fátima? [kwal**eh** oo]
play (verb) jogar [Joog**a**r]
(in theatre) a peça de teatro [p**eh**sa di t-y**a**troo]
playground o pátio de recreio [p**a**t-yoo di rikr**ay**-oo]
pleasant agradável
please se faz favor [si fash fav**oh**r], por favor [poor]
yes please sim, por favor [seeng]
could you please ...? por favor, pode ...? [pod]
please don't por favor, não faça isto [nowng f**a**sa **ee**shtoo]
pleased: pleased to meet you (said to man/woman) muito prazer em conhecê-lo/conhecê-la [mw**ee**ngtoo praz**ay**r ayng koon-yis**ay**loo]
pleasure: my pleasure de nada [di]
plenty: plenty of ... muito ... [mw**ee**ngtoo]
there's plenty of time temos muito tempo [t**ay**mooJ – t**ay**mpoo]
that's plenty, thanks (said by man/woman) chega, obrigado/obrigada [sh**ay**ga obrig**a**doo]
pliers o alicate [alik**a**t]
plug (electrical) a tomada [toom**a**da]
(for car) a vela [v**eh**la]
(in sink) a tampa do ralo [doo r**a**loo]
plumber o canalizador [kanalizad**oh**r]
p.m.* da tarde [tard]
poached egg o ovo escalfado [**oh**voo shkalf**a**doo]
pocket o bolso [oo b**oh**lsoo]
point: two point five dois vírgula cinco [d**oh**-iJ v**ee**rgoola s**ee**nkoo]
there's no point não vale a pena [nowng v**a**l-ya p**ay**na]
points (in car) os platinados [platin**a**doosh]
poisonous venenoso [vinin**oh**zoo]

police a polícia [pool**ee**s-ya]
call the police! chamem a polícia! [sh**a**mayng]

There are three different authorities with which you might come into contact, though in an emergency the first policeman you see will be able to help you. In major towns, the police force most likely to be of assistance will be the **PSP (Polícia de Segurança Pública)**, responsible among other things for incidents involving tourists. They wear distinctive blue uniforms, a beret and a badge on their jackets identifying themselves. The **Polícia Judiciária** is the force responsible for investigating crime. The **GNR (Guarda Nacional Republicana)** police the rural areas, patrol the motorways, and are responsible for overseeing all ceremonial occasions; ordinarily they wear blue-grey uniforms. You can't count on English being spoken by most of the local police personnel.
For all emergency services dial 115.

policeman o polícia [oo pool**ee**s-ya]
police station o Posto da Polícia [p**oh**shtoo]
policewoman a mulher-polícia [mool-y**eh**r]
polish (for shoes) a pomada para calçados [poom**a**da p**a**ra kals**a**doosh]
polite bem-educado [bayng idook**a**doo]
polluted contaminado [kontamin**a**doo]
pony o pónei [p**o**nay]
pool (for swimming) a piscina [pish-s**ee**na]
poor (not rich) pobre [p**o**br]
(quality) mau [mow], (**f**) má
pop music a música pop [m**oo**zika]
pop singer (man/woman) o cantor pop [kant**oh**r], a cant**o**ra pop
popular popular [poopool**a**r]
population a população [poopoolas**ow**ng]
pork a carne de porco [karn di p**oh**rkoo]
port (for boats) o porto [p**oh**rtoo]
(drink) o vinho do Porto [v**ee**n-yoo doo]

Port is produced from grapes grown in the valley of the Douro and is stored in huge wine lodges at Vila Nova de Gaia, a riverside suburb of Porto. You can visit these for tours and free tastings. Alternatively, you can try any of 300 types and vintages of port at the **Instituto do Vinho do Porto** (Port Wine Institute) in Lisbon and Porto. Even if your quest for port isn't serious enough to do either, be sure to try the dry white aperitif ports, still little known outside the country.

porter (in hotel) o porteiro [poort**ay**roo]
portrait o retrato [ritr**a**too]
Portugal Portugal [poortoog**al**]
Portuguese (adj) português [poortoog**ay**sh]
(language) português
(man) o português
(woman) a portuguesa
the Portuguese os portugueses [poortoog**ay**zish]
posh (restaurant, people) chique [sheek]
possible possível [poos**ee**vil]
is it possible to ...? é possível ...? [eh]
as ... as possible tão ... quanto possível [t**ow**ng ... kw**a**ntoo]
post (mail) o correio [koorr**ay**-oo]
(verb) pôr no correio [pohr noo]
could you post this for me? podia-me pôr isto no correio? [pood**ee**-ami – **ee**shtoo noo]
postbox a caixa do correio [kīsha doo]
postcard o postal [poosht**al**]
postcode o código postal [k**o**digoo poosht**al**]
poster (for room) o poster
(in street) o cartaz [kart**a**sh]
poste restante a posta-restante [p**o**shta risht**a**nt]
post office os correios [koorr**ay**-oosh]

Post offices are indicated by the letters **CTT (Correios e Telecomunicações)** and are normally open Monday to Friday from 9 a.m. to 6 p.m; larger ones are sometimes open on Saturday mornings as well and the main Lisbon branches have much longer opening hours. You can have poste restante (general delivery) mail sent to you at any post office in the country. Letters should be marked Posta Restante, and ideally your name should be written in capitals and underlined. To collect, you need to take along your passport – look for the counter marked **encomendas**. If you are expecting mail, ask the postal clerk to check for letters under your first name and any other initials (including Ms, etc) as well as under your surname.
To send mail abroad, you are best advised to use the more expensive **correio azul** (express mail).

potato a batata
potato chips as batatas fritas [bat**a**tash fr**ee**tash]
pots and pans as panelas e tachos [pan**eh**lazee t**a**shoosh]
pottery (objects) a loiça de barro [**loh**-isa di b**a**rroo]
pound* (money, weight) a libra [l**ee**bra]
power cut o corte de energia [kort denirJ**ee**-a]

power point a tomada [toomada]
practise: I want to practise my Portuguese quero praticar o meu português [kehroo pratikaroo may-oo poortoogaysh]
prawn a gamba
prefer: I prefer ... prefiro ... [prifeeroo]
pregnant grávida
prescription (for medicine) a receita [risayta]
see pharmacy
present (gift) o presente [prizaynt]
president (of country: man/woman) o/a presidente [prizidaynt]
pretty bonito [booneetoo]
it's pretty expensive é muito caro [mweengtoo karoo]
price o preço [praysoo]
priest o padre [padr]
prime minister (man/woman) o primeiro ministro [primayroo mineeshtroo], a primeira ministra
printed matter os impressos [imprehsoosh]
priority (in driving) a prioridade [pr-yooridad]
prison a cadeia [kaday-a]
private privado [privadoo]
private bathroom a casa de banho privativa [kaza di ban-yoo privateeva]
probably provavelmente [proovavilmaynt]
problem o problema [prooblayma]
no problem! tudo bem! [toodoo bayng]
program(me) o programa [proograma]
promise: I promise prometo [proomaytoo]
pronounce: how is this pronounced? como se pronuncia? [kohmoo si proonoonsee-a]
properly (repaired, locked etc) bem [bayng]
protection factor (of suntan lotion) o factor de protecção [fatohr di prootehsowng]
Protestant protestante [prootishtant]
public convenience a casa de banho pública [kaza di ban-yoo pooblika]
public holiday o feriado [fir-yadoo]
pudding (dessert) a sobremesa [sobrimayza]
pull puxar [pooshar]
pullover o pullover
puncture o furo [fooroo]
purple roxo [rohshoo]
purse (for money) a carteira [kartayra]
(US) a mala de mão [di]
push empurrar [aympoorrar]
pushchair o carrinho de bebé [karreen-yoo di bebeh]
put* pôr [pohr]
where can I put ...? onde posso pôr ...? [ohnd posoo]
could you put us up for the night? pode dar-nos

Pp

acomodação para uma noite? [pod **da**rnooz akoomoodas**ow**ng p**a**ra **oo**ma]
pyjamas o pijama [piJ**a**ma]

Q

quality a qualidade [kwalid**a**d]
quarantine a quarentena [kwarayn**tay**na]
quarter a quarta parte [kw**a**rta part]
quayside: on the quayside no cais [noo kīsh]
question a pergunta [pirg**oo**nta]
queue a bicha [b**ee**sha]
quick rápido [r**a**pidoo]
that was quick! que rápido que foi! [ki – foh-i]
what's the quickest way there? qual é o caminho mais rápido para lá? [kwal**eh** oo kam**ee**n-yoo mīsh r**a**pidoo]
quickly depressa [dipr**eh**sa]
quiet (place, hotel) silencioso [silayns-y**oh**zoo]
quiet! cale-se! [k**a**lsi]
quite (fairly) bastante [basht**a**nt]
(very) muito [mw**ee**ngtoo]
that's quite right está certo [shta s**eh**rtoo]
quite a lot bastante

R

rabbit o coelho [kw**ay**l-yoo]
race (for runners, cars) a corrida [koorr**ee**da]
racket (tennis, squash) a raqueta [rak**eh**ta]
radiator (of car, in room) o radiador [rad-yad**oh**r]
radio o rádio [r**a**d-yoo]
on the radio no rádio [noo]
rail: by rail por caminho de ferro [poor kam**ee**n-yoo di f**eh**rroo]
railway o caminho de ferro
rain a chuva [sh**oo**va]
in the rain à chuva
it's raining está a chover [sht**a**-a shoov**ay**r]
raincoat o impermeável [impirm-y**a**vil]
rape a violação [v-yoolas**ow**ng]
rare (uncommon) raro [r**a**roo]
(steak) mal passado [pas**a**doo]
rash (on skin) a erupção [eroops**ow**ng]
raspberry a framboesa [frambw**ay**za]
rat a ratazana
rate (for changing money) o câmbio [k**a**mb-yoo]
rather: it's rather good é bastante bom/boa [eh basht**a**nt bong/b**oh**-a]
I'd rather ... prefiro ... [prif**ee**roo]
razor (electric) a máquina de barbear [m**a**kina di barb-y**a**r]
razor blades as lâminas para barbear [l**a**minash]
read ler [layr]
ready pronto [pr**oh**ntoo]
are you ready? (said to

man/woman) estás pronto/ pronta? [shtash prohntoo]
I'm not ready yet (said by man/woman) ainda não estou pronto/pronta [a-eenda nowng shtoh]

dialogue

when will it be ready? quando estará pronto? [kwandoo shtara]
it should be ready in a couple of days deve ficar pronto em dois dias [dehv fikar – ayng doh-iJ dee-ash]

real verdadeiro [virdadayroo]
really realmente [r-yalmaynt]
I'm really sorry lamento imenso [lamayntoo imaynsoo]
that's really great isso é fantástico [eesweh fantashtikoo]
really? (doubt) de verdade? [di virdad]
(polite interest) sim? [seeng]
rear lights as luzes de trás [loozish di trash]
rearview mirror o espelho retrovisor [shpayl-yoo ritroovizohr]
reasonable (prices etc) razoável [razwavil]
receipt o recibo [riseeboo]
recently há pouco [a pohkoo]
reception (in hotel, for guests) a recepção [risehsowng]
at reception na recepção
reception desk o balcão da recepção [balkowng]
receptionist (man/woman) o/a recepcionista [risehs-yooneeshta]
recognize reconhecer [rikoon-yisayr]
recommend: could you recommend ...? podia recomendar ...? [poodee-a rikoomayndar]
record (music) o disco [deeshkoo]
red vermelho [virmayl-yoo]
red wine o vinho tinto [veen-yoo teentoo]
refund o reembolso [ri-aymbohlsoo]
can I have a refund? pode dar-me o reembolso? [pod darmoo]
region a região [riJ-yowng]
registered: by registered mail por correio registado [poor koorray-oo riJishtadoo]
registration number a matrícula [matreekoola]
relative (noun: male/female) o/a parente [paraynt]
religion a religião [riliJ-yowng]
remember: I remember lembro-me [laymbroomi]
I don't remember não me lembro [nowng mi laymbroo]
do you remember? lembra-se? [laymbrasi]
rent (noun: for apartment etc) o aluguer [aloogehr]
(verb: car etc) alugar
to rent para alugar

dialogue

I'd like to rent a car queria alugar um carro [kir**ee**-a – oong k**a**rroo]
for how long? por quanto tempo? [poor kw**a**ntoo t**ay**mpoo]
two days dois dias [d**oh**-iJ d**ee**-ash]
this is our range esta é a nossa gama [**eh**shteh-a n**o**sa]
I'll take the ... fico com o ... [f**ee**koo kongoo]
is that with unlimited mileage? é com quilometragem ilimitada? [eh kong kilomitr**a**Jayng]
it is sim [seeng]
can I see your licence, please? posso ver a sua carta de condução, por favor? [p**o**soo vayr a s**oo**-a k**a**rta di kondoos**ow**ng poor fav**oh**r]
and your passport e o seu passaporte [yoo s**ay**-oo pasap**o**rt]
is insurance included? o seguro está incluído? [oo sig**oo**roo shta inklw**ee**doo]
yes, but you pay the first 15,000 escudos sim, mas tem de pagar os primeiros quinze contos [seeng mash tayng ki pag**a**r oosh prim**ay**roosh keenz k**oh**ntoosh]
can you leave a deposit of 10,000 escudos? pode deixar um depósito de dez contos? [pod daysh**a**r oong dip**o**zitoo di dehsh]

rented car o carro de aluguer [k**a**rroo daloog**eh**r]
repair reparar
can you repair this? pode reparar isto? [pod ripar**a**r **ee**shtoo]
repeat repetir [ripit**ee**r]
could you repeat that? podia repetir? [pood**ee**-a]
reservation a reserva [riz**eh**rva]
I'd like to make a reservation queria fazer uma reserva [kir**ee**-a faz**ay**r **oo**ma]

dialogue

I have a reservation tenho uma reserva [t**ay**n-yoo **oo**ma]
yes sir, what name please? sim senhor, que nome, por favor? [seeng sin-y**oh**r ki nohm poor fav**oh**r]

reserve (verb) reservar [rizirv**a**r]

dialogue

can I reserve a table for tonight? posso reservar uma mesa para esta noite? [p**o**soo – **oo**ma m**ay**za p**a**ra **eh**shta n**oh**-it]
yes madam, for how many people? sim senhora, para

quantas pessoas? [seeng sinyora para kwantash pisoh-ash]
for two para duas [doo-ash]
and for what time? e para que hora? [i – ki-ora]
for eight o'clock para as oito horas [azoh-itorash]
and could I have your name, please? pode dizer-me o seu nome, por favor? [pod dizayrmoo say-oo nohm poor favohr]
see **alphabet** for spelling

rest: I need a rest preciso dum descanso [priseezoo doong dishkansoo]
the rest of the group o resto do grupo [rehshtoo doo groopoo]
restaurant o restaurante [rishtowrant]

Portugal is full of affordable restaurants, and servings tend to be huge. Your main course is likely to be accompanied by an enormous portion of both chips and rice. You'll often find that the smarter the restaurant, the smaller the portion. It is perfectly acceptable to ask for a half portion, **uma meia dose** [ooma may-a doz] or **uma dose** between two. Meals are often listed with prices for a half portion. It is worth checking out the **ementa turística**, too – not necessarily a 'tourist menu' as such, but more like the French menu de jour. Smarter restaurants, however, sometimes resent the law that compels them to offer the **ementa turística**, responding with stingy portions.
You will often be brought a variety of starters to nibble while ordering your meal; these are sometimes part of a set cover charge, but more often you will be charged for as much as you eat – in some places right down to each individual portion of butter. If you do not want starters, tell the waiter to take them away as soon as you take a seat.
Portuguese waiters tend to rely on a high level of honesty amongst their customers, paticularly in local bars. The most common way of working out the bill at the end of an evening is simply to count up the empty bottles and plates on the table.
Apart from straightforward restaurants – **restaurantes** – you could end up eating a meal in one of several other venues. A **tasca** is a small neighbourhood tavern; a **casa de pasto** is a cheap local dining room usually with a set three-course menu, mostly served only at lunchtime. A **cervejaria** (literally: beer house) is more informal than a restaurant, with people dropping in at all hours for a beer and a snack. In Lisbon they are often wonderful old tiled caverns, specialising in seafood. Also specialising in seafood is a **marisqueira**, occasionally very upmarket, though as often as not a

regular restaurant with a superior fishy menu.

restaurant car a carruagem restaurante [karrwaJayng rishtowrant]
rest room a casa de banho [kaza di ban-yoo]
see **toilet**
retired: I'm retired (said by man/woman) estou reformado/reformada [shtoh rifoormadoo]
return: a return to ... um bilhete de ida e volta a ... [oong bil-yayt deeda ee]
return ticket o bilhete de ida e volta
see **ticket**
reverse charge call a chamada paga no destinátario [shamada – noo dishtinatar-yoo]
reverse gear a marcha atrás [marshatrash]
revolting repugnante [ripoognant]
rib a costela [kooshtehla]
rice o arroz [arrohsh]
rich (person) rico [reekoo]
(food) forte [fort]
ridiculous ridículo [rideekooloo]
right (correct) certo [sehrtoo]
(not left) direito [diraytoo]
you were right tinhas razão [teen-yaJ razowng]
that's right está certo [shta]
this can't be right isto não pode estar certo [eeshtoo nowng pod shtar]
right! está bem! [bayng]
is this the right road for ...? esta é a estrada certa para ...? [ehshta eh a shtrada]
on the right à direita [dirayta]
turn right vire à direita [veer]
right-hand drive com volante à direita [kong voolant]
ring (on finger) o anel [anehl]
I'll ring you eu telefono-lhe [ay-oo telefohnool-yi]
ring back voltar a telefonar [telefoonar]
ripe (fruit) maduro [madooroo]
rip-off: it's a rip-off isso é um roubo [eesoo eh oong rohboo]
rip-off prices os preços exorbitantes [praysooz ezoorbitantsh]
risky arriscado [arrishkadoo]
river o rio [ree-oo]
road (in town) a rua [roo-a]
(in country) a estrada [shtrada]
is this the road for ...? é esta a estrada para ...? [ehshta]
it's just down the road é aqui perto [eh akee pehrtoo]
road accident o acidente de viação [asidaynt di v-yasowng]
road map o mapa das estradas [daz shtradash]
roadsign o sinal
rob: I've been robbed (said by man/woman) fui roubado/roubada [fwee rohbadoo]
rock a rocha [rosha]
(music) a música rock [moozika]
on the rocks (with ice) com

gelo [kong Jayloo]
roll (bread) o paposseco [papoosaykoo]
roof (of house) o telhado [til-yadoo]
(of car) o tejadilho [tiJadeel-yoo]
roof rack o porta-bagagens no tejadilho [porta bagaJayngsh]
room o quarto [kwartoo]
in my room no meu quarto [noo may-oo]

dialogue

do you have any rooms? tem quartos vagos? [tayng kwartoosh vagoosh]
for how many people? para quantas pessoas? [kwantash pisoh-ash]
for one/for two para uma/ para duas [ooma/ – doo-ash]
yes, we have rooms free sim, temos quartos vagos [seeng taymoosh]
for how many nights will it be? para quantas noites? [noh-itsh]
just for one night só para uma noite [saw – noh-it]
how much is it? quanto é o quarto? [kwantweh]
... with bathroom and ... without bathroom ... com casa de banho e ... sem casa banho [kong kaza di ban-yoo ee ... sayng]
can I see a room with bathroom? posso ver um quarto com casa de banho? [posoo vayr oong]
OK, I'll take it está bem, fico com ele [shta bayng feekoo kong ayl]

room service o serviço de quartos [sirveesoo di kwartoosh]
rope a corda
rosé (wine) rosé [roozay]
roughly (approximately) aproximadamente [aproosimadamaynt]
round: it's my round é a minha rodada [eh a meen-ya roodada]
roundabout (for traffic) a rotunda [rootoonda]
round trip ticket o bilhete de ida e volta [bil-yayt deeda ee]
see **ticket**
route o trajecto [trajehtoo]
what's the best route? qual é o melhor trajecto? [kwal eh-oo mil-yor]
rubber (material, eraser) a borracha [boorrasha]
rubber band o elástico [ilashtikoo]
rubbish (waste) o lixo [leeshoo]
(poor quality goods) o refugo [rifoogoo]
rubbish! (nonsense) que disparate! [ki dishparat]
rucksack a mochila [moosheela]
rude grosseiro [groosayroo]

ruins as ruínas [**rwee**nash]
rum o rum [roong]
a rum and Coke® uma cuba livre [**oo**ma k**oo**ba leevr]
run (verb: person) correr [koorr**ayr**]
how often do the buses run? de quanto em quanto tempo há autocarros? [di kw**a**ntoo ayng kwantoo **tay**mpoo a owtook**a**rroosh]
I've run out of money o meu dinheiro acabou [oo **may**-oo din-y**ay**roo akab**oh**]
rush hour a hora de ponta [**o**ra di p**oh**nta]

S

sad triste [treesht]
saddle a sela [s**eh**la]
safe (adj) seguro [sig**oo**roo]
safety pin o alfinete de segurança [alfin**ay**t di sigoor**a**nsa]
sail a vela [v**eh**la]
(verb) velejar [viliJ**ar**]
sailboard a prancha de windsurf [pr**a**nsha di]
sailboarding praticar windsurf [pratik**ar**]
salad a salada
salad dressing o tempero da salada [taymp**ay**roo]
sale: for sale à venda [v**ay**nda]
salmon o salmão [salm**ow**ng]
salt o sal
same: the same o mesmo [m**ay**Jmoo]
the same as this igual a este [igw**a**l a aysht]
the same again, please o mesmo, por favor [poor fav**ohr**]
it's all the same to me tanto faz [t**a**ntoo fash]
sand a areia [ar**ay**-a]
sandals as sandálias [sand**a**l-yash]
sandwich a sandes [sandsh]
sanitary napkins/towels os pensos higiénicos [p**ay**nsooz iJ-y**eh**nikoosh]
sardine a sardinha [sard**ee**n-ya]
Saturday sábado [s**a**badoo]
sauce o molho [m**oh**l-yoo]
saucepan a panela [pan**eh**la]
saucer o pires [peersh]
sauna a sauna [s**ow**na]
sausage a salsicha [sals**ee**sha]
say* dizer [diz**ayr**]
how do you say ... in Portuguese? como se diz ... em português? [k**oh**moo si deez ... ayng poortoog**ay**sh]
what did he say? o que é que ele disse? [oo k-yeh kayl dees]
he said ... ele disse ...
could you say that again? pode repetir? [pod ripit**ee**r]
scarf (for neck) o lenço de pescoço [l**ay**nsoo di pishk**oh**soo]
(for head) o lenço de cabeça [kab**ay**sa]
scenery a paisagem [pīz**a**Jayng]

schedule (US) o horário [oo orar-yoo]
scheduled flight o voo regular [voh-oo rigoolar]
school a escola [shkola]
scissors: a pair of scissors a tesoura [tizohra]
scooter a motoreta [mootoorayta]
scotch o whisky [weeshkee]
Scotch tape® a fita gomada [feeta goomada]
Scotland a Escócia [shkos-ya]
Scottish escocês [shkoosaysh]
I'm Scottish (man/woman) sou escocês/escocesa [soh – shkoosayza]
scrambled eggs os ovos mexidos [ovoosh misheedoosh]
scratch o arranhão [arran-yowng]
screw o parafuso [parafoozoo]
screwdriver a chave de fendas [shav di fayndash]
sea o mar
by the sea à beira-mar [bayra]
seafood os mariscos [mareeshkoosh]
seafood restaurant a marisqueira [marishkayra]
seafront a praia [prī-a]
on the seafront junto à praia [Joontwa]
seagull a gaivota [gīvota]
search procurar [prookoorar]
seashell a concha do mar [kohnsha doo]
seasick: I feel seasick (said by man/woman) estou enjoado/enjoada [shtoh aynJwadoo]
I get seasick enjoo sempre [aynJoh-oo saympr]
seaside: by the seaside à beira do mar [bayra doo]
seat o assento [asayntoo]
is this seat taken? este lugar está ocupado? [aysht loogar shta okoopadoo]
seat belt o cinto de segurança [seentoo di sigooransa]
sea urchin o ouriço-do-mar [ohreesoo doo]
seaweed a alga
secluded retirado [ritiradoo]
second (adj) segundo [sigoondoo]
(of time) o segundo
just a second! espere um momento! [shpayroong moomayntoo]
second class (travel) segunda classe [sigoonda klas]
second floor o segundo andar [sigoondoo]
(US) o primeiro andar [primayroo]
second-hand em segunda mão [ayng sigoonda mowng]
see* ver [vayr]
can I see? posso ver? [posoo]
have you seen the ...? viu o/a ...? [vee-oo]
I saw him this morning vi-o esta manhã [vee-oo ehshta man-yang]
see you! até logo! [ateh logoo]

SC

I see (I understand) percebo [pirs**ay**boo]
self-catering apartment o aparthotel [apartoht**eh**l]
self-service o self-service
sell vender [vaynd**ayr**]
do you sell ...? vende ...? [vaynd]
Sellotape® a fita gomada [f**ee**ta goom**a**da]
send mandar
I want to send this to England quero mandar isto para Inglaterra [k**eh**roo – **ee**shtoo paringlat**eh**rra]
senior citizen (man/woman) o cidadão de terceira idade [sidad**ow**ng di tirs**ay**ra id**a**d], a cidadã de terceira idade [sidad**a**ng]
separate separado [sipar**a**doo]
separated: I'm separated (said by man/woman) estou separado/separada [shtoh]
separately (pay, travel) separadamente [siparadam**ay**nt]
September Setembro [sit**ay**mbroo]
septic séptico [s**eh**ptikoo]
serious sério [s**eh**r-yoo]
service charge (in restaurant) a taxa de serviço [t**a**sha di sirv**ee**soo]
service station a estação de serviço [shtas**ow**ng]
serviette o guardanapo [gwardan**a**poo]
set menu a ementa fixa [em**ay**nta f**ee**ksa]
several vários [v**a**r-yoosh]
sew coser [kooz**ayr**]
could you sew this back on? podia coser-me isto? [pood**ee**-a kooz**ay**rm **ee**shtoo]
sex o sexo [s**eh**xoo]
sexy sexy [s**eh**xi]
shade: in the shade à sombra [s**oh**mbra]
shallow (water) pouco profundo [p**oh**koo proof**oo**ndoo]
shame: what a shame! que pena! [ki p**ay**na]
shampoo o champô [shamp**oh**]
shampoo and set lavagem e mise [lav**a**Jayng i m**ee**zi]
share (room, table etc) partilhar [partil-y**a**r]
sharp (knife) afiado [af-y**a**doo]
(taste) ácido [**a**sidoo]
(pain) agudo [ag**oo**doo]
shattered (very tired) estafado [shtaf**a**doo]
shaver a máquina de barbear [m**a**kina di barb-y**a**r]
shaving foam a espuma de barbear [shp**oo**ma]
shaving point a tomada para a máquina de barbear [toom**a**da p**a**ra m**a**kina]
she* ela [**eh**la]
is she here? ela está aqui? [shta ak**ee**]
sheet (for bed) o lençol [layns**o**l]
shelf a prateleira [pratil**ay**ra]
shellfish os mariscos [mar**ee**shkoosh]

sherry o vinho de Xerêz [**vee**n-yoo di shir**ay**sh]
ship o navio [nav**ee**-o]
by ship de navio [di]
shirt a camisa [kam**ee**za]
shit! merda! [m**eh**rda]
shock o choque [shok]
I got an electric shock from the ... apanhei um choque eléctrico do ... [apan-y**ay** oong – el**eh**trikoo doo]
shock-absorber o amortecedor [amoortisid**oh**r]
shocking chocante [shook**a**nt]
shoe os sapatos [sap**a**toosh]
a pair of shoes um par de sapatos [oong par di]
shoelaces os atacadores [atakad**oh**rish]
shoe polish a graxa para sapatos [gr**a**sha p**a**ra sap**a**toosh]
shoe repairer o sapateiro [sapat**ay**roo]
shop a loja [l**o**Ja]

Shops are usually open from around 8.30 a.m. to 7 p.m. and close for lunch from around 12.30 to 2.30 p.m. However, many shops in the big cities are open from around 9 a.m. to 6 p.m., and often don't close for lunch. Most shops are shut on Sunday and many close at 12.30 p.m. on Saturday, even in the main shopping district in Lisbon. Modern shopping malls, which are springing up around the larger cities, are likely to be open seven days a week from around 9 a.m. to as late as 11 p.m. or even midnight.

shopping: I'm going shopping vou às compras [voh ash k**oh**mprash]
shopping centre o centro comercial [s**ay**ntroo komayrs-y**a**l]
shop window a montra [m**oh**ntra]
shore (of sea, lake) a margem [m**a**rJayng]
short (person) baixo [b**ī**shoo]
(time, journey) curto [k**oo**rtoo]
shortcut o atalho [at**a**l-yoo]
shorts os calções [kals**oy**ngsh]
should: what should I do? que devo fazer? [ki d**ay**voo faz**ay**r]
he should be back soon ele deve voltar logo [ayl dehv voolt**a**r l**o**goo]
you should ... devia [div**ee**-a]
you shouldn't ... não devia ... [nowng]
shoulder o ombro [**oh**mbroo]
shout gritar
show (in theatre) o espetáculo [shpit**a**kooloo]
could you show me? podia mostrar-me? [pood**ee**-a mooshtr**a**rmi]
shower (in bathroom) o duche [doosh]
(of rain) o aguaceiro [agwas**ay**roo]
with shower com duche [kong]
shower gel o gel de duche

Sh

[Jehl di doosh]
shrimp a gamba
shut (verb) fechar [fishar]
when do you shut? a que horas fecha? [k-yorash fehsha]
when does it shut? a que horas fecha?
it's shut está fechado/fechada [shta fishadoo]
I've shut myself out fechei a porta e deixei a chave dentro [fishay – i dayshay a shav dayntroo]
shut up! cale-se! [kalisi]
shutter (on camera) o obturador [obtooradohr]
(on window) os postigos [pooshteegoosh]
shy tímido [teemidoo]
sick (unwell) doente [dwaynt]
I'm going to be sick (vomit) vou vomitar [voh voomitar]
side o lado [ladoo]
the other side of the street o outro lado da rua [oo ohtroo – roo-a]
sidelights as luzes de presença [aJ looziJ di prizaynsa]
side salad a salada a acompanhar [akompan-yar]
side street a rua secundária [roo-a sikoondar-ya]
sidewalk o passeio [pasay-oo]
sight: the sights of ... os centros de interesse de ... [oosh sayntroosh dintrays di]
sightseeing: we're going sightseeing vamos ver os lugares de interesse [vamoosh vayr oosh loogarish]
sightseeing tour o circuito turístico [sirkoo-eetoo tooreeshtikoo]
sign (roadsign etc) o sinal
signal: he didn't give a signal (driver, cyclist) ele não deu um sinal [ayl nowng day-oo oong]
signature a assinatura [asinatoora]
signpost o poste indicador [posht indikadohr]
silence o silêncio [silayns-yoo]
silk a seda [sayda]
silly tolo [tohloo]
silver a prata
silver foil o papel de alumínio [papehl daloomeen-yoo]
similar semelhante [simil-yant]
simple (easy) simples [seemplish]
since: since last week desde a semana passada [dayJda simana]
since I got here desde que cheguei [dayJd ki shigay]
sing cantar
singer (man/woman) o cantor [kantohr], a cantora
single: a single to ... uma bilhete simples para ... [oong bil-yayt seemplish]
I'm single (said by man/woman) sou solteiro/solteira [soh sooltayroo]
single bed a cama individual [individwal]
single room o quarto individual [kwartoo]

single ticket o bilhete simples [bil-y**ay**t s**ee**mplish]
sink (in kitchen) a lava-louça [l**a**va l**oh**sa]
sister a irmã [eerm**a**ng]
sister-in-law a cunhada [koon-y**a**da]
sit: can I sit here? posso sentar-me aqui? [p**o**soo sayntarmi ak**ee**]
is anyone sitting here? está alguém sentado aqui? [shta alg**ay**ng sayntadoo ak**ee**]
sit down sentar-se [saynt**a**rsi]
sit down sente-se [s**ay**ntsi]
size o tamanho [tam**a**n-yoo]
skin a pele [pehl]
skin-diving mergulhar [mirgool-y**a**r]
skinny magricela [magris**eh**la]
skirt a saia [sī-ya]
sky o céu [s**eh**-oo]
sleep dormir [doorm**ee**r]
did you sleep well? dormiu bem? [doorm**ee**-oo bayng]
sleeper (on train) a carruagem-cama [karrw**a**Jayng k**a**ma]
sleeping bag o saco de dormir [s**a**koo di doorm**ee**r]
sleeping car (on train) a carruagem-cama [karrw**a**Jayng k**a**ma]
sleeping pill o comprimido para dormir [komprim**ee**doo p**a**ra doorm**ee**r]
sleepy: I'm feeling sleepy estou com sono [shtoh kong s**oh**noo]
sleeve a manga

slide (photographic) o diapositivo [d-yapoozit**ee**voo]
slip (garment) a combinação [kombinas**ow**ng]
slippery escorregadio [shkoorrigad**ee**-oo]
slow lento [l**ay**ntoo]
slow down! (driving) mais devagar! [mīJ divag**a**r]
slowly devagar
very slowly muito devagar [mw**ee**ngtoo]
could you speak more slowly? pode falar mais devagar? [pod – mīJ]
small pequeno [pik**ay**noo]
smell: it smells (smells bad) cheira mal [sh**ay**ra]
smile sorrir [soorr**ee**r]
smoke o fumo [f**oo**moo]
do you mind if I smoke? importa-se que fume? [imp**o**rtasi ki f**oo**mi]
I don't smoke não fumo [nowng]
do you smoke? fuma? [f**oo**ma]
snack: just a snack só um snack [saw oong]
sneeze o espirro [shp**ee**rroo]
snorkel o snorkel
snow a neve [nehv]
it's snowing está a nevar [shta]
so: it's so good! é tão bom! [eh towng bong]
it's so expensive! é tão caro! [k**a**roo]
not so much não tanto

[nowng tantoo]
it's not so bad não é tão mau/má [eh towng mow]
so am I, so do I eu também [ay-oo tambayng]
so-so mais ou menos [mīzohmaynoosh]
soaking solution (for contact lenses) a solução para as lentes de contacto [sooloosowng paraJ layntsh di kontatoo]
soap o sabonete [saboonayt]
soap powder o detergente [deterJaynt]
sober sóbrio [sobr-yoo]

soccer

Soccer is Portugal's national sport. Even the smallest village has a **campo de futebol** for local players, while on a national level, spectator loyalty is largely split between the two teams who win most of the domestic trophies, Porto and Benfica. Support seems to defy geography, with many people in the north proclaiming undying love for the Lisbon team, Benfica, and vice versa. Most football matches have a relaxed family atmosphere and there is rarely any crowd trouble.

sock a peúga [p-yooga]
socket (electrical) a tomada [toomada]
soda (water) a soda
sofa o sofá [soofa]
soft (material etc) mole [mol]
soft-boiled egg o ovo quente [ohvoo kaynt]
soft drink a bebida não alcoólica [bibeeda nowng alko-olika]
soft lenses as lentes gelatinosas [layntsh Jilatinozash]
sole (of shoe, of foot) a sola
could you put new soles on these? pode pôr-lhes solas novas? [pod pohrl-yish solash novash]
some: can I have some water? pode trazer-me água? [trazayrm]
can I have some of this? pode dar-me um pouco disto? [darmoong pohkoo deeshtoo]
somebody, someone alguém [algayng]
something alguma coisa [algooma koh-iza]
something to eat alguma coisa para comer [koomair]
sometimes às vezes [ash vayzish]
somewhere nalguma parte [nalgooma part]
son o filho [feel-yoo]
song a canção [kansowng]
son-in-law o genro [Jaynroo]
soon em breve [ayng brev]
I'll be back soon estarei de volta em breve [shtaray di vohltayng]
as soon as possible logo que possível [logoo ki pooseevil]

sore: it's sore dói-me [**doy**mi]
sore throat a dor de garganta [dohr di]
sorry: (I'm) sorry tenho muita pena [**tay**n-yoo m**wee**ngta p**ay**na]
sorry? (didn't understand) como? [**koh**moo]
sort: what sort of ...? que tipo de ...? [ki **tee**poo di]
soup a sopa [**soh**pa]
sour (taste) azedo [az**ay**doo]
south o sul [sool]
in the south no sul [noo]
South Africa a África do Sul [doo]
South African (adj) sul-africano [soolafrik**a**noo]
I'm South African (man/woman) sou sul-africano/sul-africana [soh]
southeast o sudeste [sood**eh**sht]
southwest o sudoeste [soodw**eh**sht]
souvenir a lembrança [laymbr**a**nsa]
Spain a Espanha [shp**a**n-ya]
Spanish espanhol [shpan-y**o**l]
spanner a chave de porcas [shav di p**o**rkash]
spare part a peça sobresselente [p**eh**sa sobrisil**ay**nt]
spare tyre o pneu sobresselente [p-n**ay**-oo]
spark plug a vela [v**eh**la]
sparkling wine o vinho espumante [v**ee**n-yooshpoom**a**nt]
speak: do you speak English? fala inglês? [ingl**ay**sh]
I don't speak ... não falo ... [nowng f**a**loo]

dialogue

can I speak to Roberto? posso falar com o Roberto? [p**o**soo – kong oo]
who's calling? quem fala? [kayng]
it's Patricia é Patricia [eh]
I'm sorry, he's not in, can I take a message? desculpe, ele não está, quer deixar um recado? [dishk**oo**lp ayl nowng shta kehr daysh**a**r oong rik**a**doo]
no thanks, I'll call back later não, obrigada, ligarei mais tarde [ligar**ay** mīsh tard]
please tell him I called por favor, diga-lhe que telefonei [poor fav**oh**r d**ee**gal-yi ki telefoon**ay**]

spectacles os óculos [**o**kooloosh]
speed a velocidade [viloosid**a**d]
speed limit o limite de velocidade [lim**ee**t di]
speedometer o velocímetro [vilooss**ee**mitroo]
spell: how do you spell it? como é que se soletra? [k**oh**moo eh ki si sool**eh**tra]
see **alphabet**
spend gastar [gasht**a**r]
spider a aranha [ar**a**n-ya]

spin-dryer o secador de roupa [sikad**oh**r di r**oh**pa]
splinter a pua [p**oo**-a]
spoke (in wheel) o raio [rī-oo]
spoon a colher [kool-y**eh**r]
sport o desporto [dishp**oh**rtoo]
sprain: I've sprained my ... torci o ... [toors**ee** oo]
spring (season) a Primavera [primav**eh**ra]
(of car, seat) a mola
square (in town) a praça [pr**a**sa]
squash o squash
stairs a escada [shk**a**da]
stale (bread) duro [d**oo**roo]
stall: the engine keeps stalling o motor está sempre a falhar [oo moot**oh**r shta s**ay**mpra fal-y**a**r]
stamp o selo [s**ay**loo]

dialogue

a stamp for England, please um selo para Inglaterra, faz favor [oong s**ay**loo p**a**ra inglat**eh**rra fash fav**oh**r]
what are you sending? o que vai enviar? [oo ki vī aynv-y**a**r]
this postcard este postal [aysht poosht**a**l]

You can buy stamps at post offices (**correios**) or at tobacconists' and souvenir stands.

standby standby

star a estrela [shtr**ay**la]
(in film: man/woman) o actor principal [at**oh**r prinsip**a**l], a actriz principal [atr**ee**sh]
start o começo [koom**ay**soo]
(verb) começar [koomis**a**r]
when does it start? quando começa? [kw**a**ndoo koom**eh**sa]
the car won't start o carro não pega [oo k**a**rroo nowng p**eh**ga]
starter (of car) o motor de arranque [moot**oh**r darr**a**nk]
(food) a entrada [ayntr**a**da]
starving: I'm starving (said by man/woman) estou morto/morta de fome [shtoh m**oh**rtoo – di fohm]
state (country) o estado [sht**a**doo]
the States (USA) os Estados Unidos [sht**a**dooz oon**ee**doosh]
station a estação [shtas**ow**ng]
statue a estátua [sht**a**twa]
stay: where are you staying? (to man/woman) onde está hospedado/hospedada? [ohndsht**a** oshpid**a**doo]
I'm staying at ... (said by man/woman) estou hospedado/hospedada em ... [shtoh – ayng]
I'd like to stay another two nights gostaria de ficar mais duas noites [gooshtar**ee**-a di fik**a**r mīsh d**oo**-aJ n**oh**-itsh]
steak o bife [beef]
steal roubar [rohb**a**r]
my bag has been stolen

roubaram-me a mala [rohbarowng m-ya mala]
steep (hill) íngreme [eengrim]
steering a direcção [direhsowng]
step: on the step no degrau [digrow]
stereo a aparelhagem (de som) [aparil-yaJayng (di song)]
sterling as libras esterlinas [leebraz ishtirleenash]
steward (on plane) o comissário de bordo [koomisar-yoo di bordoo]
stewardess a hospedeira [oshpidayra]
sticking plaster o adesivo [adizeevoo]
sticky tape a fita-cola [feeta kola]
still: I'm still here ainda estou aqui [a-eenda shtoh akee]
is he still there? ele ainda está aí? [ayl – shta a-ee]
keep still! fique quieto! [feek k-yehtoo]
sting: I've been stung (said by man/woman) fui picado/picada [fwee pikadoo]
stockings as meias [may-ash]
stomach o estômago [shtohmagoo]
stomach ache a dor de estômago [dohr dishtohmagoo]
stone (rock) a pedra [pehdra]
stop parar
please, stop here (to taxi driver etc) pare aqui, por favor [par akee poor favohr]
do you stop near ...? pára perto de ...? [pehrtoo di]
stop it! pare com isso! [kong eesoo]
stopover a paragem [paraJayng]
storm a tempestade [taympishtad]
straight (whisky etc) puro [pooroo]
it's straight ahead sempre em frente [saympprayng fraynt]
straightaway em seguida [ayng sigeeda]
strange (odd) esquisito [shkizeetoo]
stranger (man/woman) o estranho [shtran-yoo], a estranha
I'm a stranger here sou de fora [soh di]
strap (on watch) a pulseira [poolsayra]
(on dress) a alça [alsa]
(on suitcase) a correia [koorray-a]
strawberry o morango [moorangoo]
stream o ribeiro [ribayroo]
street a rua [roo-a]
on the street na rua
streetmap o mapa da cidade [sidad]
string o cordel [koordehl]
strong forte [fort]
stuck emperrado [aympirradoo]
it's stuck está emperrado [shta]
student (male/female) o/a

estudante [shtoodant]
stupid estúpido [shtoopidoo]
suburb os arredores [arredorish]
subway (US) o metro [mehtroo]
suddenly subitamente [soobitamaynt]
suede a camurça [kamoorsa]
sugar o açúcar [asookar]
suit o fato [fatoo]
it doesn't suit me (jacket etc) não me fica bem [nowng mi feeka bayng]
it suits you fica-lhe bem [feekal-yi]
suitcase a mala
summer o Verão [virowng]
in the summer no Verão [noo]
sun o sol
in the sun ao sol [ow]
out of the sun à sombra [sohmbra]
sunbathe tomar banho de sol [toomar ban-yoo di]
sunblock (cream) o creme écran total [kraym ekrang tootal]
sunburn a queimadura de sol [kaymadoora di]
sunburnt queimado de sol [kaymadoo]
Sunday domingo [doomeengoo]
sunglasses os óculos de sol [okooloosh di]
sun lounger a cadeira reclinável [kadayra reklinavil]
sunny: it's sunny está (a fazer) sol [shta (a fazayr) sol]
sunroof o tejadilho de abrir [tiJadeel-yoo dabreer]
sunset o pôr do sol [pohr doo]
sunshade o chapéu de sol [shapeh-oo di]
sunshine a luz do sol [looJ doo]
sunstroke a insolação [insoolasowng]
suntan o bronzeado [bronz-yadoo]
suntan lotion a loção de bronzear [loosowng di bronz-yar]
suntanned bronzeado [bronz-yadoo]
suntan oil o óleo de bronzear [ol-yoo di]
super óptimo [otimoo]
supermarket o supermercado [soopermerkadoo]
supper o jantar [Jantar]
supplement (extra charge) o suplemento [sooplimayntoo]
sure: are you sure? tem a certeza? [tayng a sirtayza]
sure! claro! [klaroo]
surname o apelido [apileedoo]
swearword a asneira [aJnayra]
sweater a camisola [kamizola]
sweatshirt a sweatshirt
Sweden a Suécia [swehs-ya]
Swedish (adj, language) sueco [swehkoo]
sweet (taste) doce [dohs]
(dessert) a sobremesa [sobrimayza]
sweets os rebuçados [riboosadoosh]
swelling o inchaço [inshasoo]
swim nadar

I'm going for a swim vou nadar [voh]
let's go for a swim vamos nadar [vamoosh]
swimming costume o fato de banho [fatoo di ban-yoo]
swimming pool a piscina [pish-seena]
swimming trunks os calções de banho [kalsoyngsh di ban-yoo]
Swiss (adj) suíço [sweesoo]
switch o interruptor [intirooptohr]
switch off (engine, TV) desligar [diJligar]
(lights) apagar
switch on (engine, TV) ligar
(lights) acender [asayndayr]
Switzerland a Suíça [sweesa]
swollen inchado [inshadoo]

T

table a mesa [mayza]
a table for two uma mesa para duas pessoas [ooma – doo-ash pisoh-ash]
tablecloth a toalha de mesa [twal-ya di mayza]
table tennis o ténis de mesa [tehnish]
table wine o vinho de mesa [veen-yoo]
tailback (of traffic) a fila de carros [feela di karroosh]
tailor a alfaiataria [alfi-ataree-a]
take (lead) levar
(accept) aceitar [asaytar]
can you take me to the ...? pode levar-me ao ...? [pod levarmow]
do you take credit cards? aceita cartões de crédito? [asayta kartoyngsh di krehditoo]
fine, I'll take it está bem, fico com ele [shta bayng feekoo kong ayl]
can I take this? (leaflet etc) posso levar isto? [posoo – eeshtoo]
how long does it take? quanto tempo leva? [kwantoo taympoo lehva]
it takes three hours leva três horas [trayzorash]
is this seat taken? este lugar está ocupado? [aysht loogar shta okoopadoo]
hamburger to take away o hamburger para levar
can you take a little off here? (to hairdresser) pode cortar um pouco aqui? [pod koortar oong pohkoo akee]
talcum powder o pó de talco [paw di talkoo]
talk falar
tall alto [altoo]
tampons os tampões [tampoyngsh]
tan o bronzeado [bronz-yadoo]
to get a tan bronzear-se [bronz-yarsi]
tank (of car) o depósito [dipozitoo]
tap a torneira [toornayra]

tape (for cassette) a fita [**fee**ta]
tape measure a fita métrica [**meh**trika]
tape recorder o gravador [gravad**ohr**]
taste o sabor [sab**ohr**]
can I taste it? posso provar? [p**o**soo]
taxi o táxi
will you get me a taxi? pode chamar-me um táxi? [pod shamarmoong]
where can I find a taxi? onde posso encontrar um táxi? [ohnd poswaynkontrar]

dialogue

to the airport/Borges Hotel, please para o aeroporto/Hotel Borges, se faz favor [paroo-ayroop**oh**rtoo/oht**eh**l b**o**rJish si fash fav**ohr**]
how much will it be? quanto vai custar? [kw**a**ntoo vī kooshtar]
two thousand escudos dois contos [d**oh**-ish k**oh**ntoosh]
that's fine right here, thanks aqui está bem, obrigado/obrigada [akee shta bayng obrigadoo]

Lisbon's taxis are inexpensive as long as your destination is within the city limits. All taxis have meters, which are generally switched on, and tips are not expected.

taxi-driver o pracista [pras**ee**shta]
taxi rank a praça de táxis [pr**a**sa di t**a**xish]
tea (drink) o chá [sha]
tea for one/two, please chá para um/dois, por favor [oong/d**oh**-ish poor fav**ohr**]

Tea is a big drink in Portugal and you'll find wonderfully elegant **casas de chá** (literally: tea houses) dotted around the country. Tea is usually served without milk; **um chá com leite** is tea with milk, **um chá com limão** tea with lemon, but **um chá de limão** is an infusion of hot water with a lemon rind.

teabags os saquinhos de chá [sak**ee**n-yooJ di sha]
teach: could you teach me? pode ensinar-me? [pod aynsin**a**rmi]
teacher (man/woman) o professor [proofes**ohr**], a professora
team a equipa [ek**ee**pa]
teaspoon a colher de chá [kool-y**eh**r di sha]
tea towel o pano de cozinha [p**a**noo di kooz**ee**n-ya]
teenager o/a adolescente [adoolish-s**ay**nt]
telegram o telegrama

telephone o telefone [telef**oh**n]
see **phone**
television a televisão
[televiz**ow**ng]

The Portuguese are avid television watchers; it's rare to find a bar, café or restaurant without a television on in the corner, even in fairly upmarket places.

tell: could you tell him ...? pode dizer-lhe ...? [pod diz**ay**rl-yi]
temperature (weather) a temperatura [taympirat**oo**ra]
(fever) a febre [fehbr]
tennis o ténis [t**eh**nish]
tennis ball a bola de ténis [di]
tennis court o campo de ténis [k**a**mpoo]
tennis racket a raqueta de ténis [rak**eh**ta]
tent a tenda (de campismo) [t**ay**nda (di kamp**ee**Jmoo)]
term (at university, school) o período escolar [pir**ee**-oodoo shkool**ar**]
terminus (rail) o terminal [tirmin**a**l]
terrible terrível [tirr**ee**vil]
terrific (weather) esplêndido [shpl**ay**ndidoo]
(food, teacher) excelente [ish-sel**ay**nt]
than* do que [doo ki]
smaller than mais pequeno do que [mīsh pik**ay**noo]

thanks, thank you (said by man/woman) obrigado/obrigada [obrig**a**doo]
thank you very much muito obrigado/obrigada [mw**ee**ngtoo]
thanks for the lift obrigado/obrigada pela boleia [pila bool**ay**-a]
no thanks não obrigado/obrigada [nowng]

dialogue

thanks (said by man/woman) obrigado/obrigada
that's OK, don't mention it está bem, não se preocupe com isso [shta bayng nowng si pri-ook**oo**p kong **ee**soo]

that*: that ... esse/essa ... [ays/**eh**sa]
(further away) aquele/aquela ... [ak**ay**l/ak**eh**la]
that one esse/essa/isso [**ee**soo]
(further away) aquele/aquela/aquilo [ak**ee**loo]
I hope that ... espero que ... [shp**eh**ro ki]
that's nice! que bom! [bong]
is that ...? isso é ...? [eh]
that's it (that's right) certo [s**eh**rtoo]
the* o [oo], a
(**pl**) os [oosh], as [ash]

theatre o teatro [t-**ya**troo]
their* deles [**day**lish], delas [**deh**lash]
theirs* deles, delas
them* os [oosh]
(feminine) as [ash]
for them para eles/elas [aylsh/**eh**lash]
with them com eles/elas [kong]
to them para eles/elas
who? – them quem? – eles/elas [kayng]
then (at that time) então [ayn**tow**ng]
(after that) depois [dip**oh**-ish]
there ali [al**ee**], lá
over there ali adiante [ad-**ya**nt]
up there ali acima [as**ee**ma]
is there/are there ...? há ...? [a]
there is/there are ... há ...
there you are (giving something) tome lá [tohm]
thermometer o termómetro [tirm**oh**mitroo]
Thermos flask® o termo [**tay**rmoo]
these*: these men estes homens [**ay**shtiz**oh**mayngsh]
these women estas mulheres [**eh**shtaJ mool-y**eh**rish]
I'd like these queria estes/estas [kir**ee**-a **ay**shtish/**eh**shtash]
they* (male) eles [**ay**lish]
(female) elas [**eh**lash]
thick espesso [shp**ay**soo]
(stupid) estúpido [sht**oo**pidoo]
thief (man/woman) o ladrão [ladr**ow**ng], a ladra
thigh a coxa [k**oh**sha]
thin fino [f**ee**noo]
(person) magro [m**a**groo]
thing a coisa [k**oh**-iza]
my things as minhas coisas [aJ m**ee**n-yash k**oh**-izash]
think pensar [payns**ar**]
I think so acho que sim [**a**shoo ki seeng]
I don't think so acho que não [nowng]
I'll think about it vou pensar [voh]
third party insurance o seguro contra terceiros [sig**oo**roo k**oh**ntra tirs**ay**roosh]
thirsty: I'm thirsty tenho sede [**tay**n-yoo sayd]
this*: this boy este menino [aysht min**ee**noo]
this girl esta menina [**eh**shta min**ee**na]
this one este [aysht]/esta [**eh**shta]/isto [**ee**shtoo]
this is my wife esta é a minha mulher [eh a m**ee**n-ya mool-y**eh**r]
is this ...? isto é ...? [**ee**shtweh]
those*: those ... esses/essas ... [**ay**sish/**eh**sash]
(further away) aquelas/aquelas ... [ak**ay**lish/ak**eh**lash]
which ones? – those quais? – esses/essas [kwīsh]
(further away) quais? –

English → Portuguese

Th

aqueles/aquelas
thread o fio [**fee**-oo]
throat a garg**a**nta
throat pastilles as pastilhas p**a**ra a garganta [pasht**ee**l-yash]
through por, através de [atrav**eh**J di]
does it go through ...? (train, bus) p**a**ssa em ...? [ayng]
throw atir**a**r
throw away deitar f**o**ra [dayt**ar**]
thumb o polegar [pooligar]
thunderstorm a trovoada [troovw**a**da]
Thursday quinta-feira [**kee**nta f**ay**ra]
ticket o bilhete [bil-y**ay**t]

dialogue

a return to Setúbal um bilhete de ida e v**o**lta p**a**ra Setúbal [oong – **dee**dī – sit**oo**bal]
coming back when? quando v**o**lta? [**kw**andoo]
today/next Tuesday hoje/na próxima terça-feira [ohJ/na pr**o**sima t**ay**rsa f**ay**ra]
that will be 500 escudos são quinhentos escudos [sowng keen-y**ay**ntooz-shk**oo**doosh]

It's always cheaper to buy bus and tram tickets in advance (**pré-comprados**) in one of the kiosks around Lisbon and other major cities – these can be return or multiple tickets. You can also buy multiple, return or single tickets for the underground, and the same rule applies – the more trips you buy at once, the cheaper it will be.

ticket office (bus, rail) a bilheteira [bil-yit**ay**ra]
tide a maré [mar**eh**]
tie (necktie) a grav**a**ta
tight (clothes etc) apertado [apirt**a**doo]
it's too tight está demasiado apertado [shta dimaz-y**a**doo]
tights os collants [kool**a**nsh]
till a caixa [**kī**sha]
time* o tempo [**tay**mpoo]
what's the time? que horas são? [k-y**o**rash sowng]
this time esta vez [**eh**shta vaysh]
last time a última vez [**oo**ltima]
next time a próxima vez [pr**o**sima]
three times três vezes [traysh v**ay**zish]
timetable o horário [oo or**ar**-yoo]
tin (can) a l**a**ta
tinfoil o papel de alumínio [pap**eh**l daloom**ee**n-yoo]
tin-opener o abre-latas [abril**a**tash]
tiny minúsculo [min**oo**shkooloo]
tip (to waiter etc) a gorgeta [goorJ**ay**ta]

Th

Simple cafés and restaurants don't charge for service, though people generally leave small change as a tip in these places. In more upmarket restaurants, you'll either be charged or should leave around 10 per cent. Hotels include a service charge, but porters and maids expect something; cab drivers don't.

tired cansado [kans**a**doo]
I'm tired (said by man/woman) estou cansado/cans**a**da [shtoh]
tissues os lenços de papel [l**ay**nsoosh di pap**ehl**]
to: to Lisbon/London p**a**ra Lisboa/Londres [liJb**oh**-a/l**oh**ndrish]
to Portugal/England para Portugal/Inglaterra [poortoog**a**l/inglat**eh**rra]
we're going to the museum/to the post office vamos ao museo/aos correios [vam**oo**z ow moos**ay**-oo/owsh koorr**ay**-oosh]
toast (bread) a torrada [toorr**a**da]
today hoje [ohJ]
toe o dedo do pé [d**ay**doo doo peh]
together juntos [J**oo**ntoosh]
we're together (in shop etc) viemos juntos [v-y**ay**moosh J**oo**ntoosh]
toilet a casa de banho [k**a**za di b**a**n-yoo]
where is the toilet? onde é a casa de banho? [ohnd**eh**]
I have to go to the toilet tenho de ir à casa de banho [t**ay**n-yoo deer]

Ladies' toilets often charge (or a small tip might be expected) and they are usually clean. The gents' toilets may look more aesthetic (lots of ironwork) and are free, but are usually unattractive inside. A sign that says **retretes** will head you in the right direction, then it's **homens** for men and **senhoras** for women.

toilet paper o papel higiénico [pap**ehl** iJ-y**eh**nikoo]
tomato o tomate [toom**a**t]
tomato juice o sumo de tomate [s**oo**moo di toom**a**t]
tomato ketchup o ketchup
tomorrow amanhã [aman-y**a**ng]
tomorrow morning amanhã de manhã [aman-y**a**ng di man-y**a**ng]
the day after tomorrow depois de amanhã [dip**oh**-ish daman-y**a**ng]
toner (cosmetic) o tónico [t**o**nikoo]
tongue a língua [l**ee**ngwa]
tonic (water) a água t**ó**nica [**a**gwa]
tonight esta noite [**eh**shta n**oh**-it]
tonsillitis a amigdalite [ameegdal**ee**t]

too (excessively) demasiado [dimaz-y**a**doo]
(also) também [tamb**ay**ng]
too hot demasiado quente [kaynt]
too much demais [dimīsh]
me too eu também [**ay**-oo tamb**ay**ng]
tooth o dente [daynt]
toothache a dor de dentes [dohr di dayntsh]
toothbrush a escova de dentes [shk**oh**va]
toothpaste a pasta de dentes [p**a**shta]
top: on top of ... em cima de ... [ayng s**ee**ma di]
at the top no alto [noo **a**ltoo]
at the top of ... no topo de ... [t**oh**poo di]
top floor o piso superior [p**ee**zoo soopir-y**oh**r]
topless topless
torch a lanterna [lant**eh**rna]
total o total [toot**a**l]
tour a excursão [shkoors**ow**ng]
is there a tour of ...? há alguma excursão/visita guiada a ...? [alg**oo**ma – viz**ee**ta gee-**a**da]
tour guide (man/woman) o guia turístico [g**ee**-a toor**ee**shtikoo], a guia turística
tourist (man/woman) o/a turista [toor**ee**shta]
tourist information office o turismo [toor**ee**Jmoo]

You'll find a tourist office in almost any sizable town or village. The vast majority are exceptionally helpful and friendly. Aside from the help they can give you in finding a room (some will make bookings, others simply supply lists), they often have useful local maps and leaflets that you won't find in the national offices. Local tourist office opening hours are generally Monday to Saturday from 9 a.m. to 12.30 p.m. and from 2 to 6 p.m., though in Porto, Lisbon, the Algarve and other resorts they often stay open later than this, and open on Sunday too. In more out-of-the-way towns and villages, offices will be closed at weekends.

tour operator o operador turístico [opirad**oh**r toor**ee**shtikoo]
towards para
towel a toalha [tw**a**l-ya]
town a cidade [sid**a**d]
in town na cidade
just out of town junto à cidade [j**oo**ntwa]
town centre o centro da cidade [s**ay**ntroo]
town hall a câmara municipal [moonisip**a**l]
toy o brinquedo [breenk**ay**doo]
track (US) o cais [kīsh]
see **platform**
tracksuit o fato de treino [f**a**too di tr**ay**noo]

traditional tradicional [tradis-yoon**al**]
traffic o trânsito [tr**a**nzitoo]
traffic jam o engarrafamento [ayngarrafam**ay**ntoo]
traffic lights os semáforos [sim**a**fooroosh]
trailer (for carrying tent etc) o reboque [rib**o**k]
(US) a roulotte [rool**o**t]
trailer park o parque de campismo [park di kamp**ee**Jmoo]
train o comboio [komb**oy**-oo]
by train de comboio [di]

CP, the Portuguese railway company, operates all trains. Most are designated **Regional**, which means they stop at most stations en route and have first- and second-class cars. The next category up, **Intercidades**, are twice as fast and twice as expensive, and you should reserve your seat in advance if using them. The fastest, most luxurious and priciest services are the **Rápidos** (known as **Alfa**), which speed between Lisbon, Coimbra, and Porto – sometimes they have only first-class seats. Both these latter classes charge supplements for rail pass holders.
Always turn up at the station with time to spare since long queues often form at the ticket desk. If you end up on the train without first buying a ticket you could be liable for a huge supplement, or be kicked off the train at the next stop.
Train travel is inexpensive and most travellers simply buy a ticket every time they make a journey. If you're planning on a lot of train travel, using a rail pass will probably save you money.

dialogue

is this the train for Fátima? é este o comboio para Fátima? [eh **ay**shtoo]
sure com certeza [kong sirt**ay**za]
no, you want that platform there não, tem que ir à plataforma de lá [nowng tayng ki-**eer** – di]

trainers (shoes) os sapatos de treino [sap**a**toosh di tr**ay**noo]
train station a estação de comboios [shtas**ow**ng di komb**oy**-oosh]
tram o eléctrico [el**eh**trikoo]
translate traduzir [tradooz**eer**]
could you translate that? pode traduzir isto? [pod – **ee**shtoo]
translation a tradução [tradoos**ow**ng]
translator (man/woman) o tradutor [tradoot**ohr**], a tradutora
trash (waste) o lixo [**lee**shoo]
trashcan o caixote de lixo [kīsh**o**t di **lee**shoo]

travel viajar [v-yaJ**a**r]
we're travelling around estamos a viajar por aí [sht**a**mooz – poor a-**ee**]
travel agent's a agência de viagens [aJ**ay**nsya di v-y**a**Jayngsh]
traveller's cheque o cheque de viagem [shehk di v-y**a**Jayng]
tray a travessa [trav**eh**sa]
tree a árvore [**a**rvoori]
tremendous bestial [bisht-y**a**l]
trendy à m**o**da
trim: just a trim, please (to hairdresser) queria só cortar as pontas, por favor [kir**ee**-a saw koort**a**r ash p**o**ntash poor fav**oh**r]
trip (excursion) a excursão [shkoors**ow**ng]
I'd like to go on a trip to ... gostava de ir numa viagem a ... [goosht**a**va deer n**oo**ma v-y**a**Jayng]
trolley o carrinho [karr**ee**n-yoo]
trouble: I'm having trouble with ... tenho tido problemas com ... [t**ay**n-yoo t**ee**doo proobl**ay**mash kong]
trousers as calças [k**a**lsash]
true verdadeiro [virdad**ay**roo]
that's not true não é verdade [nowng eh vird**a**d]
trunk (US: of car) o porta-bagagens [p**o**rta-bag**a**Jayngsh]
trunks (swimming) os calções de banho [kals**oy**ngsh di b**a**n-yoo]
try tent**a**r
can I try it? posso experimentar? [p**o**soo shpirimaynt**a**r]
(food) posso provar? [proov**a**r]
try on experimentar
can I try it on? posso experimentar? [p**o**soo shpirimaynt**a**r]
T-shirt a T-shirt
Tuesday terça-feira [t**ay**rsa f**ay**ra]
tuna o atum [at**oo**ng]
tunnel o túnel [t**oo**nil]
turn: turn left/right vire à esquerda/direita [v**ee**ra shk**ay**rda/dir**ay**ta]
turn off: where do I turn off? onde devo vir**a**r? [ohnd d**ay**voo]
can you turn the heating off? pode desligar o aquecimento? [pod diJlig**a**r oo akesim**ay**ntoo]
turn on: can you turn the heating on? pode lig**a**r o aquecimento?
turning (in road) a curva [k**oo**rva]
TV TV [tay-vay]
tweezers a pinça [p**ee**nsa]
twice duas vezes [d**oo**-aJ v**ay**zish]
twice as much o dobro [oo d**oh**broo]
twin beds as camas separadas [k**a**mash sipar**a**dash]
twin room o quarto com duas camas [kw**a**rtoo kong d**oo**-ash]
twist: I've twisted my ankle torci o meu tornozelo

Tr

[toorsee oo may-oo toornoozayloo]
type o tipo [teepoo]
a different type of ... um tipo diferente de ... [oong – difiraynt di]
typical típico [teepikoo]
tyre o pneu [p-nay-oo]

U

ugly feio [fay-oo]
UK Reino Unido [raynooneedoo]
ulcer a úlcera [oolsira]
umbrella o guarda-chuva [gwarda shoova]
uncle o tio [tee-oo]
unconscious inconsciente [inkonsh-syaynt]
under (in position) debaixo de [dibīshoo di]
(less than) menos de [maynoosh di]
underdone (meat) mal passado [pasadoo]
underground (railway) o metro [mehtroo]
underpants as cuecas [kwehkash]
understand: I understand já percebi [Ja pirsibee]
I don't understand não percebo [nowng pirsayboo]
do you understand? está a compreender? [shta a kompr-ayndayr]
unemployed desempregado [dizaymprigadoo]
United States os Estados Unidos [shtadooz ooneedoosh]
university a universidade [oonivirsidad]
unleaded petrol a gasolina sem chumbo [gazooleena sayng shoomboo]
unlimited mileage quilometragem ilimitada [kilomitraJayng ilimitada]
unlock abrir [abreer]
unpack desfazer as malas [dishfazayr aJ malash]
until até a [ateh]
unusual pouco vulgar [pohkoo voolgar]
up acima [aseema]
up there lá em cima [ayng seema]
he's not up yet (not out of bed) ele ainda não está levantado [ayl a-eenda nowng shta levantadoo]
what's up? (what's wrong?) o que aconteceu? [oo ki akontisay-oo]
upmarket sofisticado [soofishtikadoo]
upset stomach o desarranjo intestinal [dizarranJoo intishtinal]
upside down de pernas para o ar [di pehrnash proo ar]
upstairs lá em cima [ayng seema]
urgent urgente [oorJaynt]
us* nos [noosh]
with us connosco [konohshkoo]
for us para nós [nosh]

USA os Estados Unidos [sht**a**dooz oon**ee**doosh]
use usar [ooz**ar**]
may I use ...? posso usar ...? [p**o**soo]
useful útil [**oo**til]
usual usual [oozw**al**]
the usual (drink etc) o de sempre [oo di saympr]

V

vacancy: do you have any vacancies? (hotel) têm vagas? [**tay**-ayng v**a**gash]
see **room**
vacation as férias [**feh**r-yash]
on vacation de férias [shtoh di]
vaccination a vacinação [vasinas**ow**ng]
vacuum cleaner o aspirador [ashpirad**oh**r]
valid (ticket etc) válido [v**a**lidoo]
how long is it valid for? até quando é válido? [at**eh** kw**a**ndoo]
valley o vale [val]
valuable (adj) valioso [val-y**oh**zoo]
can I leave my valuables here? posso deixar aqui os meus artigos de valor? [p**o**soo daysh**ar** ak**ee** ooJ m**ay**-ooz art**ee**goosh di val**oh**r]
value o valor
van a furgoneta [foorgoon**ay**ta]
vanilla a baunilha [bownn**ee**l-ya]
a vanilla ice cream um gelado de baunilha [oong Jil**a**doo di]
vary: it varies varia [var**ee**-a]
vase a jarra [J**a**rra]
veal a vitela [vit**eh**la]
vegetables os legumes [lig**oo**mish]
vegetarian (man/woman) o vegetariano [viJitar-y**a**noo], a vegetari**a**na

Vegetarians should note that chicken or ham is often not considered meat by the Portuguese; cheese omelettes sometimes come with ham included, and vegetable soup is often made with chicken or pork stock, with lumps of bacon floating in it. Most restaurants do good salads if requested, but again look out for the ham.

vending machine a máquina de venda [m**a**kina di v**ay**nda]
very muito [mw**ee**ngtoo]
very little for me muito pouco para mim [p**oh**koo p**a**ra meeng]
I like it very much gosto muito disso [g**o**shtoo – d**ee**soo]
vest (under shirt) a camisola interior [kamiz**o**la intir-y**oh**r]
via via [v**ee**-a]
video (film) o vídeo [v**ee**d-yoo]
video recorder o videogravador [veed-yoogravad**oh**r]

view a vista [**vee**shta]
villa a vivenda [viv**ay**nda]
village a aldeia [ald**ay**-a]
vinegar o vinagre [vin**a**gr]
vineyard a vinha [**vee**n-ya]
visa o visto [**vee**shtoo]
visit visitar [vizit**ar**]
I'd like to visit ... gostaria de visitar ... [gooshtar**ee**-a di]
vital: it's vital that ... é imprescindível que ... [eh impresh-sind**ee**vil ki]
vodka o v**o**dka
voice a voz [vosh]
voltage a tensão [tayns**ow**ng]

The voltage in Portugal is 220V. You will need an adapter for a two-pin (round) plug.

vomit vomitar [voomit**ar**]

W

waist a cintura [sint**oo**ra]
waistcoat o colete [kool**ay**t]
wait esperar [shpir**ar**]
wait for me espere por mim [shpehr poor meeng]
don't wait for me não espere por mim [nowng]
can I wait until my wife/partner gets here? posso esperar até a minha mulher/companheira chegar? [pos shpir**ar** at**eh** a m**ee**n-ya mool-y**eh**r/kompan-y**ay**ra shig**ar**]
can you do it while I wait? pode fazer isso enquanto espero? [pod faz**ay**r **ee**soo aynkw**a**ntoo shp**eh**roo]
could you wait here for me? pode esperar-me? [pod shpir**ar**mi]
waiter o empregado de mesa [aympreg**a**doo di m**ay**za]
waiter! se faz favor! [si fash fav**oh**r]
waitress a empregada de mesa [aympreg**a**da di m**ay**za]
waitress! se faz favor!
wake: can you wake me up at 5.30? pode acordar-me às cinco meia? [pod akoord**a**rmi ash s**ee**nkwee m**ay**-a]
wake-up call a chamada para despertar [sham**a**da p**a**ra dishpirt**ar**]
Wales o País de Gales [pa-**ee**J di g**a**lish]
walk: is it a long walk? é muito longe a pé? [eh mw**ee**ngtoo lohnJ a peh]
it's only a short walk é perto a pé [p**eh**rtoo]
I'll walk vou a pé [voh]
I'm going for a walk vou dar um passeio [oong pas**ay**-oo]
Walkman® o Walkman®
wall (outside) o muro [m**oo**roo]
(inside) a parede [par**ay**d]
wallet a carteira [kart**ay**ra]
wander: I like just wandering around gosto de andar a ver [g**o**shtoo dand**ar** a vayr]
want: I want a ... queria

um ... [kiree-a oong]
I don't want any ... não quero ... [nowng kehroo]
I want to go home quero ir para casa [eer para kaza]
I don't want to não quero
he wants to ele quer [ayl kehr]
what do you want? o que deseja? [oo ki disayJa]
ward (in hospital) a enfermaria [aynfirmaree-a]
warm quente [kaynt]
I'm so warm tenho tanto calor [tayn-yoo tantoo kalohr]
was*: he was (ele) era [(ayl) ehra]; (ele) estava [shtava]
she was (ela) era [(ehla)]; (ele) estava
it was era; estava
wash lavar
(oneself) lavar-se [–si]
can you wash these? pode lavar isto? [pod – eeshtoo]
washer (for bolt etc) a anilha [aneel-ya]
washhand basin o lavatório [lavator-yoo]
washing (clothes) a roupa para lavar [rohpa]
washing machine a máquina de lavar [makina di]
washing powder o detergente [deterJaynt]
washing-up liquid o detergente líquido [leekidoo]
wasp a vespa [vayshpa]
watch (wristwatch) o relógio (de pulso) [riloJ-yoo (di poolsoo)]
will you watch my things for me? pode tomar conta das minhas coisas? [pod toomar kohnta daJ meen-yash koh-izash]
watch out! cuidado! [kwidadoo]
watch strap a correia de relógio [koorray-a di riloJ-yoo]
water a água [agwa]
may I have some water? pode dar-me um pouco de água? [pod darmoong pohkoo dagwa]
waterproof (adj) à prova de água [dagwa]
waterskiing o esqui aquático [shkee akwatikoo]
wave (in sea) a onda [ohnda]
way: it's this way é por aqui [eh por akee]
it's that way é por ali [alee]
is it a long way to ...? é muito longe até ...? [mweengtoo lohnJ ateh]
no way! de maneira nenhuma! [di manayra nin-yooma]

dialogue

could you tell me the way to ...? pode indicar-me o caminho para ...? [podindikarmoo kameen-yoo]
go straight on until you reach the traffic lights siga em frente até chegar ao semáforo [seegayng fraynt ateh shigar ow semafooroo]
turn left vire à esquerda

[**vee**ra shk**ay**rda]
take the first on the right vire na primeira à direita [veer na prim**ay**ra dir**ay**ta]
see **where**

we* nós [nosh]
weak fraco [fr**a**koo]
weather o tempo [t**ay**mpoo]

dialogue

what's the weather forecast? qual é a previsão do tempo? [kwal**eh** a priviz**ow**ng doo t**ay**mpoo]
it's going to be fine vai estar bom [vī shtar bong]
it's going to rain vai chover [shoov**ay**r]
it'll brighten up later vai melhorar mais tarde [mil-yoor**a**r mīsh tard]

wedding o casamento [kazam**ay**ntoo]
wedding ring a aliança [al-y**a**nsa]
Wednesday quarta-feira [kw**a**rta f**ay**ra]
week a semana [sim**a**na]
a week (from) today de hoje a uma semana [dohJ a **oo**ma]
a week (from) tomorrow de amanhã a uma semana [daman-y**a**ng]
weekend o fim de semana [feeng di]
at the weekend no fim de semana [noo]
weight o peso [p**ay**zoo]
weird esquisito [shkiz**ee**too]
he's weird ele é esquisito [ayl eh]
welcome: welcome to ... bem vindo a ... [bayng v**ee**ndwa]
you're welcome (don't mention it) não tem de quê [nowng tayng di kay]
well: I don't feel well não me sinto muito bem [mi s**ee**ntoo mw**ee**ngtoo bayng]
she's not well ela não está bem [**eh**la – shta]
you speak English very well fala inglês muito bem [ingl**ay**sh]
well done! muito bem!
this one as well este também [aysht tamb**ay**ng]
well well! (surprise) ah sim! [seeng]

dialogue

how are you? como está? [k**oh**mo shta]
very well, thanks, and you? (said by man/woman) muito bem, obrigado/obrigada, e você? [obrig**a**doo – ee vos**ay**]

well-done (meat) bem passado [bayng pas**a**doo]
Welsh galês [gal**ay**sh]
I'm Welsh (man/woman) sou

galês/galesa [soh – galayza]

were*: **we were** éramos [ehramoosh]; estávamos [shtavamoosh]

you were você era [vosay ehra]; você estava [shtava]

they were (eles/elas) eram [(aylsh/ehlash) ehrowng]; (eles/elas) estavam [shtavowng]

west o oeste [wesht]

in the west no oeste [noo]

West Indian (adj) antilhano [antil-yanoo]

wet molhado [mool-yadoo]

what? o quê? [oo kay]

what's that? o que é isso? [oo k-yeh eesoo]

what should I do? o que devo fazer? [oo kay dayvoo fazayr]

what a view! que vista linda! [ki veeshta leenda]

what bus do I take? que autocarro devo tomar? [ki owtookarroo dayvoo toomar]

wheel a roda

wheelchair a cadeira de rodas [kadayra di rodash]

when? quando? [kwandoo]

when we get back quando nós voltarmos [nosh vooltarmoosh]

when's the train/ferry? quando é o comboio/ferry? [kwandweh o komboy-oo]

where? onde? [ohnd]

I don't know where it is não sei onde está [nowng say ohndshta]

dialogue

where is the cathedral? onde fica a catedral? [ohnd feeka]

it's over there fica ali adiante [feekalee ad-yant]

could you show me where it is on the map? pode mostrar-me onde está no mapa? [pod mooshtrarmi ohndshta noo mapa]

it's just here está bem aqui [shta bayng akee]

see **way**

which: which bus? qual autocarro? [kwal owtookarroo]

dialogue

which one? qual deles? [kwal daylish]

that one aquele [akayl]

this one? este? [aysht]

no, that one não aquele ali [nowng – alee]

while: while I'm here enquanto estou aqui [aynkwantoo shtoh akee]

whisky o whisky [weeshkee]

white branco [brankoo]

white wine o vinho branco [veen-yoo]

who? quem? [kayng]

who is it? quem é? [kayngeh]

the man who ... o homem que ... [**oh**mayng ki]
whole: the whole week toda a semana [**toh**da sim**a**na]
the whole lot tudo isto [**too**doo **ee**shtoo]
whose: whose is this? de quem é isto? [di kayng eh **ee**shtoo]
why? porquê? [poork**ay**]
why not? porque não? [nowng]
wide largo [**l**argoo]
wife: my wife a minha mulher [**mee**n-ya mool-**yeh**r]
will*: will you do it for me? fá-lo para mim? [**f**aloo p**a**ra meeng]
wind o vento [**vay**ntoo]
window a janela [Jan**eh**la]
(of shop) a montra [m**oh**ntra]
near the window ao pé da janela [ow peh]
in the window (of shop) na montra
window seat o lugar ao pé da janela [loog**a**r ow peh da Jan**eh**la]
windscreen o pára-brisas [p**a**ra-br**ee**zash]
windscreen wiper o limpa pára-brisas [l**ee**mpa]
windsurfing o windsurf
windy: it's so windy está muito vento [shta mw**ee**ngtoo v**ay**ntoo]
wine o vinho [v**ee**n-yoo]
can we have some more wine? pode trazer mais vinho? [pod traz**ay**r mīsh]

The best-known Portuguese table wines are reds from the Dão region. Among other smaller regions offering interesting red wines are **Colares** (near Sintra), **Valpaços** from Trás-os-Montes, **Reguengos** from Alentejo and **Lagoa** from the Algarve. **Bucelas** in the Estremadura offers crisp, dry white wines. **Madeira** wines are heady fortified wines, sweet or dry.

The light, slightly sparkling **vinhos verdes** – 'green wines', in age not colour – are produced in quantity in the **Minho**. They're drunk early and don't mature or improve with age, but are great with meals, especially shellfish. There are red and rosé vinhos verdes, though the whites are the most successful – **Casal Garcia** is the one you'll find most often in restaurants. Otherwise, Portuguese rosé wines are known abroad mainly through the spectacularly successful export of **Mateus Rosé**.

Portugal also produces a range of sparkling champagne-method wines: **espumantes naturais**. These are designated **bruto** (extra-dry), **seco** (fairly dry), **meio seco** (quite sweet) or **doce** (very sweet). The best of these come from the **Bairrada** region, northwest of Coimbra, though **Raposeira** wines are the most commonly available. Even the most basic of restaurants usually have a decent selection of wines, many of which are available

in half-bottles, too. The **vinho da casa** (house wine) is nearly always remarkably good value.

wine list a lista dos vinhos [**lee**shta dooJ **vee**n-yoosh]
winter o Inverno [inv**eh**rnoo]
in the winter no Inverno [noo]
winter holiday as férias de inverno [**feh**r-yash dinv**eh**rnoo]
wire o arame [ar**a**m]
(electric) o fio [**fee**-oo]
wish: best wishes com os melhores cumprimentos [kong ooJ mil-y**o**rish koomprim**ay**ntoosh]
with com [kong]
I'm staying with ... estou na casa do/da ... [shtoh na k**a**za doo]
without sem [sayng]
witness a testemunha [tishtim**oo**n-ya]
will you be a witness for me? quer ser minha testemunha? [kehr sayr m**ee**n-ya]
woman a mulher [mool-y**eh**r]

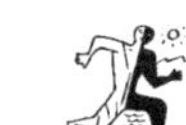

women
Portugal is rarely a dangerous place for women travellers, and only in the following few areas do you need to be particularly wary: parts of Lisbon (particularly the Cais do Sodré and the Bairro Alto by night), streets immediately around the train stations in the larger towns (traditionally the red light districts), and the Algarve, where aggressive males congregate on the pick-up. People may initially wonder why you're travelling on your own – especially inland and in the mountains, where Portuguese women never travel unaccompanied – but once they have accepted that you are a crazy foreigner you're likely to be welcomed.

wonderful (weather, holiday, person) maravilhoso [maravil-y**oh**zoo]
(meal) excelente [ish-sel**ay**nt]
won't*: it won't start não pega [nowng p**eh**ga]
wood (material) a madeira [mad**ay**ra]
woods (forest) o bosque [boshk]
wool a lã [lang]
word a pal**a**vra
work o trabalho [trab**a**l-yoo]
it's not working não funciona [nowng foons-y**oh**na]
I work in ... trabalho em ... [ayng]
world o mundo [m**oo**ndoo]
worry: I'm worried (said by man/woman) estou preocupado/preocup**a**da [shtoh pri-okoop**a**doo]
worse: it's worse está pior [shta p-yor]
worst o pior [oo]
worth: is it worth a visit? vale a pena uma visita? [val a

p**ay**na **oo**ma viz**ee**ta]
would: would you give this to ...? pode dar isto a ...? [pod dar **ee**shtwa]
wrap: could you wrap it up? pode embrulhá-lo? [aymbrool-y**a**loo]
wrapping paper o papel de embrulho [pap**eh**l daymbr**oo**l-yoo]
wrist o pulso [p**oo**lsoo]
write escrever [shkriv**ay**r]
could you write it down? pode escrever isso? [pod – **ee**soo]
how do you write it? como é que escreve isso? [k**oh**moo eh kishkr**eh**v]
writing paper o papel de carta [pap**eh**l di]
wrong: it's the wrong key não é esta a chave [nowng eh **eh**shta shav]
this is the wrong train este não é o comboio [aysht nowng eh oo komb**oy**-oo]
the bill's wrong a conta está enganada [k**oh**ntashta aynganada]
sorry, wrong number desculpe, enganei-me no número [dishk**oo**lp ayngan**ay**mi noo n**oo**miroo]
sorry, wrong room desculpe, enganei-me no quarto [kw**a**rtoo]
there's something wrong with ... passa-se qualquer coisa com ... [p**a**sasi kwalk**eh**r k**oh**-iza kong]
what's wrong? o que se passa? [oo ki si]

X-ray o raio X [r**a**-yoo sheesh]

yacht o iate [yat]
yard* a jarda [J**a**rda]
year o ano [**a**noo]
yellow amarelo [amar**eh**loo]
yes sim [seeng]
yesterday ontem [**oh**ntayng]
yesterday morning ontem de manhã [di man-y**a**ng]
the day before yesterday anteontem [anti**oh**ntayng]
yet ainda [a-**ee**nda], já [Ja]

dialogue

is it here yet? já está aqui? [Ja shta ak**ee**]
no, not yet não, ainda não [nowng a-**ee**nda nowng]
you'll have to wait a little longer yet ainda terá que esperar um pouquinho [tir**a** kishpir**a**r oong pohk**ee**n-yoo]

yoghurt o iogurte [yoog**oo**rt]
you* (pol) você [vos**ay**]
(more formal: to man/woman) o

senhor [oo sin-y**oh**r], a senh**o**ra
(fam) tu [too]
this is for you isto é para si [**ee**shtweh p**a**ra see]
(fam) isto é para ti
with you consigo [kons**ee**goo]
(fam) contigo [kont**ee**goo]

The most usual way of addressing people you don't know is to use: **o senhor** (to a man), **a senhora** (to a woman), **os senhores** (to more than one man) and **as senhoras** (to more than one woman).
Você usually indicates greater familiarity with the other person. It is used between people who feel on an equal footing.
Tu indicates intimacy. It is used among family members, close friends, and between people who belong to a particular group (for example children, students).

young jovem [J**o**vayng]
your* (pol) seu [**say**-oo], sua [s**oo**-a]
(more formal: to man/woman) do senhor [sin-y**oh**r], da senhora [sin-y**o**ra]
(fam) teu [**tay**-oo], tua [**too**-a]
yours* (pol) seu [**say**-oo], sua [s**oo**-a]
(more formal: to a man/woman) do senhor [doo sin-y**oh**r], da senhora [sin-y**o**ra]
(fam) teu [**tay**-oo], tua [**too**-a]
youth hostel o albergue da juventude [alb**eh**rg da Joovaynt**oo**d]

zero zero [z**eh**roo]
zip o fecho éclair® [fayshwaykl**eh**r]
could you put a new zip on? pode pôr um fecho éclair novo? [pod pohr oong – n**oh**voo]
zipcode o código postal [k**o**digoo pooshtal]
zoo o jardim zoológico [Jard**ee**ng zwol**o**Jikoo]
zucchini a courgette

Portuguese → English

Colloquialisms

The following are words you might well hear. You shouldn't be tempted to use any of the stronger ones unless you are sure of your audience.

bestial! [bisht-**yal**] fantastic!
burro m [**boo**rroo] thickhead
cabrão! [kabr**owng**] bastard!
está nas suas sete quintas [shta nash s**oo**-ash seht k**ee**ntash] he's/she's in his/her element
estou-me nas tintas [shtoh-mi nash t**ee**ntash] I don't give a damn
filho da puta! [p**oo**ta] son-of-a-bitch!
gajo m [**ga**Joo] bloke
grosso [gr**oh**soo] pissed
imbecil [imbes**eel**] stupid
isso é canja [eesw**eh** k**a**nJa] piece of cake (literally: this is chicken soup)
louco [l**oh**koo] nutter
maçada [mas**a**da] bother
maluco [mal**oo**koo] barmy, nuts
merda! [m**eh**rda] shit!
não faz mal [nowng faJ] it doesn't matter
não me diga! [nowng mi d**ee**ga] you don't say!
ora essa! [**o**ra **eh**sa] don't be stupid!
porreiro! [poorr**ay**roo] bloody good!
que chatice! [ki shat**ees**] oh no!, blast!
que disparate! [dishpar**a**t] rubbish!, nonsense!
que droga! [dr**o**ga] blast!
raios o partam! [**ra**-yooz oo p**a**rtowng] damn you!
rua! [r**oo**-a] get out of here!
sacana! bastard!
tolo [t**oh**loo] silly
vá à fava! go away!
vá para o caralho! [paroo kar**a**l-yoo] fuck off!
vá para o diabo! [d-y**a**boo] go to hell!
vá para o inferno! [inf**eh**rno] go to hell!

A

a the; to; her; it; to it; you
à to the
abaixo [abīshoo] below; down
mais abaixo [mīz] further down
abcesso m [absehsoo] abscess
aberto [abehrtoo] open; opened
aberto até às 19 horas open until 7 p.m.
aberto das ... às ... horas open from ... to ... o'clock
abertura f [abirtoora] opening
aborrecer [aboorrisayr] to annoy; to bore
aborrecido [aboorriseedoo] annoying; bored; annoyed
abre-garrafas m [abrigarrafash] bottle-opener
abre-latas m [abrilatash] can-opener, tin-opener
Abril [abreel] April
abrir [abreer] to open; to unlock
a abrir brevemente open soon
a/c c/o
acabar to finish
acalmar-se [–si] to calm down
acampar to camp
acaso: por acaso [poor akazoo] by chance
aceitar [asaytar] to accept; to take
acelerador m [asiliradohr] accelerator
acenda os médios switch on dipped headlights
acenda os mínimos switch on your parking lights
acender [asayndayr] to switch on; to light
acento m [asayntoo] accent
aceso [asayzoo] on, switched on
acesso m [asehsoo] access
acetona f [asitohna] nail polish remover
acho: acho que não [ashoo ki nowng] I don't think so
acho que sim [seeng] I think so
acidente m [asidaynt] accident; crash
acidente de viação [di v-ya-sowng] road accident
ácido [asidoo] sour; sharp
acima [aseema] up; above
acompanhar [akompan-yar] to accompany
aconselhar [akonsil-yar] to advise
acontecer [akontisayr] to happen
o que aconteceu? [oo ki-akontisay-oo] what has happened?, what's up?, what's wrong?
o que é que está a acontecer? [oo k-yeh kishta] what's happening?
acordado [akoordadoo] awake
acordar [akoordar] to wake, to wake up

ele já acordou? [ayl Ja akoordoh] is he awake?
acordo: de acordo com [d-ya-kohrdoo kong] according to
A.C.P. [a say pay] Portuguese Motoring Organization
acreditar to believe
acrílico m [akreelikoo] acrylic
actor m [atohr], actriz f [atreesh] actor; actress
adaptador m [adaptadohr] adapter
adega f cellar; old-style bar
adepta f [adehpta], adepto m [adehptoo] fan
adesivo m [adizeevoo] sticking plaster, Bandaid®
adeus [aday-oosh] goodbye
adeuzinho! [aday-oozeen-yoo] cheerio!
adiantado [ad-yantadoo] in advance
adiante: fica ali adiante [feekalee ad-yant] it's over there
adoecer [ad-wisayr] to fall ill
adolescente m/f [adoolish-saynt] teenager
adorar [adoorar] to adore
adorável [adooravil] lovely
adulta f [adoolta], adulto m [adooltoo] adult
advogada f [advoogada], advogado m [advoogadoo] lawyer
aeroporto m [a-ayroopohrtoo] airport
afiado [af-yadoo] sharp
afogador m choke
África f Africa
África do Sul [doo sool] South Africa
africano (m) [afrikanoo] African
afta f mouth ulcer
afundar [afoondar] to sink
agência f [aJayns-ya] agency
agência de viagens [di v-ya-Jayngsh] travel agency
agenda f [aJaynda] diary
agitar bem antes de usar shake well before using
agora [agora] now
 agora não [nowng] not just now
Agosto [agohshtoo] August
agradável [agradavil] nice, pleasant
agradecer [agradisayr] to thank
agradecido [agradiseedoo] grateful
água f [agwa] water
aguaceiro m [agwasayroo] shower
água de colónia [di] eau de toilette
água destilada f [agwa dishtilada] distilled water
água fria [free-a] cold water
água potável [pootavil] drinking water
aguardar [agwardar] to wait for
agudo [agoodoo] sharp
agulha f [agool-ya] needle
aí [a-ee] there
ainda [a-eenda] yet, still
 ainda mais ... [mīsh] even

more ...
ainda não [nowng] not yet
ainda são só ... [sowng saw] it's only ...
ajuda f [aJooda] help
ajudar to help
al. avenue
alameda f [alamayda] avenue
alarme m [alarm] alarm
alarme de incêndios [dinsaynd-yoosh] fire alarm
alavanca f lever
alavanca das mudanças [daJ moodansash] gear lever
albergaria f [albirgaree-a] luxury hotel
albergue da juventude m [albehrg da Joovayntood] youth hostel
albergue juvenil youth hostel
alça f [alsa] strap
alcunha f [alkoon-ya] nickname
aldeia f [alday-a] village
aldeia de pescadores [di pishkadohrish] fishing village
além: além de [alayng di] apart from
para além de [paralayng] beyond
alemã (f) [alimang] German
Alemanha f [aliman-ya] Germany
alemão (m) [alimowng] German
alérgico a ... [alehrJikoo] allergic to ...
Alfa high-speed train
alfabeto m [alfabehtoo] alphabet
alfaiataria f [alfī-ataree-a], alfaiate m [alfī-at] tailor
alfândega f [alfandiga] Customs
alfinete m [alfinayt] brooch; pin
alfinete de segurança m [di sigooransa] safety pin
alforreca f [alfoorrehka] jellyfish
alga f seaweed
algodão m [algoodowng] cotton
algodão em rama [ayng] cotton wool
alguém [algayng] anybody; somebody, someone
algum [algoong], alguma [algooma] some; any
alguma coisa [koh-iza] something; anything
algumas [algoomash], alguns [algoonsh] some; any
ali [alee] (over) there
ali acima [aseema] up there
ali adiante [ad-yant] over there
é por ali [eh poor] it's that way
aliança f [al-yansa] wedding ring
alicate m [alikat] pliers
alicate de unhas [doon-yash] nail clippers
alimento m [alimayntoo] food
almoçar [almoosar] to have lunch
almoço m [almohsoo] lunch
almoço embalado [almohswaymbaladoo] packed lunch

almofada f [almoofada] cushion; pillow
alojamento m [alooJamayntoo] accommodation
alpinismo m [alpineeJmoo] mountaineering
altitude f [altitood] height
alto [altoo] high; tall; loud
no alto [noo] at the top
altura f [altoora] height
altura máxima maximum headroom
alugam-se quartos rooms to let, rooms for rent
alugar [aloogar] to hire, to rent
aluga-se [alooga-si] for hire, to rent
aluguer m [aloogehr] rent
aluguer de automóveis [dowtoomovaysh] car hire, car rental
aluguer de barcos boat hire
aluguer de barracas sunshades for hire
aluguer de cadeiras beach chairs for hire
aluguer de gaivotas pedal boat hire
aluguer de parassóis beach umbrellas for hire
alvorada f [alvoorada] dawn
ama f childminder
amanhã [aman-yang] tomorrow
amanhã à tarde [tard] tomorrow afternoon
amanhã de manhã [di man-yang] tomorrow morning
amar to love
amarelo [amarehloo] yellow
amargo [amargoo] bitter
amável [amavil] kind; generous
ambos [amboosh] both
ambulância f [amboolans-ya] ambulance
ameno [amaynoo] mild
América f America
americano [amirikanoo] American
amiga f [ameega] friend
amigdalite f [ameegdaleet] tonsillitis
amigo m [ameegoo] friend
amor m [amohr] love
amortecedor m [amoortisidohr] shock-absorber
amperes mpl [ampehrish] amps
ampliação f [ampl-yasowng] enlargement
ampolas bebíveis fpl [ampohlaJ bibeevaysh] ampoules
analgésicos mpl [analJehzeekoosh] painkillers
análises de sangue fpl [analiziJ di sang] blood tests
anca f hip
âncora f anchor
andar (m) floor, storey; to walk
andar à boleia [boolay-a] to hitchhike
andar a cavalo [kavaloo] horse-riding
andar a pé [peh] to walk
anel m [anehl] ring
anilha f [aneel-ya] washer
animado [animadoo] lively

aniversário de casamento m [anivirs**a**r-yoo di kazam**ay**ntoo] wedding anniversary
aniversário natalício [natal**ee**s-yoo] birthday
ano m [**a**noo] year
Ano Novo [n**oh**voo] New Year
anteontem [anti-**oh**ntayng] the day before yesterday
antepassado m ancestor
anterior: dia anterior m [d**ee**-a antir-y**oh**r] the day before
antes [antsh] before
antibióticos mpl [antib-y**o**tikoosh] antibiotics
anticongelante m [–konJil**a**nt] antifreeze
antigo [ant**ee**goo] ancient, old
antiguidade f [antigweed**a**d] antique
anti-histamínicos mpl [–eesh-tam**ee**nikoosh] antihistamines
antilaxante m [anti-lash**a**nt] medicine for diarrhoea
antiquado [antikw**a**doo] old-fashioned
anti-séptico m [–s**eh**ptikoo] antiseptic
anúncio m [an**oo**ns-yoo] advertisement
ao [ow] to the; at the
ao norte de north of
aos [owsh] to the; at the
apagar to switch off
apagar os máximos switch headlights off
apanhar [apan-y**a**r] to get on, to catch; to pick up
apanhar banhos de sol [b**a**n-yooJ di] to sunbathe
aparelhagem (de som) f [aparel-y**a**Jayng (di song)] stereo; audio equipment
aparelho m [apar**ay**l-yoo] device
aparelho auditivo hearing aid
aparelho para a surdez [soord**ay**sh] hearing aid
aparelhos eléctricos mpl [apar**ay**l-yooz el**eh**trikoosh] electrical appliances
apartamento m [apartam**ay**ntoo] apartment, flat
aparthotel m [apartoht**eh**l] self-catering apartment
apelido m [apil**ee**doo] surname; family name
apendicite f [apendis**ee**t] appendicitis
apertado [apirt**a**doo] tight
apertar to hold tight; to fasten
apertar o cinto de segurança fasten your seatbelt
apetecer [apitis**ay**r] to feel like
apetece-me [apit**eh**simi] I feel like
apetite m [apit**ee**t] appetite
apinhado [apeen-y**a**doo] crowded
aprender [aprayndayr] to learn
apresentar [aprizent**a**r] to introduce
apressar-se [aprisa**r**si] to hurry
aproximadamente [aproosimadam**ay**nt] approximately, roughly
aquecedor m [akesid**oh**r]

heater
aquecedor eléctrico [elehtrikoo] electric fire
aquecimento m [akesimayntoo] heating
aquecimento central [sayntral] central heating
aquela [akehla], **aquele** [akayl] that, that one (further away)
aquelas [akehlash], **aqueles** [akaylish] those (further away)
aqui [akee] (over) here
aqui embaixo [aymbīshoo] down here
aqui está/estão ... [shta/shtowng] here is/are ...
aqui mesmo [mayJmoo] just here
é por aqui [eh por] it's this way
aqui tem [tayng] here you are
aquilo [akeeloo] that; that one (further away)
ar m air
árabe [arabi] Arab; Arabic
os árabes the Arabs
arame m [aram] wire
aranha f [aran-ya] spider
arco-íris m [arkoo-eereesh] rainbow
ar condicionado m [kondis-yoonadoo] air conditioning
arder [ardayr] to burn
areia f [aray-a] sand
armário m [armar-yoo] cupboard
armazém m [armazayng] warehouse; big store
aroma artificial/natural artificial/natural fragrance
arq. architect
arqueologia f [ark-yolooJee-a] archaeology
arquitecto m [arkitehtoo] architect
arraial m [arrī-al] local fair with fireworks, singing and dancing
arranhão m [arran-yowng] scratch
arranjos mpl [arranJoosh] repairs
arredores mpl [arredorish] suburb
arriscado [arrishkadoo] risky
arte f [art] art
artesanato m [artizanatoo] handicrafts, crafts
artificial [artifis-yal] artificial
artigos de bébé mpl [arteegooJ di bebeh] baby goods
artigos de campismo [kampeeJmoo] camping equipment
artigos de casa [kaza] household goods
artigos de desporto [dishpohrtoo] sports goods
artigos de luxo [looshoo] luxury goods
artigos de viagem [v-yaJayng] travel goods
artigos em cabedal [ayng kabidal] leather goods
artigos em cortiça [koorteesa] cork goods
artigos em pele [pehl] leather goods

artigos regionais regional goods, typical goods from the region
artista **m/f** [arteeshta] artist
árvore **f** [arvoori] tree
as [ash] the; them; you
às to the; at the
asa **f** wing
asa-delta **f** [aza-dehlta] hang-gliding
ascensor **m** [ashsaynsohr] lift, elevator
asma **f** [aJma] asthma
asneira **f** [aJnayra] nonsense; swearword
aspirador **m** [ashpiradohr] vacuum cleaner
aspirina **f** [ashpireena] aspirin
assaltado [asaltadoo] mugged
assar to bake; to roast
assento **m** [asayntoo] seat
assim [aseeng] this way
assim está bem [shta bayng] that'll do nicely
assim está bem? is that OK?
assinado signed
assinar to sign
assinatura **f** [asinatoora] signature
atacadores **mpl** [atakadohrish] shoelaces
atalho **m** [atal-yoo] shortcut
ataque **m** [atak] fit; attack
ataque cardíaco [kardee-akoo] heart attack
até [ateh] until
até amanhã [aman-yang] see you tomorrow
até já [Ja] see you soon
até logo! [logoo] see you!, see you later!
até mesmo ... [mayJmoo] even ...
atenção please note; caution; warning
atenção ao comboio beware of the train
atenção: portas automáticas warning: automatic doors
aterragem **f** [atirraJayng] landing
aterragem de emergência emergency landing
aterrar to land
atirar to throw
Atlântico **m** Atlantic
atletismo **m** [atleteeJmoo] athletics
atraente [atra-aynt] attractive
atrás [atrash] at the back, behind
atrás de ... [di] behind ...
atrasado [atrazadoo] late, delayed
estar atrasado [shtar] to be late
atraso **m** [atrazoo] delay
através de [atravehJ di] through
atravessar to go through, to cross
atravesse go, walk
atropelar [atropilar] to knock over, to knock down
auscultador **m** [owshkooltadohr] receiver
auscultadores **mpl** [owshkooltadohrish]

headphones
australiano (m) [owshtral-yanoo] Australian
autobanco m [owtoobankoo] cash dispenser, ATM
autocarro m [owtookarroo] coach, bus
autocarro do aeroporto [dwayroopohrtoo] airport bus
autoestrada f [owtooshtrada] motorway, highway, freeway
automático [owtoomatikoo] automatic
automóvel m [owtoomovil] car
Automóvel Clube de Portugal Portuguese Motoring Organization
av. avenue
avance go, walk
avaria f [avaree-a] breakdown
avariado [avari-adoo] damaged; faulty; out of order
avariar [avari-ar] to damage; to break down
avarias [avaree-ash] breakdown service
ave f [avi] bird
avenida f [avineeda] avenue
avião m [av-yowng] plane, airplane
de avião [dav-yowng] by plane; by air
aviso [aveezoo] warning; notice
avô m [avoh] grandfather
avó f [avaw] grandmother
azedo [azaydoo] sour
azul [azool] blue
azulejaria f [azoolayJaree-a] tile maker's workshop
azul-marinho [azool mareen-yoo] navy blue

bagagem f [bagaJayng] luggage, baggage
bagagem de mão f [di mowng] hand luggage
baía f [ba-ee-a] bay
baile m [bīli] dance
bairro m [bīrroo] district
baixo [bīshoo] low; short
balcão m [balkowng] counter
balcão de informações [dinfoormasoyngsh] information desk
balcão da recepção [risehsowng] reception desk
balde m [bowld] bucket
banco m [bankoo] bank; stool
banco de poupança [di pohpansa] savings bank
banda f band
bandeira f [bandayra] flag
banheira f [ban-yayra] bathtub, bath
banheiro m [ban-yayroo] lifeguard
banheiros [ban-yayroosh] toilets
banho m [ban-yoo] bath
banho de sol: tomar banho de sol [toomar – di] to sunbathe
barata f cockroach
barato [baratoo] cheap, inexpensive
barba f beard

barbatanas fpl [barbat**a**nash] flippers
barbeiro m [barb**ay**roo] men's hairdresser's, barber's shop
barco m [b**a**rkoo] boat
barco a motor [b**a**rkwa mooto**hr**] motorboat
barco a remos [r**ay**moosh] rowing boat
barco a vapor steamer
barco à vela sailing boat
barcos de aluguer boats for hire
barraca f beach hut
barro: louça de barro f [l**oh**sa di b**a**rroo] earthenware
barulhento [barool-y**ay**ntoo] noisy
barulho m [bar**oo**l-yoo] noise
bastante [bashtant] fairly; rather; quite (a lot)
bata (à porta) knock
batechapas bodywork repairs
bater [bat**ay**r] to hit, to knock
bateria f [batir**ee**-a] battery
baton m [bat**o**ng] lipstick
baton para o cieiro [oo s-y**ay**roo] lip salve
bêbado [b**ay**badoo] drunk
bebé m [beb**eh**] baby
beber [bib**ay**r] to drink
bebida f [bib**ee**da] drink
beco sem saída cul-de-sac, dead end
bege beige
beijar [bayJ**a**r] to kiss
beijo m [b**ay**Joo] kiss
beira: à beira do mar [b**ay**ra doo] at/by the seaside
beira-mar: à beira-mar by the sea
belga (m/f) Belgian
Bélgica f [b**eh**lJika] Belgium
beliche m [bil**ee**sh] berth, bunk; couchette; bunk beds
belo [b**eh**loo] beautiful
bem [bayng] fine, well, OK; properly
bem aqui [ak**ee**] right here
está bem [shta] that's fine
estás bem? [shtash] are you all right?
bem-educado [bayng idook**a**doo] polite
bem passado [pas**a**doo] well-done
bem-vindo [v**ee**ndoo] welcome
bem-vindo a ... welcome to ...
bengaleiro m [bengal**ay**roo] cloakroom, checkroom
berço m [b**ay**rsoo] cot
bestial! [bisht-y**a**l] fantastic!, tremendous!
bexiga f [bish**ee**ga] bladder
biberão m [bibir**ow**ng] baby's bottle
biblioteca f [bibl-yoot**eh**ka] library
bicha f [b**ee**sha] queue, line
bicicleta f [bisikl**eh**ta] bicycle, bike
bifurcação f [bifoorkas**ow**ng] fork (in road)
bigode m [big**o**d] moustache
bilha de gás f [b**ee**l-ya di gash] gas cylinder
bilhete m [bil-y**ay**t] ticket

bilhete de entrada [dayntr**a**da] admission ticket
bilhete de excursão [dishkoors**ow**ng] excursion ticket
bilhete de ida [d**ee**da] single ticket, one-way ticket
bilhete de ida e volta [d**ee**di] return ticket, round trip ticket
bilhete de lotaria [di lootar**ee**-a] lottery ticket
bilhete em aberto [bil-y**ay**tayng ab**eh**rtoo] open ticket
bilheteira f [bil-yit**ay**ra] box office, ticket office
bilhetes tickets
bilhete simples m [bil-y**ay**t s**ee**mplish] single ticket, one-way ticket
bloco de apartamentos m [bl**o**koo dapartam**ay**ntoosh] apartment block
bloco de apontamentos [dapontam**ay**ntoosh] notebook
blusa f [bl**oo**za] blouse
boa [b**oh**-a] good
boa noite [n**oh**-it] good evening; good night
Boas Festas! [b**oh**-ash f**eh**shtash] merry Christmas and a happy New Year!
boa sorte! [s**oh**rt] good luck!
boa tarde [tard] good afternoon; good evening
boate f [bwat] nightclub; disco
boa viagem! [v-y**a**Jayng] have a good journey!
boca f [b**oh**ka] mouth
bocadinho m [bookad**ee**n-yoo] little bit
bocado m [book**a**doo] piece
bochecha f [boosh**ay**sha] cheek
bóia f [b**o**-ya] buoy
boite f [bwat] nightclub; disco
bola f ball
bola de futebol [di footb**o**l] football
boleia f [bool**ay**-a] lift; ride
dar (uma) boleia a to give a lift to
bolha f [b**oh**l-ya] blister
bolinha f [bool**ee**n-ya] ball (small)
bolso m [b**oh**lsoo] pocket
bom [bong] good; fine
bom apetite! [bong apit**ee**t] enjoy your meal!
bomba f [b**oh**mba] bomb; pump
bomba de ar air pump
bomba de gasolina [di gazool**ee**na] garage, filling station, gas station; petrol pump
bombeiros mpl [bomb**ay**roosh] fire brigade
bom dia [bong d**ee**-a] good morning
boné m [boon**eh**] cap, hat
boneca f [boon**eh**ka] doll
bonito [boon**ee**too] beautiful; nice; pretty
borboleta f [borbool**ay**ta] butterfly
borda f edge
borracha f [boorr**a**sha] rubber; eraser
bosque m [boshk] woods,

forest
bota f boot (footwear)
botão m [bootowng] button
botas de borracha fpl wellingtons
bote de borracha m [bot di boorrasha] dinghy
braço m [brasoo] arm
branco [brankoo] white
Brasil m [brazeel] Brazil
brasileiro (m) [brazilayroo] Brazilian
breve [brev] brief
em breve soon
briga f [breega] fight
brigar to fight
brilhante [breel-yant] bright; brilliant
brincadeira f [breenkadayra] joke
brincos mpl [breenkoosh] earrings
brinquedo m [breenkaydoo] toy
brisa f [breeza] breeze
britânico [britanikoo] British
brochura f [broshoora] leaflet
bronquite [bronkeet] bronchitis
bronzeado (m) [bronz-yadoo] tan; suntan; suntanned
bronzeador m suntan lotion
bronzear [brohnz-yar] to tan
bronzear-se [-si] to get a tan
bugigangas mpl [booJigangash] bric-a-brac
bule m [bool] teapot
buraco m [boorakoo] hole
burro (m) [boorroo] donkey; thickhead; stupid
buscar [booshkar] to collect; to fetch
bússola f [boosoola] compass
buzina f [boozeena] horn

C

c/ with
cá here
cabeça f [kabaysa] head
cabedais mpl [kabidīsh] leather goods
cabedal m [kabidal] leather
cabeleireiro m [kabilayrayroo] hairdresser's
cabeleireiro de homens [dohmayngsh] men's hairdresser
cabeleireiro de senhoras [di sin-yorash] ladies' hairdresser
cabeleireiro unisexo [oonisehksoo] unisex salon
cabelo m [kabayloo] hair
cabide m [kabeed] coathanger
cabina f [kabeena] cabin
cabina de provas [di provash] fitting room
cabina telefónica [kabeena telefohnika] phone box, phone booth
cabos para ligar a bateria mpl [kaboosh – batiree-a] jump leads
cabra f goat
cabrão! [kabrowng] bastard!
cabrona! bastard!
caça f [kasa] game (meat); hunting
caçarola f [kasarola] saucepan

cachimbo m [kasheemboo] pipe (for smoking)
cacifo m [kaseefoo] locker
cada each; every
cadeado m [kad-yadoo] padlock
cadeia f [kaday-a] prison; chain
cadeira f [kadayra] chair
cadeira de bebé [di bebeh] highchair
cadeira de lona [lohna] deckchair
cadeira de rodas [rodash] wheelchair
cadeira reclinável [reklinavil] sun lounger
cadeirinha de bebé f [kadayreen-ya di bebeh] pushchair, buggy
caderneta f [kadayrnayta] book of tickets
café m [kafeh] café; coffee
café de esplanada [dishplanada] pavement café
cãibra f [kaymbra] cramp
cair [ka-eer] to fall
cais m [kīsh] quay; quayside; platform, (US) track
caixa f [kīsha] box; cash desk, till; cashier; cashpoint, ATM; savings bank; building society
caixa automático [owtoomateekoo] cashpoint, ATM
caixa de fusíveis [di foozeevaysh] fusebox
caixa de mudanças [moodansash] gearbox
caixa de primeiros socorros [primayroosh sookorroosh] first-aid kit
caixa de velocidades [viloosidadsh] gearbox
caixa do correio [doo koorray-oo] postbox; mailbox
caixa fechada till closed
caixote de lixo m [kīshot di leeshoo] bin, dustbin, trashcan
calçado m [kalsadoo] footwear
calcanhar m [kalkan-yar] heel (of foot)
calças fpl [kalsash] trousers, (US) pants
calções mpl [kalsoyngsh] shorts
calções de banho [di ban-yoo] swimming trunks
calculadora f [kalkooladohra] calculator
caldeira f [kaldayra] boiler
calendário m [kalendar-yoo] calendar
cale-se! [kalsi] quiet!; shut up!
calmo [kalmoo] calm
calor m [kalohr] heat
está imenso calor [shta imaynsoo] it's hot
ter calor [tayr] to be hot
cama f bed
cama de bebé [di bebeh] cot
cama de campanha [kampan-ya] campbed
cama de casal [di kazal] double bed
cama de solteiro [sooltayroo] single bed
cama dupla [doopla] double

bed
cama individual f [individw**a**l] single bed
câmara f camera
câmara de ar f [dar] inner tube
câmara de vídeo f [di v**ee**d-yoo] camcorder
câmara municipal f [moonisip**a**l] town hall
camarim m [kamar**ee**ng] dressing room
camarote m [kamar**o**t] cabin
camas separadas fpl [k**a**mash sipar**a**dash] twin beds
câmbio m [k**a**mb-yoo] bureau de change; exchange rate
câmbio do dia [doo d**ee**-a] current exchange rate
camião m [kam-y**ow**ng] truck
caminho m [kam**ee**n-yoo] path
caminho de ferro railway
Caminhos de Ferro Portugueses Portuguese Railways
camioneta f [kam-yoon**ay**ta] coach, bus; light truck
camisa f [kam**ee**za] shirt
camisa de dormir [di doorm**ee**r] nightdress
camisaria f [kamizar**ee**-a] shirt shop
camisola f [kamiz**o**la] jersey, jumper, sweater
camisola interior [intir-y**oh**r] vest (under shirt)
campainha f [kampa-**ee**n-ya] bell
campismo m [kamp**ee**Jmoo] camping
campo m [k**a**mpoo] field; countryside, country
campo de futebol [di footb**o**l] football ground
campo de golfe [golf] golf course
campo de ténis [t**eh**nish] tennis court
camurça f [kam**oo**rsa] suede
canadiano (m) [kanad-y**a**noo] Canadian
canal m canal; channel
Canal da Mancha English Channel
canalizador m [kanalizad**oh**r] plumber
canção f [kans**ow**ng] song
cancelado [kansil**a**doo] cancelled
cancelar [kansil**a**r] to cancel
candeeiro m [kand-y**ay**roo] lamp
caneca f [kan**eh**ka] mug
caneta f [kan**ay**ta] pen
caneta de feltro [di f**ay**ltroo] felt-tip pen
caneta esferográfica [shfiroogr**a**fika] ballpoint pen
canhoto [kan-y**oh**too] left-handed
canivete m [kaniv**eh**t] penknife
cano m [k**a**noo] pipe (for water)
canoa f [kan**oh**-a] canoe
canoagem f [kanw**a**Jayng] canoeing
cano de esgoto m [k**a**noo diJg**oh**too] drain
cansado [kans**a**doo] tired

cantar to sing
canto m [kantoo] corner
no canto [noo] in the corner
cantor m [kantohr], **cantora** f singer
cão m [kowng] dog
cão de guarda [gwarda] guard dog
capacete m [kapasayt] helmet
capaz: não seria capaz de ... [siree-a kapaJ di] I wouldn't be able to ...
capela f [kapehla] chapel
capelista f [kapeleeshta] haberdasher
capô m [kapoh] bonnet (of car), (US) hood
cápsula f capsule
cara f face
caranguejo m [karangayJoo] crab
caravana f caravan, (US) trailer
carburador m [karbooradohr] carburettor
careca [karehka] bald
carga máxima maximum load
carnaval m carnival
caro [karoo] expensive
carpete f [karpeht] carpet
carrinho m [karreen-yoo] trolley, (US) cart
carrinho de bagagem [di bagaJayng] luggage trolley, (US) baggage cart
carrinho de bebé [bebeh] pushchair; pram
carro m [karroo] car
de carro [di] by car
carroçaria f [karroosaree-a] bodywork
carro de aluguer m [karroo daloogehr] rented car
carro de mão [di mowng] trolley
carros de aluguer [daloogehr] car hire, car rental
carruagem f [karrwaJayng] carriage, coach
carruagem-cama f sleeper, sleeping car
carruagem para não fumadores f [nowng foomadohrish] nonsmoking carriage
carruagem restaurante [ristowrant] buffet car; restaurant car
carta f letter
carta de condução [di kondoosowng] driver's licence
carta de embarque [daymbark] boarding pass
carta de identidade [didentidad] ID card
cartão m [kartowng] card; pass; identity card; business card; cardboard
cartão bancário [bankar-yoo] cheque card
cartão de crédito [di krehdeetoo] credit card
cartão de débito [dehbeetoo] charge card
cartão de embarque [daymbark] boarding pass
cartão de garantia [di garantee-a] cheque card
cartão de telefone [di telefohn]

phonecard
cartão de visitas [di vizeetash] business card
cartão Eurocheque Eurocheque card
carta por correio expresso [poor koorray-oo shprehsoo] express letter
cartas letters
carta verde [vayrd] green card (car insurance)
cartaz m [kartash] poster
carteira f [kartayra] purse; wallet
carteirista m/f [kartayreeshta] pickpocket
carteiro m postman
casa f [kaza] home; house
em casa [ayng] at home
na sua casa [soo-a] at your place
estar na casa do/da [shtar ... doo] to stay with
ir para casa to go home
casaco m [kazakoo] jacket; coat
casaco de malha [di mal-ya] cardigan
casa de antiguidades f [kaza dantigweedadsh] antique shop
casa de banho [di ban-yoo] bathroom; toilet, rest room
casa de banho dos homens [dooz ohmayngsh] gents' toilet, men's room
casa de banho privativa [privateeva] private bathroom
casa de banho pública [pooblika] public convenience
casa de fados [di fadoosh] restaurant where traditional Portuguese fado songs are sung
casa de hóspedes [doshpidsh] guesthouse
casa de jantar [di Jantar] dining room
casa de pasto [pashtoo] canteen-style eating place, usually open at lunchtime and serving a cheap three-course menu
casa de saúde [disa-ood] clinic; nursing home
casado [kazadoo] married
casal m [kazal] couple
casamento m [kazamayntoo] wedding
casar-se [kazarsi] to get married
casas de banho mpl [kazaJ di ban-yoo] toilets, rest rooms
caseiro [kazayroo] home-made
caso m [kazoo] case
em caso de in case of
castanho [kashtan-yoo] brown
castelo m [kashtehloo] castle
catarata f waterfall; cataract
catedral f [katidral] cathedral
categoria f [katigooree-a] category
católico (m) [katolikoo] Catholic
catorze [katohrz] fourteen
causa f [kowza] cause
por causa de [poor – di] because of
cautela take care

cavaleiro m [kavalayroo] horseman
cavalheiro m [kaval-yayroo] gentleman
cavalheiros mpl [kaval-yayroosh] gents' toilet, men's room
cavalo m [kavaloo] horse
cave f [kav] cellar; basement
caveira f [kavayra] skull
caverna f [kavehrna] cave
cavilha f [kaveel-ya] tent peg
c/c current account
CE f [say eh] EC
cedo [saydoo] early
mais cedo [mĭsh] earlier
cego [sehgoo] blind
cem [sayng] hundred
cemitério m [simitehr-yoo] cemetery
centígrado m [senteegradoo] centigrade
centímetro m [senteemitroo] centimetre
cento e ... [sayntwee] one hundred and ...
central [sen-tral] central
central de correios f [di koorray-oosh] main post office
centro m [sayntroo] centre
centro comercial [komayrs-yal] shopping centre
centro da cidade [sidad] city centre, town centre
centro de enfermagem [dingfirmaJayng] clinic
centro de informação turística [dinfoormasowng tooreestika] tourist information office
centro de turismo [di tooreeJmoo] tourist information
cerâmicas fpl [siramikash] ceramics
cerca f [sayrka] fence
cerimónia f [sirimohn-ya] ceremony
de cerimónia [di] formal
certamente [sirtamaynt] certainly
certamente que não [ki nowng] certainly not
certeza: de certeza [di sirtayza] definitely
de certeza que não [ki nowng] definitely not
tem a certeza? [tayng] are you sure?
com certeza [kong] certainly, of course, sure
certidão f [sirtidowng] certificate
certo [sehrtoo] correct, right; sure
cervejaria f [sirvayJaree-a] beer house serving food
cesto m [sayshtoo] basket
cesto de compras [di komprash] shopping basket
céu m [seh-oo] sky
chaleira f [shalayra] kettle
chamada f [shamada] call
chamada de longa distância [di lohnga dishtans-ya] long-distance call
chamada internacional [internas-yoonal] international call
chamada interurbana

[interoorb**a**na] long-distance call
chamada local [look**a**l] local call
chamada paga no destinatário [noo dishtinat**a**r-yoo] collect call, reverse charge call
chamada para despertar [dishpirt**a**r] wake-up call
chamar [sham**a**r] to call
chamar-se [–si] to be called
como se chama? [k**oh**moo si sh**a**ma] what's your name?
champô m [shamp**oh**] shampoo
chão m [showng] ground; floor
no chão [noo] on the floor; on the ground
chapa da matrícula f [sh**a**pa da matr**ee**koola] licence plate
chapelaria f [shapilar**ee**-a] hat shop
chapéu m [shap**eh**-oo] hat
chapéu de sol [di] beach umbrella, sunshade
charcutaria f [sharkootar**ee**-a] delicatessen
charuto m [shar**oo**too] cigar
chateado [shat-y**a**doo] bored
chave f [shav] key
chave de fendas [di f**ay**ndash] screwdriver
chave de porcas [p**o**rkash] spanner
chave inglesa [ingl**ay**za] wrench; spanner
chaveiro m [shav**ay**roo] keyring
check-in: fazer o check-in to check in
chávena f [sh**a**vena] cup
chefe da estação m [shehf dishtas-**ow**ng] station master
chega [sh**ay**ga] that's plenty; that's enough
chegada f [shig**a**da] arrival
chegadas arrivals
chegar [shig**a**r] to arrive, to get in; to reach
cheio [sh**ay**-oo] full
cheirar [shayr**a**r] to smell
cheiro m [sh**ay**roo] smell
cheque de viagem m [shehk di v-y**a**Jayng] traveller's cheque
chinês (m) [shin**ay**sh] Chinese
chique [sheek] posh; chic
chocante [shook**a**nt] shocking
choque m [shok] shock
chorar [shoor**a**r] to cry
chover [shoov**ay**r] to rain
está a chover it's raining
chumbo m [sh**oo**mboo] lead; filling
chupa-chupa m [sh**oo**pa-sh**oo**pa] lollipop
chupeta f [shoop**ay**ta] dummy
churrascada f [shoorrashk**a**da] barbecue
chuva f [sh**oo**va] rain
Cia. company
ciclismo m [sikl**ee**Jmoo] cycling
ciclista m/f [sikl**ee**shta] cyclist
cidadã/cidadão de terceira idade f/m [sidad**a**ng/sidad**ow**ng di tirs**ay**ra id**a**d] senior citizen
cidade f [sid**a**d] town; city; town centre
fora da cidade out of town

cidade antiga [anteega] old town
ciência f [s-yayns-ya] science
cigarro m [sigarroo] cigarette
cima: em cima de ... [ayng seema di] on top of ...
lá em cima up there; upstairs
cinco [seenkoo] five
cinquenta [sinkwaynta] fifty
cinto m [seentoo] belt
cinto de salvação [di salvasowng] lifebelt
cinto de segurança [sigooransa] seatbelt
cintura f [sintoora] waist
cinzeiro m [sinzayroo] ashtray
cinzento [sinzayntoo] grey
circuito turístico m [sirkoo-eetoo tooreeshtikoo] sightseeing tour
circule pela direita/esquerda keep right/left
círculo m [seerkooloo] circle
ciumento [s-yoomayntoo] jealous
claro [klaroo] pale; light; clear;
claro! sure!, of course!
claro que não [ki-nowng] of course not
é claro [eh] of course
classe f [klas] class
classe económica [ekoonohmika] economy class
clima m [kleema] climate
clínica f [kleenika] clinic
clínica médica clinic
clínica veterinária veterinary clinic
clube m [kloob] club
clube de golfe [di golf] golf club
clube de ténis [di tehnish] tennis club
cobertor m [koobirtohr] blanket
cobra f snake
cobrar to cash
cobrir to cover
código m [kodigoo] code
código da estrada highway code
código postal m [pooshtal], cod. postal postcode, zip code
coelho m [kwayl-yoo] rabbit
cofre m safe
coisa f [koh-iza] thing
cola f glue
colar m [koolar] necklace
colarinho m [koolareen-yoo] collar
colchão m [koolshowng] mattress
colchão de praia [di prī-a] beach mat
colecção f [koolehsowng] collection
colégio m [koolehJ-yoo] college
colete m [koolayt] waistcoat
colete de salvação [di salvasowng] life jacket
colher f [kool-yehr] spoon
colher de chá f [di sha] teaspoon
colisão f [kooleezowng] crash
collants mpl [koolansh] tights, pantyhose
com [kong] with
comandante m [koomandant] captain
combinação f [kombinasowng]

combination; slip, underskirt
comboio m [komb**oy**-oo] train
de comboio [di] by train
comboio rápido express train
começar [koomes**ar**] to begin, to start
começo m [koom**ay**soo] start, beginning
comédia f [koom**eh**d-ya] comedy
comer [koom**ay**r] to eat
comerciante m/f [koomayrs-y**a**nt] business person
comichão f [koomish**ow**ng] itch
comida f [koom**ee**da] food; meal
comida congelada [konJil**a**da] frozen food
comida de bebé f [di beb**eh**] baby food
comidas fpl food; meals
comissão m [koomis**ow**ng] commission
comissário de bordo m [koomis**ar**-yoo di b**o**rdoo] steward
como [k**oh**moo] how; like; since, as
como? what?, pardon (me)?, sorry?
como é? [eh] what's it like?
como está? [shta] how are you?, how do you do?
como este [kohmw**ay**sht] like this
como vai? [vī] how are things?
companheira f [kompan-y**ay**ra] partner, girlfriend
companheiro m [kompan-y**ay**roo] partner, boyfriend
companhia f [kompan-y**ee**-a] company
companhia aérea [a-**eh**r-ya] airline
compartimento m [kompartim**ay**ntoo] compartment
completamente [komplitam**ay**nt] completely
completo [kompl**eh**too] full
complicado [komplik**a**doo] complicated
compra f [k**oh**mpra] purchase
comprar [kompr**ar**] to buy
compras fpl [k**oh**mprash] shopping
ir às compras [eer ash] to go shopping
compreender [kompr-yaynd**ay**r] to understand
comprido [kompr**ee**doo] long
comprimento m [komprim**ay**ntoo] length
comprimido m [komprim**ee**doo] tablet
comprimido para dormir [doorm**ee**r] sleeping pill
computador m [kompootad**oh**r] computer
Comunidade Europeia European Community
concerto m [kons**ay**rtoo] concert
concessionário m [konsis-yoon**ar**-yoo] agent
concha f [k**oh**nsha] shell
concha do mar [doo] seashell
concordar [konkoord**ar**] to agree

concordo [konk**o**rdoo] I agree
condições fpl [kondis**oy**ngsh] conditions, terms
condução f [kondoos**ow**ng] driving; transport
condução enquanto embriagado [aynkw**a**ntoo aymbr-yag**a**doo] drunken driving
condutor m [kondoot**oh**r], condutora f driver
conduza com cuidado drive carefully
conduzir [kondooz**ee**r] to lead; to drive
cone de gelado m [kohn di Jil**a**doo] ice-cream cone
confecções de criança fpl [konfehs-**oy**ngsh di kr-y**a**nsa] children's wear
confecções de homem [d**oh**mayng] menswear
confecções de senhora [di sin-y**o**ra] ladies' wear
confeitaria [konfaytar**ee**-a] sweet shop, candy store
conferência f [konfir**ay**ns-ya] conference
confirmar [konfirm**a**r] to confirm
confortável [konfoort**a**vil] comfortable
confusão f [konfooz**ow**ng] confusion, mix-up
congelador m [konJilad**oh**r] freezer
congestionamento m [konJisht-yoonam**ay**ntoo] traffic congestion
conhecer [kon-yis**ay**r] to know

connosco [kon**oh**shkoo] with us
consciente [konsh-sy**ay**nt] conscious
consertar [konsirt**a**r] to fix, to mend
conservar afastado da luz solar directa store away from direct sunlight
conservar no frio store in a cold place
consigo [kons**ee**goo] with you
constipação f [konshtipas**ow**ng] cold
constipado: estou constipado [shtoh konshtip**a**doo] I have a cold
consulado m [konsool**a**doo] consulate
consulta f [kons**oo**lta] appointment
consultório m [konsoolt**o**r-yoo] surgery, doctor's office
consultório dentário dental surgery
consumir dentro de ... dias to be consumed within ... days
conta f [k**oh**nta] bill; account
conta bancária [bank**a**r-ya] bank account
contactar to contact
contaminado [kontamin**a**doo] polluted
conta-quilómetros m [konta-kil**oh**mitroosh] speedometer
contar to count; to tell
contente [kont**ay**nt] happy; glad, pleased
contigo [kont**ee**goo] with you

conto **m** [kohntoo] tale, story; a thousand escudos
contra against
contraceptivo **m** [kontrasipteevoo] contraceptive
contra-indicações **fpl** contraindications
contrário [kontrar-yoo] opposite
controlo de passaportes passport control
contusão **f** [kontoozowng] bruise
conveniente [konvin-yaynt] convenient
convento **m** [konvayntoo] convent
conversação **f** [konversasowng] conversation
convés **m** [konvehsh] deck
convidada **f** [konvidada], convidado **m** [konvidadoo] guest
convidar [konvidar] to invite
convir [konveer] to suit; to be convenient
convite **m** [konveet] invitation
copo **m** [kopoo] glass; cup
cor **f** [kohr] colour
coração **m** [koorasowng] heart
corajoso [kooraJohzoo] brave
corda **f** rope
cordeiro **m** [koordayroo] lamb
cordel **m** [koordehl] string
cor de laranja [kohr di laranJa] orange (colour)
cor de rosa [roza] pink
corpo **m** [kohrpoo] body
corredor **m** [koorridohr] corridor
correia **f** [koorray-a] strap
correia da ventoinha [da ventooween-ya] fan belt
correia de relógio [di riloJ-yoo] watch strap
correio **m** [koorray-oo] post, mail; post office
pôr no correio [pohr noo] to post, to mail
correio aéreo [a-ehr-yoo] airmail
correio azul [azool] express mail
correio expresso [shprehsoo] express mail, special delivery
correio registado [riJishtadoo] registered mail
correios **mpl** [koorray-oosh] post office
Correios de Portugal S.A. National Mail Service
corrente **f** [koorraynt] chain; current
corrente de ar [koorraynt dar] draught
correr [koorrayr] to run
correspondente **m/f** [koorrishpondaynt] penfriend
corrida **f** [koorreeda] race
cortado [koortadoo] cut; blocked
cortar to cut
corte **m** [kort] cut
corte de cabelo [di kabayloo] haircut
corte de energia [denirJee-a] power cut
corte e brushing [ee] cut and blow-dry

cortiça f [koor**tee**sa] cork
cortiças fpl [koor**tee**sash] cork goods
cortina f [koor**tee**na] curtain
cortinados mpl [koortin**a**doosh] curtains
coser [kooz**ay**r] to sew
cosméticos mpl [kooJm**eh**tikoosh] cosmetics, make-up
costa f [k**o**shta] coast
na costa on the coast
costas fpl [k**o**shtash] back (of body)
costela f [koosht**eh**la] rib
cotação cambial f [kootas**ow**ng kamb-y**a**l] exchange rate
cotovelo m [kootoov**ay**loo] elbow
couro m [k**oh**roo] leather
coxa f [k**oh**sha] thigh
coxia f [koosh**ee**-a] aisle
cozer [kooz**ay**r] to cook
cozinha f [kooz**ee**n-ya] kitchen
cozinhar [kozeen-y**a**r] to cook
cozinheiro m [kozeen-y**ay**roo] cook
CP [say pay] Portuguese Railways
crédito m [kr**eh**ditoo] credit
creme m [kraym] cream, lotion
creme amaciador [amas-yad**oh**r] conditioner
creme de barbear [di barb-y**a**r] shaving cream
creme de base [baz] foundation cream
creme de limpeza [leemp**ay**za] cleansing lotion
creme écran total [ekr**a**ng toot**a**l] sunblock
creme hidratante [kraymeedrat**a**nt] moisturizer
crer [krayr] to believe
criada f [kr-y**a**da] maid
criada de quarto [di kw**a**rtoo] chambermaid
criança f [kr-y**a**nsa] child
crianças children; children crossing
cru, crua [kroo, kr**oo**-a] raw
cruzamento m [kroozam**ay**ntoo] junction, crossroads
cruzamento perigroso dangerous junction
cruzar [krooz**a**r] to cross
cruzeiro m [krooz**ay**roo] cruise
cruzeta f [krooz**ay**ta] coathanger
Cruz Vermelha Red Cross
CTT [say tay tay] National Mail Service
cuecas fpl [kw**eh**kash] underpants; pants, panties
cuecas de mulher [kw**eh**kaJ di mool-y**eh**r] pants, panties
cuidado m [kwid**a**doo] care
cuidado! look out!, be careful!, take care!
cuidado com o cão beware of the dog
cuidadoso [kwidad**oh**zoo] careful
cujo [k**oo**Joo] of which; whose
culpa f [k**oo**lpa] fault
é culpa minha/dele it's my/his fault
culpado [koolp**a**doo] guilty

cumprimento m [koomprimayntoo] compliment
com os melhores cumprimentos with best wishes
cunhada f [koon-yada] sister-in-law
cunhado m [koon-yadoo] brother-in-law
curar [koorar] to cure
curso m [koorsoo] course
curso de línguas [di leengwash] language course
curto [koortoo] short
curva f [koorva] turning; bend
curva perigosa dangerous bend
custar [kooshtar] to charge; to cost
cutelaria f [kootilaree-a] cutlery shop
c/v basement

D

d. right
da of the; from the
dá he/she/it gives; you give
damas f [damash] ladies' toilets, ladies' room
damos [damoosh] we give
dança f [dansa] dance
dança folclórica [foolklorika] folk dancing
dançar [dansar] to dance
dão [downg] they give; you give
daqui [dakee] from now
dar to give
das [dash] of the; from the
dás you give
data f date
data de validade [di validad] expiry date
de [di] from; of; by; in
de autocarro [dowtookarroo] by bus
de avião [dav-yowng] by air
de carro [di karroo] by car
de manhã [di man-yang] in the morning
debaixo de ... [dibīshoo di] under ...
decepcionado [disips-yoonadoo] disappointed
decepcionante [disips-yonant] disappointing
decidir [disideer] to decide
décimo [dehsimoo] tenth
decisão f [disizowng] decision
declaração f [diklarasowng] statement
dedo m [daydoo] finger
dedo do pé [doo peh] toe
defeito m [difaytoo] fault, defect
deficiente [difis-yaynt] disabled
deficientes físicos mpl disabled
degrau m [digrow] step
deitar fora [daytar] to throw away
deitar-se [daytarsi] to lie down; to go to bed
deixar [dayshar] to leave (behind); to let
deixar cair [ka-eer] to drop

dela [de**h**la] her; hers
delas [de**h**lash] their; theirs
dele [dayl] his
deles [**day**lish] their; theirs
delicioso [dilis-y**oh**zoo] lovely, delicious
demais [dimĪsh] too much
demasiado [dimaz-y**a**doo] too
demasiado grande too big
dê-me [**day**mi] give me
demora f delay
dentadura postiça f [dentad**oo**ra poosht**ee**sa] dentures
dente m [daynt] tooth
dentista m/f [dent**ee**shta] dentist
dentro de ... [**day**ntroo] inside ...
dentro de ... dias [di ... **dee**-ash] in ... days' time
dentro de um momento [doong moom**ay**ntoo] in a minute
dentro de casa [di k**a**za] indoors
departamento m [dipartam**ay**ntoo] department
depende [dip**ay**nd] it depends
depende de ... [di] it depends on ...
depois [dip**oh**-ish] then, after that; afterwards
depois de ... [di] after ...
depois de amanhã [daman-**yang**] the day after tomorrow
depósito m [dip**o**zitoo] deposit; tank
depósito de bagagem [di bag**a**Jayng] left luggage (office), baggage checkroom
depósitos mpl deposits
depressa [dipr**eh**sa] quickly
deprimido [diprim**ee**doo] depressed
dê prioridade give way, yield
derrubar [dirroob**ar**] to knock over
desafio de futebol m [dizaf**ee**-oo di footb**o**l] football match
desagradável [dizagrad**a**vil] unpleasant
desaparecer [dizaparis**ay**r] to disappear
desapontado [dizapont**a**doo] disappointed
desarranjo intestinal m [dizarr**a**nJoo intishtin**a**l] upset stomach
descansar [dishkans**ar**] to relax
descanso m [dishk**a**nsoo] rest
descer [dishs**ay**r] to go down; to get off
descobrir [dishkoobr**ee**r] to find out, to discover
descolagem f [dishkool**a**Jayng] take-off
descolar [dishkool**ar**] to take off, to unglue
descontar [dishkont**ar**] to cash
desconto m [dishk**oh**ntoo] discount
descrição f [dishkris**ow**ng] description
desculpar-se [dishkoolp**ar**si] to apologize
desculpas fpl [disk**oo**lpash] apologies
desculpe [dishk**oo**lp] I'm sorry,

excuse me, pardon (me)
desde [**day**Jdi] since; from
desejar [dis**ay**Jar] to want
que deseja? [ki dis**ay**Ja] how can I help you?
desempregado [dizaympig**a**doo] unemployed
desenho m [dis**ay**n-yoo] drawing; pattern
desenvolver [disaynvolv**ayr**] to develop
desfazer as malas [dishfaz**ayr** aJ m**a**lash] to unpack
desfiladeiro m [dishfilad**ay**roo] pass
desfolhada f [disfool-y**a**da] party held at threshing time
desgarradas fpl [diJgarr**a**dash] improvised popular songs
cantar à desgarrada to sing impromptu in competition
desinfectante m [dizinfet**a**nt] disinfectant
desligado [diJlig**a**doo] off, switched off
desligar [diJlig**ar**] to turn off; to switch off
desligue o motor switch off your engine
desmaiar [diJmī-**ar**] to faint; to collapse
desmaquilhador de olhos m [dishmakil-yad**ohr** d**o**l-yoosh] eye make-up remover
desocupar antes das ... vacate before ...
desodorizante m [dizohdooriz**a**nt] deodorant
despacha-te! [dishp**a**shat] hurry up!
despertador m [dishpirtad**ohr**] alarm clock
desporto m [dishp**oh**rtoo] sport
desportos náuticos mpl [dishp**oh**rtoosh n**ow**tikoosh] water sports
destinatário m addressee
destino m [disht**ee**noo] destination
desvio m [diJv**ee**-oo] detour, diversion
detergente m [deterJ**ay**nt] soap powder, washing powder
detergente líquido [l**ee**kidoo] washing-up liquid
detergente para lavar a louça [l**oh**sa] washing-up liquid
detestar [ditisht**ar**] to hate
detestável [ditisht**a**vil] obnoxious
Deus [d**ay**-oosh] God
devagar [divag**ar**] slow; slowly
deve [dehv] you must, you have to
dever (m) [div**ayr**] duty; to owe; to have to
devia [div**ee**-a] you should
devolver [divolv**ayr**] to give back
dez [dehsh] ten
dezanove [dizan**o**v] nineteen
dezasseis [dizas**ay**sh] sixteen
dezassete [dizas**eh**t] seventeen
Dezembro [dez**ay**mbroo] December
dezoito [diz**oh**-itoo] eighteen
dia m [d**ee**-a] day
diabética (f) [d-yab**eh**tika],

diabético (**m**) [d-yab**eh**tikoo] diabetic
dia de anos m [**dee**-a d**a**noosh] birthday
dialecto m dialect
diamante m [d-yam**a**nt] diamond
diapositivo m [d-yapooozit**ee**voo] slide
diária f [d-y**a**r-ya] cost per day
diariamente [d-yar-yam**ay**nt] daily
diário (**m**) [d-y**a**r-yo] diary; daily
diarreia f [d-yarr**ay**-a] diarrhoea
dias de semana weekdays
dias verdes cheap travel days
dicionário m [dis-yoon**a**r-yoo] dictionary
dieta f [d-y**eh**ta] diet
diferença f [difir**ay**nsa] difference
diferente [difir**ay**nt] different
difícil [dif**ee**sil] difficult, hard
dificuldade f [difikoold**a**d] difficulty
digo I say
diluir num pouco de água dissolve in a little water
Dinamarca f [dinam**a**rka] Denmark
dinamarquês [dinamark**ay**sh] Danish
dinheiro m [deen-y**ay**roo] money; cash
dirá [dir**a**] he/she will say; you will say
dirão [dir**ow**ng] they will say; you will say
dirás [dir**a**sh] you will say
direcção f [direhs**ow**ng] direction; steering
directo [dir**eh**too] direct
direi [dir**ay**] I will say
direita: à direita [dir**ay**ta] on the right
à direita (de) [di] on the right (of)
vire à direita [veer] turn right
direito [dir**ay**too] straight; right (not left)
direitos mpl [dir**ay**toosh] rights
livre de direitos [leevr di] duty-free
diremos [dir**ay**moosh] we will say
disco m [d**ee**shkoo] disco; record
discoteca f [dishkoot**eh**ka] disco; record shop
disjuntor principal m [diJoont**oh**r preensip**a**l] mains switch
disquete f [dishk**eh**t] disk, diskette
disse [dees] I/he/she/it/you said
dissemos [dis**ay**moosh] we said
disseram [dis**eh**rowng] you/they said
disseste [dis**eh**sht] you said
distância f [disht**a**ns-ya] distance
distribuição f [dishtribweess**ow**ng] delivery
distribuidor m [dishtribweed**oh**r] distributor
dito [d**ee**too] said
DIU m [d**ee**-oo] IUD, coil

divertido [divir**tee**doo] fun, amusing, enjoyable
divertir-se [divir**tee**rsi] to enjoy oneself
divisas fpl foreign currency
divorciado [divoors-y**a**doo] divorced
dizer [diz**ayr**] to say; to tell
o que quer dizer? [oo ki kehr] what do you mean?
do of the; from the
dobro [d**oh**broo] twice as much
doce [dohs] sweet
documento m [dookoom**ay**ntoo] document
doença f [dw**ay**nsa] disease, illness
doente [dwaynt] ill, sick, unwell
doer [dwayr] to hurt
doido [d**oh**-idoo] crazy, mad
dois [d**oh**-ish] two
doloroso [dooloor**oh**zoo] painful
domingo [doom**ee**ngoo] Sunday
domingos e dias feriados Sundays and public holidays
Dona Mrs
dona f [d**oh**na] owner; respectful way of addressing a woman, precedes the first name
donde [dohnd] where from
donde é? [dohnd**eh**] where do you come from?
dono m [d**oh**noo] owner
do que [doo ki] than
dor f [dohr] ache, pain
dor de cabeça [di kab**ay**sa] headache
dor de dentes [dayntsh] toothache
dor de estômago [dishtohmagoo] stomach ache
dor de garganta [di garg**a**nta] sore throat
dor de ouvidos [dohv**ee**doosh] earache
dormidas rooms to let (in a private house)
dormir [doorm**ee**r] to sleep
a dormir asleep
dor nas costas f [dohr nash k**o**shtash] backache
dos of the; from the
dose f [doz] portion
dose para crianças f [doz kr-y**a**n-sash] children's portion
dou [doh] I give
doutor m [doht**oh**r], **doutora f** [doht**o**ra] doctor
doutro modo [d**oh**troo m**o**doo] otherwise
doze [dohz] twelve
droga f [dr**o**ga] drugs, narcotics
drogaria f [droogar**ee**-a] drugstore, shop selling toiletries
dto. right
duas vezes [d**oo**-aJ v**ay**zish] twice
duche m [doosh] shower
com duche [kong] with shower
dunas fpl [d**oo**nash] sand dunes
duplo [d**oo**ploo] double

durante [doorant] during
duro [dooroo] hard; stale
duzentas [doozayntash], **duzentos** [doozayntoosh] two hundred
dúzia f [dooz-ya] dozen

E

e [ee] and
e. left
é [eh] he/she/it is; you are
é ...? is he/she/it ...?; are you ...?
écran m [ekrang] screen
edifício m [idifees-yoo] building
edredão m [idridowng] duvet
efervescente [ifirvish-saynt] effervescent, sparkling
eh! hey!
eixo m [ayshoo] axle
ela [ehla] she; her; it
elas [ehlash] they; them
elástico m [ilashtikoo] elastic; elastic band
ele [ayl] he; him; it
electricidade f [eletrisidad] electricity
electricista m [eletriseeshta] electrician
eléctrico (m) [elehtrikoo] electric; tram, streetcar
electro-domésticos mpl [doomehshtikoosh] electrical appliances
eles [aylish] they; them
elevador m [elevadohr] lift, elevator
em [ayng] in; at; on
embaixada f [aymbīshada] embassy
embaixo [aymbīshoo] down, downstairs; underneath
embaixo de ... [di] underneath ...
lá embaixo down there
embalagem económica f economy pack
embalagem familiar family pack
embaraçoso [aymbarasohzoo] embarrassing
embora [aymbora] although
ir embora to go away
embraiagem f [aymbrī-aJayng] clutch
embrulhar [aymbrool-yar] to wrap
embrulho m [aymbrool-yoo] parcel
ementa f [emaynta] menu
ementa fixa [feeksa] set menu
ementa turística [tooreestika] today's menu, set menu
emergência f [emirJayns-ya] emergency
emergências casualty, emergencies
emocionante [emoos-yoonant] exciting
emperrado [aympirradoo] stuck
empoeirado [aympoo-ayradoo] dusty
empolha f [aympohl-ya] blister
empregada f [aympregada] waitress
empregada de balcão [di

balk**ow**ng] barmaid
empregada de mesa [m**ay**za] waitress
empregada de quarto [kw**a**rtoo] chambermaid, maid
empregado [aympreg**a**doo] **m** employee
empregado (de mesa) **m** [di m**ay**za] waiter
emprego **m** [aympr**ay**goo] job
empresa **f** [aympr**ay**za] company, firm
emprestado: pedir emprestado [pideer aymprisht**a**doo] to borrow
emprestar [aymprisht**a**r] to lend
empurrar [aympoorr**a**r] to push
E.N. national highway
encantador [aynkantad**oh**r] lovely
encaracolado [aynkarakool**a**doo] curly
encerrado [aynsayrr**a**doo] closed
encher [aynsh**ay**r] to fill up, to fill
encomenda **f** [aynkoom**ay**nda] package; parcel
encomendas **fpl** parcels, parcels counter
encontrar [aynkontr**a**r] to find; to meet
encravado [aynkrav**a**doo] jammed
endereço **m** [ayndir**ay**soo] address
enevoado [inivw**a**doo] foggy; misty; cloudy
enfarte **m** [aynf**a**rt] heart attack
enfermaria **f** [aynfirmar**ee**-a] hospital ward
enfermeira **f** [aynfirm**ay**ra], **enfermeiro** **m** [aynfirm**ay**roo] nurse
enganado [ayngan**a**doo] wrong
enganar-se [ayngan**a**rsi] to be wrong, to make a mistake
enganei-me [ayngan**ay**m] I've made a mistake
engarrafamento **m** [ayngarrafam**ay**ntoo] traffic jam
engolir [ayngool**ee**r] to swallow
engraçado [ayngras**a**doo] funny, amusing
enjoado [aynJw**a**doo] seasick
enorme [en**o**rm] enormous
enquanto [aynkw**a**ntoo] while
ensinar [aynsin**a**r] to teach
então [aynt**ow**ng] then, at that time
entrada **f** [ayntr**a**da] entrance, way in; starter, appetizer; admission charge
entrada livre admission free
entrada proibida no entry
entrar [ayntr**a**r] to go in, to enter
entre! come in!
entre [ayntr] among; between
entrega ao domicílio delivery service
entregar [ayntrig**a**r] to deliver
entrevista [ayntriv**ee**shta] appointment
entupido [ayntoop**ee**doo] blocked
envelope **m** [aynvil**o**p] envelope
envelope de avião **m** [dav-y**ow**ng] airmail envelope

envergonhado [aynvirgoon-y**a**doo] ashamed
enviar [aynv-y**a**r] to send
enviar posteriormente to forward
enxaqueca f [aynshak**ay**ka] migraine
época f [**eh**pooka] season; age
equipa f [ek**ee**pa] team
equipamento m [ekipam**ay**ntoo] equipment
era [**eh**ra] I was; he/she/it was; you were
eram [**eh**rowng] they were; you were
éramos [**eh**ramoosh] we were
eras [**eh**rash] you were
ermida f [erm**ee**da] chapel
errado [err**a**doo] wrong
erro m [**ay**rroo] mistake, error
erupção f [eroops**ow**ng] rash
ervanário m [ervan**a**r-yoo] herbalist
és [ehsh] you are
esc. escudo (Portuguese unit of currency)
escada f [shk**a**da] ladder; stairs
escadas fpl [shk**a**dash] stairs
escadas rolantes [rool**a**ntsh] escalator
escala f [shk**a**la] intermediate stop
escalar [shkal**a**r] to climb
escocês (m) [shkoos**ay**sh] Scottish; Scotsman
escocesa (f) [shkoos**ay**za] Scottish; Scots woman
Escócia f [shk**o**s-ya] Scotland
escola f [shk**o**la] school
escola de línguas f [di l**ee**ngwash] language school
escolher [shkool-y**ay**r] to choose
esconder [shkond**ay**r] to hide
escorregadio [shkoorrigad**ee**-oo] slippery
escova f [shk**oh**va] brush
escova de cabelo [di kab**ay**loo] hairbrush
escova de dentes [dayntsh] toothbrush
escova de unhas [d**oo**n-yash] nailbrush
escrever [shkriv**ay**r] to write
escrito por ... [shkr**ee**too poor] written by ...
por escrito in writing
escritório m [shkrit**o**r-yoo] office
escudo m [shk**oo**doo] escudo (Portuguese unit of currency)
escurecer [shkooores**ay**r] to get dark
escuro [shk**oo**roo] dark
escutar [shkoot**a**r] to listen (to)
esferográfica f [shfiroogr**a**fika] ballpoint pen
Espanha f [shp**a**n-ya] Spain
espanhóis: os espanhóis [shpan-**oy**sh] the Spanish
espanhol [shpan-y**o**l] Spanish
espantoso [shpant**oh**zoo] amazing, astonishing
especialidade f [shpis-yalid**a**d] speciality
especialmente [shpis-yalm**ay**nt] especially
espectáculo m [shpit**a**kooloo] show

espelho **m** [shp**ay**l-yoo] mirror
espelho retrovisor [ritroovizo**hr**] rearview mirror
esperar [shpir**ar**] to expect; to hope; to wait
espero que não [shp**eh**roo ki nowng] I hope not
espero que sim [s**ee**ng] I hope so
espere [shpehr] wait
espere pelo sinal wait for the tone
esperto [shp**eh**rtoo] clever
espesso [shp**ay**soo] thick
espetáculo **m** [shpit**a**kooloo] show
espigados **mpl** [shpig**a**doosh] split ends
espingarda **f** [shpeeng**a**rda] gun
espirrar [shpirr**ar**] to sneeze
espirro **m** [shp**ee**rroo] sneeze
esplanada **f** [shplan**a**da] esplanade; pavement café
esplêndido [shpl**ay**ndidoo] terrific
esposa **f** [shp**oh**za] wife
espuma de barbear **f** [shp**oo**ma di barb-y**ar**] shaving foam
esq. left
esquadra da polícia **f** [shkw**a**rda da pool**ee**s-ya] police station
esquecer [shkis**ayr**] to forget
esqueci-me [shkis**ee**mi] I forget
esquerda: à esquerda [shk**ay**rda] on the left (of), to the left
vire à esquerda [v**ee**ra] turn left
esquerdo [shk**ay**rdoo] left
esqui aquático **m** [shkee akw**a**tikoo] waterskiing
esquisito [shkiz**ee**too] weird, odd, strange
essa [**eh**sa] that; that one
essas [**eh**sash] those
esse [ays] that
essencial [esayns-y**al**] essential
esses [**ay**sish] those
esta [**eh**shta] this; this one
está [shta] hello (on the phone); he/she/it is; you are
ele está? [ayl] is he in?
está ... it is ...
está ...? is it ...?; hello? (on the telephone)
está bem [bayng] that's fine, all right
estação **f** [shtas**ow**ng] station; season
estação alta high season
estação baixa [bīsha] low season
estação de autocarros [dowtook**a**rroosh] bus station
estação de caminho de ferro [di kam**ee**n-yoo di f**eh**rroo] railway station
estação de camionetas [kam-yoon**ay**tash] bus station, coach station
estação de comboios [kombo**y**-oosh] train station
estação de serviço [di sirv**ee**soo] service station
estação dos autocarros [dooz owtook**a**rroosh] bus station, coach station

estacionamento **m** [shtas-yoonam**ay**ntoo] car park, parking lot
estacionamento privado [priv**a**doo] private parking
estacionamento proibido no parking
estacionamento reservado aos hóspedes parking reserved for patrons, patrons only
estacionar [shtas-yoon**a**r] to park
estadia **f** [shtad**ee**-a] stay
estádio **m** [sht**a**d-yoo] stadium
estado **m** [sht**a**doo] state
Estados Unidos (da América) **mpl** [sht**a**dooz oon**ee**dooJ (dam**eh**rika)] United States (of America)
estafado [shtaf**a**doo] shattered, exhausted
estalagem **f** [shtal**a**Jayng] luxury hotel
estamos [sht**a**moosh] we are
estância **f** [sht**a**ns-ya] timber yard
estão [shtowng] they are; you are
estar [shtar] to be
estará [shtar**a**] he/she/it/you will be
estarão [shtar**ow**ng] you/they will be
estarás [shtar**a**sh] you will be
estarei [shtar**ay**] I will be
estaremos [shtar**ay**moosh] we will be
estas [**eh**shtash] these

estás [shtash] you are
estátua **f** [sht**a**twa] statue
estava [sht**a**va] I/he/she/it/you used to be
estavam [sht**a**vam] you/they used to be
estávamos [sht**a**vamoosh] we used to be
estavas [sht**a**vash] you used to be
este [**ay**sht] this; this one
este **m** [ehsht] east
estendal **m** [shtend**a**l] clothes line
estes [**ay**shtish] these
esteve [sht**ay**v] he/she/it was; you were
estive [sht**ee**v] I was
estivemos [shtiv**ay**moosh] we were
estiveram [shtiv**eh**rowng] they were; you were
estiveste [shtiv**eh**sht] you were
estômago **m** [sht**oh**magoo] stomach
estou [shtoh] I am
estrada **f** [shtr**a**da] road
estrada nacional [nas-yoon**a**l] national highway
estrada principal [preensip**a**l] main highway
estragado [shtrag**a**doo] faulty; out of order
estragar [shtrag**a**r] to damage
estrangeira (**f**), estrangeiro (**m**) [shtranJ**ay**roo] foreign; foreigner
no estrangeiro [noo] abroad
estranha (**f**) [shtr**a**n-ya],

estranho (**m**) [shtr**a**n-yoo] stranger; peculiar; funny; strange
estreia **f** [shtr**ay**-a] first showing
estreito [shtr**ay**too] narrow
estrela **f** [shtr**ay**la] star
estudante **m/f** [shtood**a**nt] student
estupendo [shtoop**ay**ndoo] amazing
estúpido [sht**oo**pidoo] stupid
etiqueta **f** [etik**ay**ta] label
eu [**ay**-oo] I
EUA USA
eu mesmo [**ay**-oo m**ay**Jmoo] myself
Europa **f** [ay-oor**o**pa] Europe
europeia (**f**) [ay-ooroop**ay**-a], europeu (**m**) [ay-ooroop**ay**-oo] European
exactamente! [ezatam**ay**nt] exactly!
exacto [ez**a**too] accurate, correct
exagerar [ezagir**a**r] to exaggerate
exame **m** [ez**a**m] exam, test
exausto [ez**ow**shtoo] exhausted, tired
excelente [ish-sel**ay**nt] excellent; lovely
excepto [ish-s**eh**too] except
excepto aos domingos Sundays excepted
excesso de bagagem **m** [ish-s**eh**soo di bag**a**Jayng] excess baggage
excursão **f** [shkoors**ow**ng] coach trip; trip
excursão com guia [kong] guided tour
excursão organizada [organiz**a**da] package holiday
excursões **fpl** [shkoors**oy**ngsh] excursions
exemplo **m** [ez**ay**mploo] example
por exemplo [poor] for example
exigir [eziJ**ee**r] to demand
Exmo. Sr. (Excelentíssimo Senhor) Dear Sir
experiente [shpir-y**ay**nt] experienced
experimentar [shpirimaynt**a**r] to try; to try on
explicar [shplik**a**r] to explain
exposição **f** [shpoozis**ow**ng] exhibition
extensão **f** [shtens**ow**ng] extension; extension lead
extintor **m** [shtint**oh**r] fire extinguisher
extraordinário [shtra-ohrdin**a**r-yoo] extraordinary
extremamente [shtremam**ay**nt] extremely

F

F cold
fábrica **f** [f**a**brika] factory
fabricado em ... made in ...
faca **f** [f**a**ka] knife
fácil [f**a**sil] easy
faço [f**a**soo] I do

factor de protecção m [fatohr di prootesowng] protection factor
factura f [fatoora] invoice
fadista m/f [fadeeshta] singer of traditional Portuguese fado songs
fado m [fadoo] traditional Portuguese song, usually sad and romantic
faiança f [fī-ansa] glazed earthenware
faixa f [fīsha] lane
falar to speak; to talk
fala ...? do you speak ...?
não falo inglês I don't speak English
falido [faleedo] broke; bankrupt
falso [falsoo] fake; false
falta missing
faltar to be lacking; to be missing
família f [fameel-ya] family
famoso [famohzoo] famous
fantástico [fantashtikoo] fantastic
fará [fara] he/she/it/you will do
farão [farowng] you/they will do
farás [farash] you will do
farei [faray] I will do
faremos [faraymoosh] we will do
farmácia f [farmas-ya] pharmacy, chemist's
farmácias de serviço fpl [di sirveesoo] emergency pharmacies, duty chemists
faróis máximos mpl [faroyJ masimoosh] headlights
faróis médios dipped headlights
faróis mínimos [meenimoosh] sidelights
farol m headlight; lighthouse
farto [fartoo] fed up
fato m [fatoo] suit
fato de banho [di ban-yoo] swimming costume
fato de treino [traynoo] tracksuit
favorito [favooreetoo] favourite
favor: por favor [favohr] please
se faz favor [si fash] please
é favor fechar a porta please close the door
favor não incomodar please do not disturb
fazem-se chaves keys cut here
fazer [fazayr] to do; to make
fazer a barba to shave
fazer amor [amohr] to make love
fazer as malas [aJ malash] to pack
fazer bicha [beesha] to queue, to stand in line
fazer brushing to blow-dry
fazer mudança [moodansa] to change (trains)
fazer surf to surf
fazer vela [vehla] to sail
fazer windsurf to windsurf
faz favor [fash favohr] please, excuse me
febre f [fehbr] temperature,

fever
febre dos fenos [fehbr doosh faynoosh] hayfever
febril [febreel] feverish
fechado [fishadoo] shut, closed; reserved; overcast
fechado à chave [fishadwa shav] locked
fechado até ... closed until ...
fechado para balanço closed for stocktaking
fechado para férias closed for holidays
fechado para obras closed for repairs
fechadura f [fishadoora] lock
fechar [fishar] to close; to shut
fechar à chave [shav] to lock
fecho m [fayshoo] handle
fecho éclair® zip, zipper
feio [fay-oo] ugly
feira f [fayra] funfair; trade fair
feiras das vilas local village fairs
feito [faytoo] made; done
feito à mão [faytwa mowng] hand-made
feliz [fileesh] happy
feliz aniversário! [fileez anivirsar-yoo] happy birthday!
Feliz Ano Novo! [anoo nohvoo] Happy New Year!
felizmente [filiJmaynt] fortunately
Feliz Natal! [fileeJ] Merry Christmas!
feminista (f) [femineeshta] feminist
feriado m [fir-yadoo] public holiday
férias fpl [fehr-yash] holiday; vacation
de férias [di] on holiday; on vacation
férias de inverno fpl [dinvehrnoo] winter holiday
férias grandes fpl [grandsh] summer holidays
ferida f [fireeda] wound
ferido [fireedoo] injured
ferragens fpl [firraJayngsh] ironmongery, hardware
ferramenta f [firramaynta] tool
ferro m [fehrroo] iron
ferro de engomar m [dayngoomar] iron
festa f [fehshta] party
Boas Festas! [boh-ash fehshtash] merry Christmas and a happy New Year
festas dos santos populares feast days of saints
Fevereiro [fivrayroo] February
fez [faysh] he/she/it did, he/she/it has done; you did, you have done
fibras naturais natural fibres
ficar [fikar] to remain, to stay
ficam dois [feekowng doh-ish] there are two left
onde fica ...? [feeka] where is ...?
ficar com [kong] to keep
fígado m [feegadoo] liver
filha f [feel-ya] daughter
filho m [feel-yoo] son
filho da puta! [poota] son-of-a-bitch!

filme **m** [feelm] film; movie
filme colorido **m** [koolooreedoo] colour film
filtro **m** [feeltroo] filter
filtros de café **mpl** [feeltroosh di kafeh] filter papers
fim **m** [feeng] end
no fim de ... [noo – di] at the end of ...
no fim eventually
fim de autoestrada end of motorway/highway
fim de estação end of season
fim de semana [di simana] weekend
finalmente [finalmaynt] at last
fino [feenoo] thin; fine
fio **m** [fee-oo] lead; thread; wire
fio de fusível **m** [di foozeevil] fuse wire
fio dentário **m** [dentar-yoo] dental floss
fita **f** [feeta] tape, cassette
fita-cola **f** sticky tape
fita elástica **f** [elashtika] rubber band
fita gomada [goomada] Sellotape®, Scotch tape®
fita métrica [mehtrika] tape measure
fiz [feesh] I did, I have done
fizemos [fizaymoosh] we did, we have done
fizeram [fizehrowng] you/they did, they have done
fizeste [fizehsht] you did, you have done
flertar [flirtar] to flirt
flor **f** [flohr] flower
floresta **f** [floorehshta] forest
fluentemente [flwentimaynt] fluently
fogão **m** [foogowng] cooker
fogo **m** [fohgoo] fire
fogos de artifício **mpl** [fogoosh dartifees-yoo] fireworks
fogueira **f** [foogayra] fire, campfire
foi [foh-i] it was, he/she went, he/she has left
folha **f** [fohl-ya] leaf; sheet
folha de prata silver foil
folheto **m** [fool-yaytoo] brochure; leaflet
fome [fohm] hunger
tenho fome [tayn-yoo] I'm hungry
tens fome? [taynsh] are you hungry?
fomos [fohmoosh] we were, we have been; we went, we have gone
fonte **f** [fohnt] fountain
fora: lá fora outside
do lado de fora [doo ladoo di] outside
fora de casa [di kaza] outdoors
foram [fohrowng] you/they were, you/they have been; you/they went, you/they have gone
forcados **mpl** [foorkadoosh] group of men who wrestle with the bull during a bullfight

forma: em forma [ayng **for**ma] fit
de qualquer forma [di kwal**kehr**] anyway
formiga f [foor**mee**ga] ant
forno m [**foh**rnoo] oven
forte [fort] strong; rich
fósforos mpl [**fo**shfooroosh] matches
foste [fohsht] you were, you have been; you went, you have gone
fotocópias fpl [footoo**ko**p-yash] photocopies
fotografar [footoogra**far**] to photograph
fotografia f [footoogra**fee**-a] photograph; photographic goods
fotógrafo m [foo**to**grafoo] photographer
fraco [**fra**koo] weak
fractura f [fra**too**ra] fracture
frágil [**fra**Jil] fragile
fralda f [**fral**da] nappy, diaper
fraldas descartáveis fpl [dishkar**ta**vaysh] disposable nappies/diapers
França f [**fran**sa] France
francês (m) [fran**saysh**] French; Frenchman
francesa (f) [fran**say**za] French; French woman
franquia f [fran**kee**-a] postage
free-shop f duty-free shop
frente f [fraynt] front
em frente [ayng] in front
em frente a [fraynta] opposite; in front of
na frente at the front
frequência f [frik**way**ns-ya] frequency
frequentado [frikwaynt**a**doo] busy
frequente [frik**waynt**] frequent
frequentemente [frikwayn-tem**aynt**] frequently
fresco [**fray**shkoo] fresh; cool
frigideira f [friJid**ay**ra] frying pan
frigorífico m [frigoo**ree**fikoo] fridge
frio [**free**-oo] cold
tenho frio [**tay**n-yoo] I'm cold
fritar [fri**tar**] to fry
fronha da almofada f [**froh**n-ya dalmoo**fa**da] pillow case
fronteira f [fron**tay**ra] border, frontier
frutaria f [froota**ree**-a] fruit shop
fuga f [**foo**ga] leak
fui [fwee] I went, I have gone; I was, I have been
fumadores mpl [foomad**oh**rish] smokers, smoking
fumar [foo**mar**] to smoke
fuma? [**foo**ma] do you smoke?
não fumo [nowng] I don't smoke
fumo m [**foo**moo] smoke
funcionar [foons-yo**nar**] to work
não funciona [nowng] out of order
fundo (m) [**foo**ndoo] deep; bottom
funil m [foo**neel**] funnel

furado [fooradoo] flat (tyre)
furgão m [foorgowng] van
furgoneta f [foorgoonayta] van
furioso [foor-yohzoo] furious
furo m [fooroo] puncture
fusível m [foozeevil] fuse
futebol m [footbol] football
futuro m [footooroo] future
no futuro [noo] in future

G

gado m [gadoo] cattle
gajo m [gaJoo] guy
galão m [galowng] gallon; milky coffee in a tall glass
galeria de arte f [galiree-a dart] art gallery
Gales m [galish] Wales
galês (m) [galaysh] Welsh; Welshman
galesa (f) [galayza] Welsh; Welsh woman
gama f range
ganhar [gan-yar] to win; to earn
ganso m [gansoo] goose
garagem f [garaJayng] garage
garantia f [garantee-a] guarantee
garfo m [garfoo] fork
garganta f throat
garrafa f bottle
garraiadas fpl [garrī-adash] bull-running
gás m [gash] gas
gás Cidla® m camping gas
gasóleo m [gazol-yoo] diesel
gasolina f [gazooleena] petrol, gasoline
gasolina-normal three-star petrol, regular gas
gasolina sem chumbo [sayng shoomboo] unleaded petrol
gasolina-super [sooper] four-star petrol
gás para campismo m [gash para kampeeJmoo] camping gas
gastar [gashtar] to spend
gato m [gatoo] cat
gaveta f [gavayta] drawer
G.B. [Jay bay] Great Britain
geada f [J-yada] frost
gelado (m) [Jiladoo] frozen; ice cream; ice lolly
gelataria f [Jilataree-a] ice-cream parlour
gel de duche m [Jehl di doosh] shower gel
gelo [Jayloo] ice
gel para o cabelo m [Jehl par-oo kabayloo] hair gel
gémeos mpl [Jaym-yoosh] twins
gengiva f [JenJeeva] gum
genro m [Jaynroo] son-in-law
gente f [Jaynt] people
toda a gente [tohda] everyone
genuíno [Jinweenoo] genuine
geral [Jeral] general
geralmente [Jeralmaynt] usually
gerente m/f [Jeraynt] manager; manageress
gesso m [Jaysoo] plaster cast
ginásio m [Jinaz-yoo] gym
gira-discos m [jeera-

deeshkoosh] record player
glutão [glootowng] greedy
G.N.R. [Jay en err] branch of the Portuguese police
golfe m [golf] golf
Golfo da Biscáia m [gohlfoo da bishkī-a] Bay of Biscay
gordo [gohrdoo] fat
gorduroso [goordoorohzoo] greasy
gorgeta f [goorJayta] tip
gostar [gooshtar] to like
gosta de ...? [goshta di] do you like ...?
gosto [goshtoo] I like, I like it
gostoso [gooshtohzoo] tasty; pleasant; nice
gota f [gohta] drop
gotas para os olhos fpl [gohtash parooz ol-yoosh] eye drops
governo m [goovayrnoo] government
Grã-Bretanha f [gran britan-ya] Great Britain
gradualmente [gradwalmaynt] gradually
grama m gram(me)
gramática f [gramatika] grammar
grande [grand] large, big
grandes armazéns mpl [grandz armazayngsh] department store
granizo m [graneezoo] hail
gratuito [gratoo-eetoo] free (of charge)
gravador (de cassetes) m [gravadohr (di kasehtsh)] tape recorder
gravata f tie, necktie
grave [grav] nasty
grávida pregnant
graxa para sapatos f [grasha para sapatoosh] shoe polish
Grécia f [grehs-ya] Greece
grego (m) [graygoo] Greek
grelhador m [gril-yadohr] grill
gripe f [greep] flu
gritar [gritar] to shout
grosseiro [groosayroo] rude
grosso [grohsoo] pissed
grupo m [groopoo] group, party
grupo de sange [di sang] blood group
guarda m/f [gwarda] caretaker
guarda-chuva m [gwarda shoova] umbrella
Guarda Fiscal Customs police
Guarda Nacional Republicana branch of the Portuguese police
guardanapo m [gwardanapoo] napkin, serviette
guardar [gwardar] to keep
guerra f [gehrra] war
guia f [gee-a] guide, courier
guia turística f [tooreeshtika], guia turístico m [tooreeshtikoo] tour guide
guichet m [geeshay] window; ticket window

H

h is not pronounced in Portuguese

H gents', men's room
há ... [a] there is ..., there are ...
há ...? is there...?, are there ...?
há uma semana [ooma simana] a week ago
há pouco [pohkoo] recently
há vagas vacancies, rooms free
hábito m [abeetoo] custom; habit
hall m lobby
H.C. state hospital
hemorróidas fpl [emoorroydash] piles
hepatite f [epateet] hepatitis
hipermercado m [eepermerkadoo] hypermarket
história f [ishtor-ya] history; story
hoje [ohJ] today
Holanda f [olanda] Netherlands, Holland
holandês (**m**) [olandaysh] Dutch; Dutchman
holandesa (**f**) [olandayza] Dutch; Dutch woman
homem m [ohmayng] man
homens mpl [ohmayngsh] men; gents' toilet, men's room
honesto [onehshtoo] honest
hora f [ora] hour; time
hora de chegada [di shigada] arrival time
hora de partida [parteeda] departure time
hora de ponta [pohnta] rush hour
hora local local time
horário m [orar-yoo] timetable, (US) schedule
horário das consultas [dash konsooltash] surgery hours, (US) office hours
horas fpl [orash] hours; o'clock
às seis horas [ash sayz orash] at six o'clock
que horas são? [k-yorash sowng] what's the time?
horas de abertura fpl [orash dabirtoora] opening times
horas de visita fpl [di vizeeta] visiting hours
horrível [orreevil] awful, dreadful, horrible
hortelã-pimenta f [ortilang pimaynta] peppermint
hospedado [oshpidadoo]:
estar hospedado em [shtar – ayng] to be a guest at, to stay at
hospedaria f [oshpidaree-a] guesthouse
hospedar-se [oshspidarsi] to stay
hóspede m/f [oshpidi] guest
hospedeira (de bordo) f [oshpidayra (di bordoo)] stewardess, air hostess
Hospital Civil m state hospital
hospitalidade f [oshpitalidad]

hospitality
houve [ohv] there has been
húmido [oomeedoo] damp; humid
humor m [oomohr] mood; humour
hydroplano m [idrooplanoo] hydrofoil

I

iate m [yat] yacht
ida: bilhete de ida [bil-yayt deeda] single ticket, one-way ticket
idade f [eedad] age
que idade tem? [keedad tayng] how old are you?
ideia f [iday-a] idea
idiota m [id-yota] stupid
ignição f [ignisowng] ignition
igreja f [igrayJa] church
igual [igwal] same
ilha f [eel-ya] island
imediatamente [imid-yatamaynt] immediately, at once
imenso [imaynsoo] immensely, a lot
imitação f [imitasowng] imitation
impermeável m [impirm-yavil] raincoat
importante [impoortant] important
importar to matter, to be important; to import
importa-se de ...? [importasi] will you ...?
importa-se se ...? [si] do you mind if ...?
não me importo [nowng mimportoo] I don't mind
importuno [importoonoo] annoying
impossível [impooseevil] impossible
imprescindível [impresh-sindeevil] vital
impressionante [impris-yoonant] impressive
impresso m [imprehsoo] form, document
impressos mpl [imprehsoosh] printed matter
incêndio m [insaynd-yoo] fire
inchaço m [inshasoo] lump, swelling
inchado [inshadoo] swollen
incluído [inklweedoo] included
incluir [inklweer] to include
inconsciente [inkonsh-syaynt] unconscious
inconstante [inkonshtant] changeable
incrível [inkreevil] incredible
indiano (m) [ind-yanoo] Indian
indicações indications
indicador m [indikadohr] indicator
indicativo m [indikateevoo] dialling code, area code
indigestão f [indiJishtowng] indigestion
indústria f [indooshtr-ya] industry
infecção f [infehsowng] infection

infeccioso [infehs-y**oh**zoo] infectious
infectado [infeht**a**doo] septic
infelizmente [infiliJm**ay**ngt] unfortunately
inflamação f [inflamas**ow**ng] inflammation
inflamável inflammable
informação f [infoormas**ow**ng] information, piece of information
informações fpl [infoorm-as**oy**ngsh] directory enquiries; information
Inglaterra f [inglat**eh**rra] England
inglês (m) [ingl**ay**sh] English; Englishman
em inglês [ayng] in English
inglesa (f) [ingl**ay**za] English; English woman
ingleses: os ingleses [ingl**ay**zish] the English
ingredientes mpl [ingrid-y**ay**ntsh] ingredients
íngreme [**ee**ngrim] steep
início m [in**ee**s-yoo] beginning
no início [noo] at the beginning
início de autoestrada start of motorway/highway
injecção f [inJehs**ow**ng] injection
inocente [inoos**ay**nt] innocent
insecto m [ins**eh**too] insect
insistir [insisht**ee**r] to insist
insolação f [insoolas**ow**ng] sunstroke
insónia f [ins**o**n-ya] insomnia
Instituto do Vinho do Porto m Port Wine Institute
inteiro [int**ay**roo] whole
inteligente [intiliJ**ay**nt] intelligent, clever
Intercidades fast train, Intercity train
interdito a menores de ... anos no admission to those under ... years of age
interessado [intris**a**doo] interested
interessante [intris**a**nt] interesting
internacional [internas-yoon**a**l] international
interpretar [interprit**a**r] to interpret
intérprete m/f [int**eh**rprit] interpreter
interruptor m [intiroopt**oh**r] switch
interruptor de ligar/desligar m [di lig**a**r/diJlig**a**r] on/off switch
intervalo m [interv**a**loo] interval
intoxicação alimentar f [intoksikas**ow**ng] food poisoning
introduza a moeda na ranhura insert coin in slot
inundação f [inoondas**ow**ng] flood
Inverno m [inv**eh**rnoo] winter
ir [eer] to go
ir buscar [booshk**a**r] to get, to fetch
Irlanda f [eerl**a**nda] Ireland
Irlanda do Norte f [eerl**a**nda doo nort] Northern Ireland

irlandês (m) [eerlandaysh] Irish; Irishman
irlandesa (f) [eerlandayza] Irish; Irishwoman
irmã f [eermang] sister
irmão m [eermowng] brother
isqueiro m [ishkayroo] cigarette lighter
isso [eesoo] that; that one
isso é ... [eh] that's ...
isso é ...? is that ...?
isto [eeshtoo] this; this one
isto é ...? [eeshtweh] is this ...?
Itália f [ital-ya] Italy
italiana (f) [ital-yana] Italian,
italiano (m) [ital-yanoo] Italian

J

já [Ja] ever; already
Janeiro [Janayro] January
janela f [Janehla] window
jantar (m) [Jantar] evening meal, dinner; supper; to have dinner
jarda f [Jarda] yard
jardim m [Jardeeng] garden
jardim público [pooblikoo] park
jardim zoológico [zwoloJikoo] zoo
jarra f [Jarra] vase
jarro m [Jarroo] jug; jar
joalharia f [Jwal-yaree-a] jewellery
joalheiro m [Jwal-yayroo] jeweller
joelho m [Jwayl-yoo] knee
jogar [Joogar] to play
jogar fora to throw away
jogo m [Johgoo] game, match
jóias fpl [Jo-yash] jewellery
jornal m [Joornal] newspaper
jovem [Jovayng] young
jovens mpl [Jovayngsh] young people
judaico [Joodīkoo] Jewish
Julho [Jool-yoo] July
Junho [Joon-yoo] June
junta da culatra f [Joonta da koolatra] cylinder head gasket
junto da ... [Joontoo da] beside the ...
juntos [Joontoosh] together
justo [Jooshtoo] just, fair

L

lá over there, there
lã f [lang] wool
lábios mpl [lab-yoosh] lips
laca f hair spray
lado m [ladoo] side
do outro lado [doo-ohtroo] opposite
do outro lado de ... [doo ohtroo ladoo di] across the ...
ladra f, ladrão m [ladrowng] thief
lago m [lagoo] lake; pond
lama f mud
lamentar [lamayntar] to regret, to be sorry
lâminas para barbear fpl [laminash para barb-yar] razor blades
lâmpada f light bulb

lanterna **f** [lant**eh**rna] torch, flashlight
lápis **m** [lapsh] pencil
lápis para as sobrancelhas [p**a**rash sobrans**ay**l-yash] eyebrow pencil
lápis para os olhos [p**a**rooz **o**l-yoosh] eyeliner
largo (**m**) [l**a**rgoo] wide; square
lata **f** can; tin
lata de gasolina **f** [di gazool**ee**na] petrol can
lavabos **mpl** [lav**a**boosh] toilets, rest rooms
lavagem a seco **f** [lav**a**Jayng a s**ay**koo] dry-cleaning
lavagem automática [owtoom**a**tika] carwash
lavagem e mise [ee m**ee**z] shampoo and set
lava-louça **f** [l**a**va l**oh**sa] sink
lavandaria **f** [lavandar**ee**-a] laundry (place)
lavandaria automática [owtoom**a**tika] launderette
lavar to wash
lavar à mão [mowng] to handwash
lavar a roupa [r**oh**pa] to do the washing
lavar e pentear [paynt-y**a**r] wash and set
lavar na máquina machine wash
lavar-se [–si] to wash (oneself)
lavatório **m** [lavat**o**r-yoo] washhand basin
lavrador **m** [lavrad**oh**r] farmer
laxativo **m** [lashat**ee**voo] laxative
lei **f** [lay] law
leitaria **f** [laytar**ee**-a] shop selling dairy products
leite de limpeza **m** [layt di leemp**ay**za] skin cleanser
leitor de CDs **m** [layt**oh**r di say daysh] CD-player
lembrança **f** [laymbr**a**nsa] gift; souvenir
lembrar-se [–si] to remember
lembra-se? [l**ay**mbrasi] do you remember?
não me lembro [n**ow**ng mi l**ay**mbroo] I don't remember
lenço **m** [l**ay**nsoo] handkerchief
lenço de cabeça [di kab**ay**sa] headscarf
lenço de pescoço [pishk**oh**soo] scarf (for neck)
lençol **m** [layns**o**l] sheet
lenços de papel **mpl** [l**ay**nsoosh di pap**eh**l] tissues, paper handkerchiefs, Kleenex®
lentes de contacto **fpl** [layntsh di kont**a**too] contact lenses
lentes gelatinosas [Jilatin**o**zash] soft lenses
lentes rígidas [r**ee**Jidash] hard lenses
lentes semi-rígidas [simir**ee**Jidash] gas permeable lenses
lento [l**ay**ntoo] slow
leque **m** [lehk] fan (handheld)
ler [layr] to read
lésbica **f** [l**eh**Jbika] lesbian

La

leste m [lehsht] east
no leste [noo] in the east
letra f [laytra] letter
letra de imprensa block letters
levada m country walkway along irrigation channels on Madeira
levantar-se [livantarsi] to get up
levante o auscultador lift the receiver
levar to take; to carry
para levar to take away, to go (food)
leve [lehv] light (not heavy)
Lg. square
lhe [l-yi] (to) him; (to) her; (to) you
lhes [l-yaysh] (to) them; (to) you
libra f [leebra] pound
libras esterlinas fpl [leebraz ishtirleenash] pounds sterling
lição f [lisowng] lesson
licença f [lisaynsa] licence; permit
com licença [kong] excuse me
licenciatura f [lisayns-yatoora] degree
liceu m [lisay-oo] secondary school, high school
ligação f [ligasowng] connection
ligação com ... connects with ...
ligadura f [ligadoora] bandage
ligar to turn on, to switch on
lima de unhas f [leema doon-yash] nailfile
limite de velocidade m [limeet di viloosidad] speed limit
limpa pára-brisas m [leempa parabreezash] windscreen wiper
limpar [leempar] to clean
limpeza a seco f [leempayza a saykoo] dry-clean; dry-cleaning
limpo [leempoo] clean
língua f [leengwa] language; tongue
linha f [leen-ya] line
liquidação sale
liquidação total clearance sale
Lisboa [liJboh-a] Lisbon
liso [leezoo] plain
lista f [leeshta] list
lista telefónica [telefohnika] phone book, telephone directory
litro m [leetroo] litre
livraria f [livraree-a] bookshop, bookstore
livre [leevr] free, vacant
livro m [leevroo] book
livro de cheques [di shehksh] cheque book
livro de expressões [dishprisoyngsh] phrasebook
livro de moradas [di mooradash] address book
livro-guia m [gee-a] guidebook
lixívia f [lisheev-ya] bleach
lixo m [leeshoo] rubbish, trash; litter
local de encontro m [lookal

daynk**oh**ntroo] meeting place
localidade f [lookalid**ad**] place
loção f [loos**ow**ng] lotion
loção de bronzear f [di bronz-y**ar**] suntan lotion
loção écran total f [ekr**a**ng toot**al**] sunblock
loção para depois do sol f [dip**oh**-ish doo] aftersun cream
locomotiva f [lokoomoot**ee**va] engine
logo [l**o**goo] immediately, at once
logo que possível [ki poos**ee**vil] as soon as possible
loiça f [l**oh**-isa] crockery
loiça de barro [di b**a**rroo] pottery
loja f [l**o**Ja] shop
loja de aluguer de automóveis [daloog**eh**r dowtoom**o**vaysh] car hire, car rental
loja de antiguidades f [dantigweed**a**dsh] antique shop
loja de artesanato [dartizan**a**too] craft shop, handicrafts shop
loja de artigos fotográficos [dart**ee**goosh fotogr**a**fikoosh] camera shop
loja de brinquedos [di breenk**ay**doosh] toyshop
loja de desportos [dishp**o**rtoosh] sports shop
loja de ferragens [di firr**a**Jayngsh] hardware store
loja de fotografia [footoograf**ee**-a] photography shop
loja de lembranças [laymbr**a**nsash] gift shop
loja de malas [m**a**lash] handbag shop
loja de peles [pehlsh] furrier
loja de produtos naturais [prood**oo**toosh natoor**ī**sh] health food shop
Londres [l**oh**ndrish] London
longe [lohnJ] far
ao longe [ow] in the distance
fica longe? [f**ee**ka] is it far away?
lotação esgotada all tickets sold
louça: lavar a louça [l**oh**sa] to wash the dishes
louça de barro f [di b**a**rroo] earthenware
louco [l**oh**koo] nutter
louro [l**oh**roo] blond
lua f [l**oo**-a] moon
lua-de-mel f [l**oo**-a di mehl] honeymoon
lugar m [loog**ar**] greengrocer's; seat; place
em outro lugar [ayng **oh**troo] elsewhere
lugar ao pé da janela [ow peh da Jan**eh**la] window seat
lugar de corredor [di koorid**oh**r] aisle seat
lugar de vegetais [di vigit**ī**sh] greengrocer's
lugares em pé standing room
lugares reservados a cegos, inválidos, grávidas e acompanhantes de crianças com menos de 4 anos seats reserved for the blind, disabled, expectant mothers

and those with children under four
lume **m** [**loom**] light; fire
luvas **fpl** [**loo**vash] gloves
luxo **m** [**loo**shoo] luxury
de luxo [di] de luxe
luxuoso [loosh-w**oh**zoo] luxurious
luz **f** [loosh] light
luz do sol **f** [looJ doo] sunshine
luzes de presença **fpl** [**loo**ziJ di priz**ay**nsa] sidelights
luzes de trânsito traffic lights
luzes de trás [**loo**zish di trash] rear lights
Lx Lisbon

M

M. underground, (US) subway
má bad; nasty
macaco **m** [mak**a**koo] jack
maçada **f** [mas**a**da] bother
maçador [masad**oh**r] boring
maçaneta **f** [masan**ay**ta] door knob
machão **m** [mash**ow**ng] macho
machista [mash**ee**shta] sexist
maço **m** [m**a**soo] packet
madeira **f** [mad**ay**ra] wood
madrasta **f** [madr**a**shta] stepmother
madrugada **f** [madroog**a**da] dawn
de madrugada [di] at dawn
maduro [mad**oo**roo] ripe
mãe **f** [mayng] mother
magricela [magris**eh**la] skinny
magro [m**a**groo] slim; thin
Maio [**mī**-oo] May
maior [mī-**o**r] greater; bigger, larger
o maior the biggest
a maior parte (de) [part (di)] most (of)
maioria: a maioria dos/das ... [mī-ooree-a doosh/dash] most ...
mais [mīsh] more
mais alguma coisa? [mīz alg**oo**ma k**oh**-iza] anything else?
mais de ... [mīJ di] more than ..., over ...
mais ... do que ... more ... than ...
mais um/uma [mīz oong/**oo**ma] an extra one
não há mais [nowng a mīsh] there's none left
mais longe [mīJ lohnJ] further
mais nada no more; nothing else
mais ou menos [mīz oh m**ay**noosh] about, approximately, more or less; average, so-so
mais tarde [mīsh tard] later, later on
mal hardly; badly
mala **f** bag; suitcase; handbag
fazer as malas [faz**ay**r aJ m**a**lash] to pack one's bags
mala de mão [di mowng] handbag, (US) purse
mal cozido [kooz**ee**doo] not cooked, undercooked
mal-entendido **m** [malayntayndeedoo]

misunderstanding
maluco [mal**oo**koo] barmy, nuts
mamã f [mam**a**ng] mum
mamar: dar de mamar a to breastfeed
mancha f spot
mandar to send
manga f sleeve
manhã f [man-y**a**ng] morning
às sete da manhã [ash seht] at seven a.m.
de manhã [di] in the morning
esta manhã [**eh**shta] this morning
manivela do motor f [maniv**eh**la doo mot**oh**r] crankshaft
manta f blanket
mantenha-se à direita, caminhe pela esquerda (cars) keep to the right, (pedestrians) walk on the left
mão f [mowng] hand
mapa m map
mapa da cidade m [sid**a**d] street map
mapa das estradas m [daz shtr**a**dash] road map
maquilhagem f [makil-y**a**Jayng] make-up
máquina f [m**a**kina] machine
máquina de barbear [di barb-y**a**r] electric shaver
máquina de lavar [lav**a**r] washing machine
máquina de venda [di v**ay**nda] vending machine
máquina fotográfica [footoogr**a**fika] camera
mar m sea
maravilhoso [maravil-y**oh**zoo] wonderful
marca f make, brand name
marcação f [markas**ow**ng] appointment
marcar to dial
marca registada registered trademark
marcha f [m**a**rsha] candlelit procession
marcha atrás [marshatr**a**sh] reverse gear
Março [m**a**rsoo] March
marco de correio m [m**a**rkoo di koor**ay**-oo] letterbox, mailbox
maré f [mar**eh**] tide
margem f [m**a**rJayng] shore
marido m [mar**ee**doo] husband
marisqueira f [marishk**ay**ra] seafood restaurant
marque o número desejado dial the number you require
Marrocos m [marr**o**koosh] Morocco
martelo m [mart**eh**loo] hammer
mas [mash] but
matar to kill
maternidade f [maternid**a**d] maternity hospital
matrícula f [matr**ee**koola] registration number
mau [mow] bad; nasty
maxila f [maks**ee**la] jaw
me me; to me; myself
mecânico m [mek**a**nikoo] mechanic
média: em média [ayng m**eh**d-

ya] on average
médica f [mehdika] doctor
medicamento m [midikamayntoo] drug
médico m [mehdikoo] doctor
medida f [mideeda] size
médio [mehd-yoo] medium; medium-rare
de tamanho médio [di taman-yoo] medium-sized
Mediterrâneo m [miditirran-yoo] Mediterranean
medo m [maydoo] fear
meia dúzia f [may-a dooz-ya] half a dozen
meia hora f [ora] half an hour
meia-noite f [noh-it] midnight
meia pensão f [paynsowng] half board, American plan
meias fpl [may-ash] stockings; socks
meias collants stockings
meias de vidro [di veedroo] hosiery
meio m [may-oo] middle; half
no meio [noo] in the middle
meio bilhete m [bil-yayt] half fare
meio-dia m [may-oo dee-a] midday, noon
ao meio-dia [ow] at midday
mel m [mehl] honey
melhor [mil-yor] best; better
melhorar [mil-yorar] to improve
mencionar [mayns-yoonar] to mention
menina f [mineena] girl; young lady
menino m boy
menor [minor] smaller
menos [maynoosh] less
menos de [di] under, less than
menos do que [doo ki] less than
pelo menos at least
mentir [maynteer] to lie
menu de preço fixo [di praysoo feeksoo] fixed-price menu
menu turístico [tooreeshtikoo] tourist menu
mercado m [mirkadoo] market
mercearia f [mirs-yaree-a] grocery store
merceeiro m [mirs-yayroo] grocery store
merda! [mehrda] shit!
mergulhar [mirgool-yar] to dive
mergulho m [mirgool-yoo] skin-diving
mês m [maysh] month
mesa f [mayza] table
mesma [mayJma], **mesmo** [mayJmoo] same; myself
o/a mesmo/mesma the same
ele mesmo himself
mesmo se ... [mayJmo si] even if ...
metade f [mitad] half
metade do preço [doo praysoo] half price
metro m [mehtroo] metre; underground, (US) subway
metropolitano m underground, (US) subway
meu [may-oo] my; mine
meu próprio ... [propr-yoo] my own ...

meus [may-oosh] my; mine
mexer [mishayr] to move
microondas f [mikroo-ohndash] microwave (oven)
mil [meel] thousand
milha f [meel-ya] mile
milhão m [mil-yowng] million
milímetro m [mileemitroo] millimetre
mim [meeng] me
minha [meen-ya], minhas [meen-yash] my; mine
ministério m [minishtehr-yoo] ministry, government department
minúsculo [minooshkooloo] tiny
minuto m [minootoo] minute
míope [mee-oopi] shortsighted
miradouro m scenic view, vantage point
missa m [meesa] mass
misturar [mishtoorar] to mix
mobília f [moobeel-ya] furniture
mochila f [moosheela] rucksack, backpack
moda f fashion
na moda fashionable
modas para senhoras fpl [modash para sin-yorash] ladies' fashions
moderno [moodehrnoo] modern
moeda f [mwehda] coin
moinho (m) [moo-een-yoo] mill; dull (pain)
mola f spring (in seat); peg
mola de roupa [di rohpa] clothes peg
mola para o cabelo [paroo kabayloo] hairgrip
mole [mol] soft
molhado [mool-yadoo] wet
momento m [moomayntoo] moment
um momento [oong] hold on, just a moment
montanha f [montan-ya] mountain
montar a cavalo [kavaloo] to go horse-riding
monte m [mohnt] hill
montra f [mohntra] shop window
monumento m [moonoomayntoo] monument
monumento nacional national monument
morada f [moorada] address
morar [moorar] to live
mordedura f [moordedoora] bite
morrer [moorrayr] to die
morte f [mort] death
morto [mohrtoo] dead
morto de fome [di fohm] starving
mosca f [mohshka] fly
mosquito m [mooshkeetoo] mosquito
mosteiro m [mooshtayroo] monastery
mostrar [mooshtrar] to show
mota f, motocicleta f [mootoosiklehta] motorbike
motor m [mootohr] engine
motor de arranque [darrank] starter motor

motoreta f [mootoor**ay**ta] scooter
motorista m/f [mootoor**ee**shta] driver; motorist
motorizada f [mootooriz**a**da] moped
mourisco [mohr**ee**shkoo] Moorish
mouro m [m**oh**-ooroo] Moor
 os mouros the Moors
móveis de cozinha mpl kitchen furniture
muçulmano [moosoolm**a**noo] Muslim
mudança f [mood**a**nsa] gear(s)
mudar [mood**a**r] to move
mudar de roupa [di r**oh**pa] to get changed
mudar em ... change at ...
muitas vezes [mw**ee**ngta v**ay**zish] often
muito [mw**ee**ngtoo] a lot, lots; plenty of; much; very (much); quite
 muito mais [mīsh] a lot more
 não muito [nowng] not (very) much; not a lot; not too much
 muito tempo [t**ay**mpoo] a long time
 muito bem [bayng] very well
 muito bem! well done!
 muito prazer [praz**ay**r] how do you do?, nice to meet you
 muito prazer em conhecê-lo [ayng koon-yis**ay**loo] very pleased to meet you
muitos mpl [mw**ee**ngtoosh] many
muletas fpl [mool**ay**tash] crutches
mulher f [mool-y**eh**r] woman; wife
mulher-polícia f [pool**ee**s-ya] policewoman
multa f [m**oo**lta] fine
multa por uso indevido penalty for misuse
multidão f [mooltid**ow**ng] crowd
mundo m [m**oo**ndoo] world
muro m [m**oo**roo] wall
músculo m [m**oo**shkooloo] muscle
museu m [mooz**ay**-oo] museum
música f [m**oo**zika] music
música folclórica [foolkl**o**rika] folk music
música pop pop music
música rock rock (music)
músico m [m**oo**zikoo] musician

N

n. number
na in the; at the; on the
 na casa do Américo at Américo's
 na quinta-feira by Thursday
 na televisão on television
nacional [nas-yoon**a**l] national
nacionalidade f [nas-yoonalid**a**d] nationality
nada nothing
 mais nada [mīJ] nothing else
 de nada my pleasure, don't mention it

nada a declarar nothing to declare
nadador salvador f [nadad**oh**r salvad**oh**r] lifeguard
nadar to swim
nalguma parte [nalg**oo**ma part] somewhere
namorada f [namoor**a**da] girlfriend
namorado m [namoor**a**doo] boyfriend
não [nowng] no; not
não aconselhável a menores de ... anos not recommended for those under ... years of age
não beber do not drink
não congelar do not freeze
não contém ... does not contain ...
não engolir do not swallow
não engomar do not iron
não exceder a dose indicada do not exceed the dose indicated
não faz mal [faJ m**a**l] it doesn't matter, never mind; it's OK
não fumar no smoking
não funciona out of order
não há vagas no vacancies
não ingerir do not swallow
não me diga! [mi d**ee**ga] you don't say!
não mexer do not touch
não ... nada nothing; not ... anything
não ... nenhum [nin-y**oo**ng] none; not ... any
não ... ninguém [ning**ay**ng] nobody, no-one; not ... anybody, not ... anyone
não ... nunca [n**oo**nka] never
não pendurar do not hang, dry flat
não pisar a relva please keep off the grass
não secar na máquina do not spin-dry
não sei [say] I don't know
não tem de quê [tayng di kay] don't mention it, you're welcome
não torcer do not wring
nariz m [nar**ee**sh] nose
nas [nash] in the; at the; on the
nascer [nash-s**ay**r] to be born
nasci em ... [nash-s**ee** ayng] I was born in ...
Na. Sra. (Nossa Senhora) Our Lady
natação f [natas**ow**ng] swimming
Natal m Christmas
natural [natoor**a**l] natural
natureza f [natoor**ay**za] nature
náuseas fpl [n**ow**z-yash] nausea
navio m [nav**ee**-o] ship
de navio [di] by ship
necessário [nisis**a**r-yoo] necessary
negativo m [nigat**ee**voo] negative
negócio m [nig**o**s-yoo] deal; business
nem eu [nayng **ay**-oo] nor do I
nem ... nem ... [nayng] neither ... nor ...

nenhum [nin-y**oo**ng], nenhuma [nin-y**oo**ma] none; no ...
de maneira nenhuma! [di man**ay**ra] no way!
de nenhum modo [m**o**doo] not in the least
nenhum deles [daylsh] neither of them
neo-zelandês m [n**eh**-o ziland**ay**sh], neo-zelandesa f [ziland**ay**za] New Zealander
nervoso [nirv**oh**zoo] nervous
neta f [n**eh**ta] granddaughter
neto m [n**eh**too] grandson
nevar [niv**a**r] to snow
neve f [nehv] snow
névoa f [n**eh**vwa] mist
nevoeiro m [nivw**ay**roo] fog
ninguém [ning**ay**ng] nobody, no-one
nível de óleo m [n**ee**vil d**o**l-yoo] oil level
no [noo] in; in the; at the; on the
no alto at the top
no fundo de at the bottom of
no hotel at the hotel
no sábado on Saturday
no. number
nódoa f [n**o**dwa] stain
noite f [n**oh**-it] evening; night
à noite in the evening; at night
de noite at night
esta noite [**eh**shta] this evening; tonight
noite de Santo António 13th June: Saint's day with music, fireworks and processions
noite de São João 24th June: Saint's day with music, fireworks and processions
noite de São Pedro 29th June: Saint's day with music, fireworks and processions
noiva (f) [n**oh**-iva] engaged; fiancée
noivo (m) [n**oh**-ivoo] engaged; fiancé
nojento [nooJ**ay**ntoo] disgusting; filthy
nome m [nohm] name
nome de solteira [di soolt**ay**ra] maiden name
nome próprio [pr**o**pr-yoo] Christian name, first name
nono [n**oh**noo] ninth
nora f daughter-in-law
nordeste m [noord**eh**sht] northeast
noroeste m [noorw**eh**sht] northwest
norte m [nort] north
ao norte [ow] to the north
no norte [noo] in the north
Noruega f [noorw**eh**ga] Norway
norueguês (m) [noorweg**ay**sh], norueguesa (f) [noorweg**ay**za] Norwegian
nos [noosh] in the; at the; on the; us; to us; ourselves
nós [nosh] we; us
No. Sr. (Nosso Senhor) Our Lord
nossa, nossas [n**o**sash], nosso [n**o**soo], nossos [n**o**soosh] our; ours

nota f note; banknote, (US) bill
notas falsas fpl [notash falsash] forged banknotes
notícias fpl [nootees-yash] news
noutro [nohtroo] in another; on another
nova morada f [moorada] forwarding address
Nova Zelândia [ziland-ya] New Zealand
nove [nov] nine
novecentas [novesayntash], **novecentos** [novesayntoosh] nine hundred
Novembro [noovaymbroo] November
noventa [noovaynta] ninety
novidades fpl [noovidadsh] news
novo [nohvoo] new
nu [noo], **nua** [noo-a] naked
num [noong], **numa** [nooma] in a
número m [noomiroo] number
número de telefone [di telefohn] phone number
número de voo [noomiroo di voh-oo] flight number
nunca [noonka] never
nuvem f [noovayng] cloud

NO

o [oo] the; him; it; to it; you
objectiva f [obJeteeva] lens (of camera)
objectos de escritório mpl office supplies
objectos perdidos lost property, lost and found
obliterador m [oblitiradohr] ticket-stamping machine
obra f work
obras (na estrada) fpl roadworks
obrigada, obrigado [obrigadoo] thanks, thank you
muito obrigado/obrigada [mweengtoo] thank you very much
observar [obsirvar] to watch
obturador m [obtooradohr] shutter
óbvio [obv-yoo] obvious
Oceano Atlântico [os-yanoo atlantikoo] Atlantic Ocean
oculista m [okooleeshta] optician
óculos mpl [okooloosh] glasses, spectacles
óculos de sol [di] sunglasses
óculos protectores [prootetohrish] goggles
ocupado [okoopadoo] engaged; busy; occupied
oeste m [wesht] west
no oeste [noo] in the west
ofender [ofayndayr] to offend
ofensivo [ofaynseevoo] offensive
oferecer [ofrisayr] to get; to offer
oferta especial special offer
oiço [oh-isoo] I hear
oitavo [oh-itavoo] eighth
oitenta [oh-itaynta] eighty

oito [**oh**-itoo] eight
oitocentas [oh-itoos**ay**ntash], oitocentos [oh-itoos**ay**ntoosh] eight hundred
olá! [ool**a**] hi!, hello!
óleo m [**o**l-yoo] oil
óleo de bronzear [di brohnz-y**ar**] suntan oil
oleoso [ol-y**oh**zoo] oily
olhar para [ol-y**ar**] to look at
olho m [**oh**l-yoo] eye
ombro m [**oh**mbroo] shoulder
onda f [**oh**nda] wave
onde? [ohnd] where?
onde é? [ohnd**eh**] where is it?
onde está? [ohnd shta] where is it?
onde vai? [vī] where are you going?
de onde? [dohnd] where from?
de onde é? [dohnd-**eh**] where are you from?
ontem [**oh**ntayng] yesterday
ontem à noite [n**oh**-it] last night
ontem de manhã [di man-y**a**ng] yesterday morning
onze [ohnz] eleven
operação f [opiras**ow**ng] operation
operador turístico m [opirad**oh**r tooreeshtikoo] tour operator
oposto [op**oh**shto] opposite
optimista [otim**ee**shta] optimistic
óptimo [**o**timoo] super
óptimo! great!, good!, excellent!
o que [oo kay] what
o que é isso? [oo k-yeh **ee**soo] what's this?
ora essa! [**o**ra **eh**sa] don't be stupid!
orelha f [or**ay**l-ya] ear
organizar [organiz**ar**] to organize
orgulhoso [orgool-y**oh**zoo] proud
orquestra f [ork**eh**shtra] orchestra
os [oosh] the; them; you
osso m [**oh**soo] bone
otorrinolaringologista ear, nose and throat specialist
ou [oh] or
ou ... ou ... either ... or ...
ouriço-do-mar m [ohr**ee**soo doo] sea urchin
ourivesaria f [ohrivezar**ee**-a] jeweller's
ouro m [**oh**roo] gold
ousar [ohz**ar**] to dare
Outono [oht**oh**noo] autumn, (US) fall
no Outono [noo] in the autumn, in the fall
outra coisa [**oh**tra k**oh**-iza] something else
outras localidades [**oh**traJ lookalid**a**dsh] other places
outra vez [**oh**tra vaysh] again
outro [**oh**troo] different, another; other
Outubro [oht**oo**broo] October
ouvir [ohv**ee**r] to hear
ao ouvir o sinal... when you

hear the tone ...
ovelha f [ov**ay**l-ya] sheep

P

P. square
pá f spade
pacote m [pak**o**t] carton; pack
padaria f [padar**ee**-a] bakery
padeiro m [pad**ay**roo] baker
padrasto m [padr**a**shtoo] stepfather
padre m [padr] priest
pagamento m [pagam**ay**ntoo] payment
pagamento a pronto cash payment
pagar to pay
pagar em dinheiro [ayng deen-**yay**roo] to pay cash
página f [p**a**Jina] page
páginas amarelas [p**a**Jinaz amar**eh**lash] yellow pages
pai m [pī] father
painel m [pīn**eh**l] dashboard; panel
país m [pa-**ee**sh] country; nation; homeland
pais mpl [pīsh] parents
paisagem f [pīz**a**Jayng] scenery
País de Gales m [pa-**ee**J di g**a**lish] Wales
palácio m [pal**a**s-yoo] palace
palavra f word
palco m [p**a**lkoo] stage
pálido [p**a**lidoo] pale
panela f [pan**eh**la] pan, saucepan
panfleto m [panfl**ay**too] leaflet
pano m [p**a**noo] fabric, cloth
pano de cozinha [di kooz**ee**n-ya] tea towel
pano de loiça [l**oh**-isa] dishcloth
pantufas fpl [pant**oo**fash] slippers
papá m dad
papeira f [pap**ay**ra] mumps
papéis waste paper
papel m [pap**eh**l] paper
papelaria f [papelar**ee**-a] stationer
papel de alumínio [daloom**ee**n-yoo] aluminium foil
papel de carta [di] writing paper, notepaper
papel de embrulho [daymbr**oo**l-yoo] wrapping paper
papel higiénico [iJ-y**eh**nikoo] toilet paper
par m pair
um par de ... [oong par di] a couple of ...; a pair of ...
para into; for; to; towards
para onde? [**oh**nd] where to?
para alugar [paraloog**a**r] for hire; to rent
parabéns! [parab**ay**ngsh] congratulations!; happy birthday!
pára-brisas m [parabr**ee**zash] windscreen
pára-choques m [parash**o**ksh] bumper
parafuso m [paraf**oo**zoo] screw
paragem f [par**a**Jayng] stop
paragem do autocarro f [doo

owtookarroo] bus stop
parapentismo m [parapaynteeJmoo] para-gliding
parar to stop
pare! [par] stop!
pare com isso! [kong eesoo] stop it!
parecer [paresayr] to look like
parede f [parayd] wall
páre, escute e olhe stop, look and listen
parente m/f [paraynt] relative
parque de campismo m [park di kampeeJmoo] campsite; caravan site, (US) trailer park
parque de estacionamento [shtas-yonamayntoo] car park, parking lot
parque de estacionamento subterrâneo [soobtirran-yoo] underground car park/parking lot
parque para roulotes [roolotsh] caravan site, (US) trailer park
parque recreativo [rekr-yateevoo] amusement park
parte f [part] part
em parte nenhuma [nin-yooma] nowhere
em toda a parte [tohda] everywhere
parte posterior [pooshteriohr] back (part)
particular [partikoolar] private
partida f [parteeda] departure
partido (m) [parteedoo] broken; party (political)
partilhar [partil-yar] to share
partir [parteer] to break; to leave
a partir de [di] from
Páscoa f [pashkwa] Easter
passadeira de peões f [pasadaira di p-yoyngsh] pedestrian crossing, (US) crosswalk
passado (m) [pasadoo] past
no ano passado [noo anoo] last year
semana passada [simana] last week
passageira f [pasaJayra], passageiro m [pasaJayroo] passenger
passagem de nível m [pasaJayng] level crossing, (US) grade crossing
passagem de peões pedestrian crossing, (US) crosswalk
passagem subterrânea underpass
passaporte m [pasaport] passport
passar to pass
o que se passa? [oo ki si] what's happening?; what's wrong?
passar a ferro [a fehrroo] to iron
pássaro m [pasaroo] bird
passatempo m [–taympoo] hobby
passe (m) go, walk, cross now; weekly or monthly ticket
passeio m [pasay-oo] pavement, sidewalk; walk

ir a dar um passeio to go for a walk
pasta f [pashta] briefcase
pasta de dentes [di dayntsh] toothpaste
pastelaria f [pashtilaree-a] cake shop, café selling cakes
pastilha elástica f [pashteel-ya elashtika] chewing gum
pastilhas de mentol fpl [pashteel-yaJ di] mints
pastilhas para a garganta throat pastilles
patinar [patinar] to skid; to skate
patins de gelo mpl [pateenJ di Jayloo] ice skates
pátio de recreio m [pat-yoo di rikray-oo] playground
patrão m [patrowng] boss
pavilhão desportivo sports pavilion
Pç. square
pé m [peh] foot
a pé on foot
ir a pé to walk
estar de pé [di] to stand
ao pé de [ow ... di] near
peão m [p-yowng] pedestrian
peça de teatro f [pehsa di t-yatroo] play
peça sobresselente f [sobrisilaynt] spare part
pechincha f [pisheensha] bargain
pedaço m [pidasoo] piece
pedir [pideer] to ask; to order
pedir emprestado [aymprishtadoo] to borrow
pedra f [pehdra] stone, rock
pega f [pehga] handle; action of wrestling with the bull during a bullfight
pegar [pigar] to catch
peito m [paytoo] breast; bust; chest
peixaria f [paysharee-a] fishmonger's
pela [pila] through the; by the; about the
pelas [pilash] through the; by the; about the
pelas três horas by three o'clock
pele f [pehl] skin; leather; suede; fur
peleiro m [pilayroo] furrier
película aderente f [pileekoola adiraynt] clingfilm
pelo [piloo] through the; by the; about the
pelos [piloosh] through the; by the; about the
pena: é uma pena [eh ooma payna] it's a pity
que pena! [ki] what a pity!
não vale a pena [nowng val-ya] there's no point
tenho muita pena [mweengta] I'm so sorry
pensão f [paynsowng] guesthouse
pensão completa [komplehta] full board
pensar [paynsar] to think
penso m [paynsoo] dressing; Elastoplast®, Bandaid®
pensos higiénicos mpl

[**pay**nsooz iJ-**yeh**nikoosh] sanitary napkins/towels
pente m [paynt] comb
peões mpl [p-yoyngsh] pedestrians
pequeno [pik**ay**noo] little, small
pequeno almoço m [alm**oh**soo] breakfast
perceber [pirsib**ay**r] to understand
percebo [pirs**ay**boo] I understand, I see
perdão [pird**ow**ng] sorry
perder [pird**ay**r] to lose; to miss
perdido [pird**ee**doo] lost
perdidos e achados lost property, lost and found
perfeito [pirf**ay**too] perfect
perfumaria f [pirfoomar**ee**-a] perfume shop
pergunta f [pirg**oo**nta] question
perguntar [pirgoont**ar**] to ask
perigo m [pir**ee**goo] danger
perigo de desmoronamento danger of landslides
perigo de incêndio beware of starting fires
perigo de morte extreme danger
perigo, parar danger: stop
perigoso [pirig**oh**zoo] dangerous
período m [pir**ee**-oodoo] period
período escolar [shkool**ar**] term
permanente f [pirman**ay**nt] perm
permitido [pirmit**ee**doo] allowed
permitir to allow
perna f [p**eh**rna] leg
(de) pernas para o ar [(di) p**eh**rnash proo ar] upside down
persianas fpl [pirs-y**a**nash] blinds
pertencer [pirtaynss**ay**r] to belong
perto [p**eh**rtoo] near
perto daqui [dak**ee**] nearby, near here
perto de [di] next to
perturbar [pirtoorb**ar**] to disturb
peruca f [pir**oo**ka] wig
pesadelo m [pizad**ay**loo] nightmare
pesado [piz**a**doo] heavy
pesca f [p**eh**shka] fishing
pescar [pishk**ar**] to fish
pesca submarina f [soob-mar**ee**na] underwater fishing
pescoço m [pishk**oh**soo] neck
peso m [p**ay**zoo] weight
peso líquido net weight
peso neto net weight
pessoa f [pis**oh**-a] person
pessoal m [pisoo-**al**] staff, employees
peúga f [p-y**oo**ga] sock
piada f [p-y**a**da] joke
picada f [pik**a**da] bite; sting
picada de insecto [dins**eh**too] insect bite
picado [pik**a**doo] stung
picante [pik**a**nt] hot, spicy
picar [pik**ar**] to sting; to chop finely
picar o bilhete stamp/punch your ticket
pijama m [piJ**a**ma] pyjamas

pilha f [peel-ya] battery
pílula f [peeloola] pill
pinça f [peensa] tweezers
pincel m [peensehl] paintbrush
pintado de fresco wet paint
pintar [peentar] to paint
pintura f [peentoora] picture
pior [p-yor] worse; worst
o pior the worst
piquenique m [pikineek] picnic
pires m [peersh] saucer
piscina f [pish-seena] swimming pool
piscina coberta [koobehrta] indoor pool
piscina infantil [infanteel] children's pool
piso m [peezoo] floor, storey; surface
piso escorregadio slippery road surface
piso irregular uneven road surface
piso superior [soopir-yohr] top floor
pista f runway
pistola f [pishtola] gun
plano (m) [planoo] plan; flat (adj)
planta f plant
plástico m [plashtikoo] plastic
plataforma f [plataforma] platform, (US) track
plateia f [platay-a] audience; ground floor of auditorium
platinados mpl [platinadoosh] points
P.M.P. (por mão própria) deliver by hand
pneu m [pnay-oo] tyre
pneu sobresselente [soobrisilaynt] spare tyre
pó m [paw] dust; powder
pobre [pobr] poor
pode [pod] you can/he/she can
pode (você) ...? [vosay] can you ...?
pode-se ...? [podsi] is it OK to ...?
pode dar-me ...? [pod darmi] can I have a ...?, may I have ...?
poder [poodayr] to be able to
pó de talco m [paw di talkoo] talcum powder
podia ...? [poodee-a] could you ...?
podre [pohdr] rotten
põe [poyng] he/she/it puts; you put
põem [poh-ayng] you/they put
pões [poyngsh] you put
polegada f [pooligada] inch
polegar m [pooligar] thumb
polícia m [poolees-ya] police; policeman
Polícia de Segurança Pública branch of the Portuguese police responsible for public order
polícia de trânsito traffic warden
Polícia Judiciária branch of the police force responsible for investigating crime
poliéster polyester
política f politics

político political
polvo **m** [**poh**lvoo] octopus
pomada **f** [poo**ma**da] ointment
pomada para calçados [kalsa**doo**sh] shoe polish
pomos [**poh**moosh] we put
pónei **m** [**po**nay] pony
ponho [**poh**n-yoo] I put
pontão **m** [pon**tow**ng] jetty
ponte **f** [pohnt] bridge; crown
ponto de encontro meeting point
população **f** [poopoola**sow**ng] population
por [poor] through; by
por avião by airmail
por noite [**noh**-it] per night
pôr [pohr] to put
porca **f** [**po**rka] nut (for bolt)
porção **f** [poor**sow**ng] portion
porcaria **f** [poorka**ree**-a] dirt; mess
porcelana **f** [poorsi**la**na] china
por cento [**say**ntoo] per cent
porco **m** [**poh**rkoo] pig
pôr do sol **m** [pohr doo] sunset
por favor [poor fav**oh**r] please
porque [poor**kay**] because; why
porque não? [nowng] why not?
porreiro! [poorr**ay**roo] bloody good!
porta **f** door; gate
porta-bagagens **m** [baga**J**ayngsh] boot, (US) trunk
porta-bagagens na capota, porta-bagagens no tejadilho [noo tiJa**dee**l-yoo] roof rack
porta-bebés **m** [be**beh**sh] carry-cot
porta de embarque **f** [daymb**ark**] gate
portagem toll
porta-moedas **m** [mw**eh**dash] purse
porta nº ... gate number ...
portão **m** [poor**tow**ng] gate
portão de embarque [daymb**ark**] gate (at airport)
porteiro **m** [poort**ay**roo] doorman, porter
porteiro da noite [**noh**-it] night porter
Porto **m** [**poh**rtoo] Oporto
porto **m** harbour, port
Portugal Telecom National Telecommunications Service
português (**m**) [poortoog**ay**sh] Portuguese; Portuguese man
em português in Portuguese
os portugueses the Portuguese
portuguesa (**f**) [poortoog**ay**za] Portuguese; Portuguese woman
posologia **f** dose
possível [poo**see**vil] possible
posso [**po**soo] I can
posso ...? can I ...?
posso ter ...? [tayr] can I have ...?
postal **m** [pooshta**l**] postcard
posta-restante **f** [**po**shta rishtant] poste restante, (US) general delivery
poste indicador **m** [posht indikad**oh**r] signpost

posterior: parte posterior f [pooshtir-y**oh**r] back (part)
postigos mpl [pooshtee**ee**goosh] shutters
Posto da Polícia m [p**oh**shtoo da pool**ee**s-ya] police station
posto de enfermagem first-aid post
posto de socorros first-aid centre
pouco [p**oh**koo] a little
um pouco [oong] a little bit
um pouco caro [k**a**roo] a bit expensive
um pouco disto [d**ee**shtoo] some of this
pouco vulgar [voolg**a**r] unusual
poucos [p**oh**koosh] few; a few
pouquinho: um pouquinho [oong pohk**ee**n-yoo] a little bit
pousada f [pohs**a**da] state-owned hotel, often a historic building
praça f [pr**a**sa] square; market
praça de táxis [di t**a**xish] taxi rank
praça de touros [t**oh**roosh] bullring
pracista m [pras**ee**shta] taxi-driver
praia f [prī-a] seafront; beach
na praia on the beach
prancha à vela f [pr**a**nsha v**eh**la] sailboard
prancha de saltos [di s**a**ltoosh] diving board
prancha de windsurf sailboard
prata f [pr**a**ta] silver
prateleira f [pratil**ay**ra] shelf
praticar [pratik**a**r] to practise
praticar jogging to go jogging
praticar windsurf to windsurf
prático [pr**a**tikoo] practical
prato m [pr**a**too] course, dish; plate
prazer: (muito) prazer em conhecê-lo/conhecê-la [(mw**ee**ngtoo) praz**ay**r aing koon-yis**ay**loo] pleased to meet you
precipício m [prisip**ee**s-yoo] cliff
precisar [prisiz**a**r] to need
preciso de ... [pris**ee**zoo di] I need ...
preço m [pr**ay**soo] price; charge
pré-comprado bought in advance
preço de custo cost price
preço por dia [poor d**ee**-a] price per day
preço por pessoa [pis**oh**-a] price per person
preço por semana [sim**a**na] price per week
preços reduzidos reduced prices
preencher [pri-aynsh**ay**r] to fill in
preferir [prifir**ee**r] to prefer
prefiro ... [prif**ee**roo] I prefer ...
prego m [pr**eh**goo] nail (metal); roll with a thin slice of meat
preguiçoso [prigis**oh**zoo] lazy
prendas fpl [pr**ay**ndash] gifts
prender [pr**ay**ndayr] to arrest
preocupação f [pri-ookoo-pas**ow**ng] worry

preocupado [pri-ookoopa**d**oo] worried
preocupar-se com to worry about
pré-pagamento choose your food, drink etc then pay at the cash desk before being served
preparar [pripar**ar**] to prepare
presente m [priz**ay**nt] present, gift
preservativo m [prizirvat**ee**voo] condom
presidente m/f [prizid**ay**nt] president
pressa: estou com pressa [shtoh kong pr**eh**sa] I'm in a hurry
não há pressa [nowng a] there's no hurry
pressão f [pris**ow**ng] tyre pressure
pressão arterial [artiri-**al**] blood pressure
presta: não presta [nowng pr**eh**shta] it's no good
prestável [preshtt**a**vil] helpful
preto [pr**ay**too] black
preto e branco black and white
previsão do tempo f [priviz**ow**ng doo t**ay**mpoo] weather forecast
prima f [pr**ee**ma] cousin
Primavera f [primav**eh**ra] spring
primeira: a primeira vez [prim**ay**ra vaysh] the first time
primeira à esquerda [a-shk**ay**rda] first on the left
primeira classe [klas] first class
primeiro [prim**ay**roo] first
primeiro andar m first floor, (US) second floor
primeiro ministro m [prim**ay**roo min**ee**shtroo] prime minister
primeiro piso first floor, (US) second floor
primeiros socorros mpl [prim**ay**roosh sook**o**rroosh] first aid
primo m [pr**ee**moo] cousin
princesa f [preens**ay**za] princess
principal [preensip**al**] main
principalmente [preensipalm**ay**nt] mostly
príncipe m [pr**ee**nsipi] prince
principiante m/f [preensip-y**a**nt] beginner
princípio: ao princípio [ow preens**ee**p-yoo] at first
prioridade f right of way; priority
dar prioridade give way, yield
prisão f [priz**ow**ng] jail
prisão de ventre [di vayntr] constipation
privado [priv**a**doo] private
problema m [proobl**ay**ma] problem
procissão f [proosis**ow**ng] candlelit procession held to celebrate feast days and Good Friday
procurar [prookoor**ar**] to look for; to search
produto m [prood**oo**too] product
produtos alimentares

[alimayntarish] foodstuffs
produtos de beleza [di belayza] beauty products
produtos de limpeza [leempayza] household cleaning materials
professor m [proofesohr], **professora** f [proofesohra] teacher
programa m [proograma] program(me)
proibida a entrada a ... no admittance to ...
proibida a entrada a cães no dogs
proibida a entrada a menores de ... anos no admittance to those under ... years of age
proibida a inversão de marcha no U-turns
proibida a paragem no stopping
proibida a passagem no access
proibido [proo-ibeedoo] forbidden
proibido ... no ...
proibido acampar no camping
proibido a pessoas estranhas ao serviço personnel only
proibido estacionar no parking
proibido fazer lume no campfires
proibido fumar no smoking
proibido nadar no swimming
proibido pescar no fishing
proibido tirar fotografias no photography
proibido tomar banho no bathing
proibido ultrapassar no overtaking
prometer [proomitayr] to promise
pronto [prohntoo] ready
pronto a vestir ready-to-wear
pronto-socorro m [prohntoo sookohrroo] breakdown service
pronunciar [proonoons-yar] to pronounce
propósito: de propósito [di proopozitoo] deliberately
própria: a sua própria [soo-a propr-ya], **o seu próprio** [oo say-oo propr-yoo] his/her/its/your/their own
propriedade privada private property
proteger [prootiJayr] to protect
proteger do calor e humidade store away from heat and damp
protestante (m/f) [prootishtant] Protestant
prova: à prova de água [dagwa] waterproof
provar [proovar] to try; to try on; to taste
provavelmente [proovavilmaynt] probably
próxima sessão às ... horas next showing at ... o'clock
próximo [prosimoo] near; next
o/a ... mais próximo/próxima [mīJ] the nearest ...

próximo de [di] next to
ps. weight
P.S.P. branch of the Portuguese police
pua f [poo-a] splinter
público (m) [pooblikoo] audience; public
pular [poolar] to jump
pulga f [poolga] flea
pulmões mpl [poolmoyngsh] lungs
pulseira f [poolsayra] bracelet; watchstrap
pulso m [poolsoo] wrist
pura lã pure wool
pura lã virgem pure new wool
puxar [pooshar] to pull
puxar (a alavanca) em caso de emergência pull (lever) in case of emergency
puxe pull

Q hot
quais? [kwīsh] which?; which ones?
qual? [kwal] which?
qual deles? [daylsh] which one?
qualidade f [kwalidad] quality
qualquer [kwalkehr] any
qualquer coisa [koh-iza] anything
qualquer medicamento deve estar fora do alcance das crianças keep all medicines out of the reach of children
quando? [kwandoo] when?
quantia f [kwantee-a] amount
quanto? [kwantoo] how much?
quanto custa? [kooshta] how much does it cost?
quanto é? [kwantweh] how much is it?
quantos? [kwantoosh] how many?
quarenta [kwaraynta] forty
quarentena f [kwarayntayna] quarantine
quarta-feira f [kwarta fayra] Wednesday
quarta parte f [part] quarter
quarto (m) [kwartoo] bedroom; room; quarter; fourth
quarto andar fourth floor, (US) fifth floor
quarto com duas camas [kong doo-ash kamash] twin room
quarto de banho das senhoras [di ban-yoo dash sin-yorash] ladies' toilets, ladies' room
quarto de casal [di kazal] double room
quarto de hotel [dohtehl] hotel room
quarto duplo [doopIoo] double room
quarto individual [individwal] single room
quarto para duas pessoas [doo-ash pisoh-ash] double room
quarto para uma pessoa [ooma] single room
quase [kwaz] almost, nearly

quase nunca [**noo**nka] hardly ever
quatro [kw**a**troo] four
quatrocentas [kwatros**ay**ntash], quatrocentos [kwatros**ay**ntoosh] four hundred
que that; than
o que? what?
o que é isso? [oo k-yeh **ee**soo] what's that?
que ...! what a ...!
que bom! [ki bong] that's nice!
quê? [kay] what?
quebrar [kibr**a**r] to break
quebre em caso de emergência break in case of emergency
queda f [k**eh**da] fall
queda de pedras falling stones
queda de rochas falling rocks
queimado [kaym**a**do] burnt
queimado de sol [di] sunburnt
queimadura f [kaymad**oo**ra] burn
queimadura de sol f sunburn
queimar [kaym**a**r] to burn
queixas complaints
queixo m [k**ay**shoo] chin
quem? [kayng] who?
de quem? [di] whose?
de quem é isto? [eh **ee**shtoo] whose is this?
quem é? [kayng**eh**] who is it?
quem fala? who's calling?
quente [kaynt] warm; hot
quer ...? [kehr] would you like ...?, do you want...?
querer [kir**ay**r] to want
queria [kir**ee**-a] I want; I'd like
queria ...? could I have ...?
quero [k**eh**roo] I want
não quero I don't want (to)
não quero nada I don't want anything
quieto [k-y**eh**too] still
quilo m [k**ee**loo] kilo
quilometragem ilimitada [kilomitr**a**Jayng ilimit**a**da] unlimited mileage
quilómetro m [kil**o**mitroo] kilometre
quinhentas [keen-y**ay**ntash], quinhentos [keen-y**ay**ntoosh] five hundred
quinta f [k**ee**nta] farm
quinta-feira f [k**ee**nta f**ay**ra] Thursday
quinto [k**ee**ntoo] fifth
quinze [keenz] fifteen
quinzena f [keenz**ay**na] fortnight
quiosque m [k-yoshk] kiosk
quiosque de jornais [di Joornīsh] newspaper kiosk

R

R. street
rabo m tail; backside, behind
radiador m [rad-yad**oh**r] radiator
Radiodifusão Portuguesa Portuguese Radio
radiografia f [rad-yoograf**ee**-a] X-ray
Radiotelevisão Portuguesa

Portuguese Television
rainha f [ra-**ee**n-ya] queen
raio m [rī-oo] ray, beam; spoke
raio X m [**ra**-yoo sheesh] X-ray
rapariga f [rapar**ee**ga] girl
rapaz m [rap**a**sh] boy
Rápido m [**ra**pidoo] express (train)
rápido fast, quick
raqueta f [rak**eh**ta] racket
raqueta de ténis tennis racket
raro [**ra**roo] rare, uncommon
ratazana f [ratazana] rat
rato m [**ra**too] mouse
razão f [raz**ow**ng] reason
tinhas razão [**tee**n-yaJ raz**ow**ng] you were right
razoável [razw**a**vil] reasonable
r/c ground floor, (US) first floor
R.D.P. Portuguese Radio
realmente [r-yalm**ay**nt] really
reaver [r-yav**ay**r] to get back
rebentado [ribent**a**doo] burst
reboque m [rib**o**k] trailer (for carrying tent etc)
rebuçado m [riboos**a**doo] sweet, candy
recado m [rik**a**doo] message
deixar um recado [daysh**a**r oong] to leave a message
receber [risib**ay**r] to receive
receita f [ris**ay**ta] recipe; prescription
recepção f [risehs**ow**ng] reception
recepcionista m/f [risehs-yoon**ee**shta] receptionist
recibo m [ris**ee**boo] receipt
reclamação f [riklamas**ow**ng] complaint
reclamação de bagagens [di bag**a**Jayngsh] baggage claim
reclamações complaints
reclamar [riklam**a**r] to complain
recomendar [rikoomaynd**a**r] to recommend
reconhecer [rikoon-yis**ay**r] to recognize
rede f [rayd] net; hammock
redondo [rid**oh**ndoo] round
reembolsar [ri-aymbools**a**r] to refund
reembolso m [ri-aymb**oh**lsoo] refund
refeição f [rifays**ow**ng] meal
reformada (f) [rifoorm**a**da] pensioner; retired
reformada de terceira idade f [di tirs**ay**ra id**a**d] senior citizen
reformado (m) [rifoorm**a**doo] pensioner; retired
reformado de terceira idade m senior citizen
refugo m [rif**oo**goo] rubbish
reg. registered
região f [riJ-y**ow**ng] region; area
da região local
Regional local train, usually stopping at most stations
registado [riJisht**a**doo] registered
registos registered mail
reg.to. regulation
regulamento m regulation
rei m [ray] king

Reino Unido m [raynooneedoo] United Kingdom
relâmpago m [rilampagoo] lightning
religião f [riliJ-yowng] religion
relógio m [riloJ-yoo] clock; watch, wristwatch
relógio de pulso [di poolsoo] watch, wristwatch
relojoaria f [rilooJwaree-a] watchmaker's shop
relva f [rehlva] grass
relvado m [relvadoo] lawn
rem. sender
remar to row
remédio m [rimehd-yoo] medicine
remetente m/f sender
renda f [raynda] lace
reparar [riparar] to fix, to repair
repele-insectos m [ripehl insehtoosh] insect repellent
repele-mosquitos m [moosh-keetoosh] mosquito repellent
repelente de insectos eléctrico m [ripilaynt dinsehtoosh elehtrikoo] electric mosquito killer
repetir [ripiteer] to repeat
repousar [ripohzar] to rest
repouso m [ripohzoo] rest
representante m/f [riprizayntant] agent
repugnante [ripoognant] revolting
rés de chão m [rehJ doo showng] ground floor, (US) first floor
reserva f [rizehrva] reservation
reserva de lugares [di loogarish] seat reservation
reservado [rizirvadoo] reserved
reservar [rizirvar] to book, to reserve
reservas reservations
residencial m [rizidayns-yal] bed and breakfast hotel
respirar [rishpirar] to breathe
responder [rishpondayr] to answer
responsável [rishponsavil] responsible
resposta f [rishposhta] answer
ressaca f [risaka] hangover
restaurante m [rishtowrant] restaurant
resto m [rehshtoo] rest, remainder
retalho m [rital-yoo] oddment
retirado [ritiradoo] secluded
retrato m [ritratoo] portrait
retretes fpl [ritrehtsh] toilets, rest rooms
retrosaria f [ritroozaree-a] haberdasher
reumatismo m rheumatism
reunião f [r-yoon-yowng] meeting
revelação de filmes f [rivilasowng di feelmsh] film processing
revisor m [rivizohr] ticket inspector
revista f [riveeshta] magazine
ribeiro m [ribayroo] stream
rico [reekoo] rich
ridículo [rideekooloo] ridiculous
rímel m [reemil] mascara

rinque de patinagem m [reenk di patina**J**ayng] ice rink
rins mpl [reengsh] kidneys
rio m [**ree**-oo] river
rir [reer] to laugh
R.N. National bus/coach service
rocha f [**ro**sha] rock
rochedo m [roosh**ay**doo] cliff
roda f [**ro**da] wheel
rodada f [roo**da**da] round
Rodoviária Nacional National bus/coach service
rolha f [**roh**l-ya] cork
romance m [roo**mans**] novel
roncar [ron**kar**] to snore
rosa f [**ro**za] rose
rótulo m [**ro**tooloo] label
rotunda f [roo**toon**da] roundabout
roubado [rohb**a**doo] robbed
roubar [rohb**ar**] to steal
roubo m [**roh**boo] burglary; theft; rip-off
roulotte f [roo**lot**] caravan, (US) trailer
roupa f [**roh**pa] clothes
roupa de cama [di **ka**ma] bed linen
roupa de homens [d**oh**mayngsh] menswear
roupa de senhoras [sin-**y**orash] ladies' wear
roupa interior [intir-**yohr**] underwear
roupão m [rohp**ow**ng] dressing gown
roupa para lavar laundry, washing
roxo [**roh**shoo] purple
R.T.P. Portuguese Television
rua f [**roo**-a] road; street
rua! get out of here!
rua principal [preensip**a**l] main road
rua secundária [sikoond**a**r-ya] side street
rua sem saída cul-de-sac, dead end
rubéola f [roob**eh**-ola] German measles
ruínas fpl [rw**ee**nash] ruins
ruivo [**roo**-ivoo] red-headed

S

S ladies' toilets, ladies' room
S. saint
S/ without
sábado [**sa**badoo] Saturday
saber [sab**ayr**] to know; to be able to
sabia [sab**ee**-a] I knew
não sabia [nowng] I didn't know
sabonete m [saboon**ayt**] soap
sabor m [sab**ohr**] taste; flavour
saboroso [saboor**oh**zoo] tasty, delicious
sacana! bastard!
saca-rolhas m [**sa**karr**oh**l-yash] corkscrew
saco m [**sa**koo] bag
saco de compras [di k**oh**mprash] shopping bag
saco de dormir [doorm**eer**] sleeping bag

saco (de) plástico [plashtikoo] plastic bag
sacos de lixo **mpl** [sakoosh] bin liners
saia **f** [sī-ya] skirt
saia! get out!
saída **f** [sa-eeda] departure; exit
saída de emergência [demirJayns-ya] emergency exit
saio [sī-oo] I get off; I go out; I leave
sair [sa-eer] to get off, to get out; to go out; to leave
sais de banho **mpl** [sīJ di ban-yoo] bath salts
saiu [sa-ee-oo] he/she is out; he/she has gone out
sala **f** lounge
sala de chá tea room
sala de convívio [di konveev-yoo] lounge
sala de embarque [daymbark] departure lounge
sala de espera [dishpehra] lounge, departure lounge
sala de estar [dishtar] living room
sala de jantar [di Jantar] dining room
salão de beleza **m** [salowng di belayza] beauty salon
salão de cabeleireiro [di kabilayrayroo] hairdressing salon
saldos **mpl** [saldoosh] sale
salgado [salgadoo] savoury; salty
salto **m** [saltoo] heel (of shoe)
sandálias **fpl** [sandal-yash] sandals
sangrar to bleed
sangue **m** [sang] blood
santinho! [santeen-yoo] bless you!
são [sowng] healthy; they are; you are
sapataria **f** [sapataree-a] shoe shop
sapateira **f** [sapatayra] crab
sapateiro **m** [sapatayroo] shoe repairer's
sapateiro rápido [rapidoo] heel bar
sapatos **mpl** [sapatoosh] shoes
sapatos de treino [di traynoo] trainers
sarampo **m** [sarampoo] measles
sardinhada **f** [sardin-yada] party where grilled sardines are eaten
S.A.R.L. (Sociedade Anónima de Responsabilidade Limitada) limited company
satisfeito [satisfaytoo] satisfied, full
saudável [sowdavil] healthy
saúde [sa-ood] health
saúde! cheers!
à sua saúde! [soo-a] your health!
se [si] if; yourself; himself; herself; themselves; yourselves; itself; oneself
secador de cabelo **m** [sikadohr di kabayloo] hairdryer
secador de roupa [di rohpa]

spin-dryer

secar [si**kar**] to dry

secar com secador (de mão) [kong sikad**ohr** (di mowng)] to blow-dry

secção f [sehks**ow**ng] section; department

secção de crianças [di kry-**a**nsash] children's department

secção de perdidos e achados [di pird**ee**dooz ee-ash**a**doosh] lost property office, lost and found

seco [**say**koo] dry

secreto [sikr**eh**too] secret

século m [**seh**kooloo] century

seda f [**say**da] silk

sede: ter sede [tayr sayd] to be thirsty

se faz favor [si fash fav**ohr**] please; excuse me

seguida: em seguida [ayng sig**ee**da] straight away

seguinte [sig**ee**ngt] following; next

dia seguinte m the day after

seguir [sig**eer**] to follow

seguir pela direita [pila dir**ay**ta] keep to your right

seguir pela esquerda [pilashk**ay**rda] keep to your left

segunda classe [sig**oo**nda klas] second class

segunda-feira f [sig**oo**nda f**ay**ra] Monday

segunda mão: em segunda mão [sig**oo**nda mowng] second-hand

segundo (m) [sig**oo**ndoo] second

segundo andar m second floor, (US) third floor

segurar [sigoor**ar**] to hold

seguro (m) [sig**oo**roo] insurance; safe; sure

seguro de viagem [di v-y**a**Jayng] travel insurance

sei [say] I know

seis [saysh] six

seiscentas [sayshs**ay**ntash], **seiscentos** [sayshs**ay**ntoosh] six hundred

sela f [**seh**la] saddle

selo m [**say**loo] stamp

selvagem [silv**a**Jayng] wild

sem [sayng] without

semáforos mpl [sim**a**fooroosh] traffic lights

semana f [sim**a**na] week

na próxima semana [pr**o**sima] next week

Semana Santa Easter

sem chumbo [sayng sh**oo**mboo] leadfree, unleaded

sem conservantes does not contain preservatives

sem corantes does not contain artificial colouring

sem corantes nem conservantes does not contain artificial colouring or preservatives

semelhante [simil-y**a**nt] similar

sem pensão no meals served

sempre [saympr] always

sempre em frente [**say**mprayng fraynt] straight ahead

sem preservativos does not contain preservatives
senha f [**sayn**-ya] ticket; receipt
Senhor [sin-**yohr**] Mr
senhor (**m**) sir; gentleman; you
o senhor [oo] you
os senhores [oosh sin-**yoh**rish] you
do senhor [doo] your; yours
dos senhores [doosh sin-**yoh**rish] your; yours
Senhora [sin-**yo**ra] Mrs
senhora madam; lady; you
a senhora you
as senhoras [ash sin-**yo**rash] you
da senhora, das senhoras your; yours
senhoras ladies' toilet, ladies' room
sensato [saynsa**too**] sensible
sensível [sayn**see**vil] sensitive
sentar-se [sayn**tar**si] to sit, to sit down
como se sente? [**koh**moo si saynt] how are you feeling?
sente-se [**sayn**tsi] sit down
sentido proibido no entry
sentido único one way
sentimento m [sayntim**ayn**too] feeling
sentir [sayn**teer**] to feel
separadamente [siparadam**ayn**t] separately
separado [sipar**a**doo] separate; separated
ser [sayr] to be
será [sir**a**] he/she/it/you will be
serão [sir**ow**ng] you/they will be
serás [sir**a**sh] you will be
serei [sir**ay**] I will be
seremos [sir**ay**moosh] we will be
sério [**seh**r-yoo] serious
serve-se ... das ... horas às ... horas ... served from ... o'clock until ... o'clock
serviço m [sir**vee**soo] service
serviço automático direct dialling
serviço de quartos [di kw**ar**toosh] room service
serviço de urgências [doorJ**ay**ns-yash] casualty department
serviço expresso express service
serviço incluído service included
serviço internacional international service
serviço permanente 24-hour service
servir [sir**veer**] to serve
sessenta [ses**ayn**ta] sixty
sete [seht] seven
setecentas [setes**ayn**tash], **setecentos** [setes**ayn**toosh] seven hundred
Setembro [sit**ay**mbroo] September
setenta [set**ayn**ta] seventy
setentrional [setayntr-yoon**al**] northern

sétimo [sehtimoo] seventh
seu [say-oo], seus [say-oosh] his; her; hers; its; your; yours; their; theirs
sexo m [sehxoo] sex
sexta-feira f [sayshta fayra] Friday
Sexta-Feira Santa Good Friday
sexto [sayshtoo] sixth
S.f.f. please
si [see] you
SIDA f [seeda] AIDS
siga-me [seegami] follow me
significar [signifikar] to mean
silêncio m [silayns-yoo] silence
silencioso [silayns-yohzoo] quiet
sim [seeng] yes; it is
sim? really?
ah sim! [seeng] well well!
simpático [simpatikoo] friendly
simples [seemplish] simple, easy
sinagoga f [sinagoga] synagogue
sinal m sign; signal; roadsign
sinal de alarme [dalarm] emergency alarm
sincero [sinsehroo] sincere
sino m [seenoo] bell
sintético [sintehtikoo] synthetic
sinto-me [seentoomi] I feel
sinto-me bem [bayng] I'm OK, I'm fine
sítio m [seet-yoo] place
noutro sítio [nohtroo] somewhere else
só [saw] alone; just; only
sobrancelha f [soobransayl-ya] eyebrow
sobre [sohbr] about, concerning; on
sobretudo m [soobritoodoo] overcoat
sobrinha f [soobreen-ya] niece
sobrinho m [soobreen-yoo] nephew
sóbrio [sobr-yoo] sober
sociedade f [soos-yaydad] society; company
socorro! [sookohrroo] help!
sofá m [soofa] sofa; couch
sofisticado [soofishtikadoo] sophisticated; upmarket
sogra f mother-in-law
sogro m [sohgroo] father-in-law
sogros mpl [sogroosh] in-laws
soirée evening performance
sol m sun
ao sol [ow] in the sun
está (a fazer) sol [shta (a fazayr)] it's sunny
solteiro (m) [sooltayroo] single; bachelor
solto [sohltoo] loose
solução de limpeza f [sooloosowng di leempayza] cleaning solution
solução para as lentes de contacto [paraJ layntsh di kontaktoo] soaking solution
soluços mpl [sooloosoosh] hiccups
sombra f [sohmbra] shade; shadow
à sombra in the shade
sombra para os olhos [parooz

ol-yoosh] eye shadow
somente [somaynt] only; just
somos [sohmoosh] we are
sonho m [sohn-yoo] dream
sonífero m [sooneefiroo] sleeping pill
sono m [sohnoo] sleep
estar com sono [shtar kong] to be sleepy
sopé: no sopé do ... [noo soopeh doo] at the bottom of ...
só pode vender-se mediante receita médica available only on prescription
sorrir [soorreer] to smile
sorriso m [soorreezoo] smile
sorte f [sort] luck
sou [soh] I am
sou de ... [di] I am from ...
soutien m [soot-yang] bra
sozinha [sozeen-ya], sozinho [sozeen-yoo] by myself
Sr. Mr
Sra. Mrs
Sto. saint
sua [soo-a] his; her; hers; its; your; yours; their; theirs
suar [soo-ar] to sweat
suas [soo-ash] his; her; hers; its; your; yours; their; theirs
suave [swav] delicate; mild
subir [soobeer] to go up
subitamente [soobitamaynt] suddenly
sucesso m [soosehsoo] success
sudeste m [soodehsht] southeast
sudoeste m [soodwehsht] southwest
Suécia f [swehs-ya] Sweden
sueca (f) [swehka], sueco (m) [swehkoo] Swedish; Swede
suficiente [soofis-yaynt] enough
suficientemente [soofis-yayntimaynt] enough
Suíça f [sweesa] Switzerland
suíça (f) [sweesa], suíço (m) [sweesoo] Swiss
sujidade f [sooJidad] dirt
sujo [sooJoo] dirty
sul m [sool] south
no sul [noo] in the south
sul-africana (f) [soolafrikana], sul-africano (m) [soolafrikanoo] South African
supermercado m [soopermerkadoo] supermarket
suplemento m [sooplimayntoo] supplement, extra charge
supositório m [soopoozitor-yoo] suppository
surdo [soordoo] deaf
surpreendente [soorpr-yayndaynt] surprising
surpresa f [soorprayza] surprise

T

tabacaria f [tabakaree-a] tobacconist; tobacco store; tobacco goods; newsagent
tabaco m [tabakoo] tobacco
taberna m [tabehrna] pub
tabuleiro m [taboolayroo] tray
talheres mpl [tal-yehrish]

cutlery
talho m [**tal**-yoo] butcher's shop
talvez [talv**ay**sh] maybe, perhaps
talvez não [nowng] perhaps not
tamanho m [tam**a**n-yoo] size
também [tamb**ay**ng] also, too, as well
eu também [**ay**-oo] so am I; so do I; me too
tampa f cap, lid
tampa do ralo f [doo r**a**loo] plug (in sink)
tampões mpl [tamp**oy**ngsh] tampons
tanto [**ta**ntoo] so much
tanto faz [fash] it's all the same to me
tão [towng] so
tão ... como ... as ... as ...
tão ... quanto [kw**a**ntoo] as ... as
tão ... quanto possível [pooseevil] as ... as possible
tapete m [tap**ay**t] carpet
tarde f [tard] afternoon; late
à tarde in the afternoon
esta tarde [**eh**shta] this afternoon
da tarde p.m.
três da tarde 3 p.m.
tarifa f [tar**ee**fa] charges
tasca f [**ta**shka] small tavern serving food
taxa de serviço f [**ta**sha di sirv**ee**soo] service charge
te [ti] you; to you; yourself
teatro m [t-y**a**troo] theatre
tecido m [tis**ee**doo] cloth, material
tecto m [**teh**too] ceiling
tejadilho m [tiJad**ee**l-yoo] car roof
tel. telephone
teleférico m [telef**eh**rikoo] cable car
telefonar [telefoon**ar**] to call, to phone
telefone m [telef**oh**n] telephone
telefone de cartão [di kart**ow**ng] cardphone
telefone público [p**oo**blikoo] payphone
Telefones de Lisboa e Porto S.A. telephone company for Lisbon and Oporto
telefonista m/f [telefoon**ee**shta] operator
telemóvel m [telem**o**vil] mobile phone
televisão f [televiz**ow**ng] television
telhado m [til-y**a**doo] roof
tem [tayng] he/she/it has; you have
tem ...? have you got any ...?, do you have ...?
ele/ela tem de ... he/she must ...
têm [**tay**-ayng] you/they have
temos [**tay**moosh] we have
temos que ... [ki] we've got to ..., we must ...
temperatura f [taympirat**oo**ra] temperature

Portuguese → English

Te

tempestade f [taympishta**d**] storm
tempo m [**tay**mpoo] time; weather
a tempo on time
por quanto tempo? [poor kw**a**ntoo] for how long?
tenda (de campismo) f [**tay**nda (di kamp**ee**Jmoo)] tent
tenho [**tay**n-yoo] I have; I am; I have to
não tenho [nowng] I don't have any
tenho de/que ... [di/ki] I must ...
ténis m [**teh**nish] tennis
ténis de mesa [di m**ay**za] table tennis
tens [taynsh] you have
tensão f [taynsowng] tension; voltage
tensão arterial alta [artir-ya**l**] high blood pressure
tentar [tayntar] to try
tépido [**teh**pidoo] lukewarm
ter [tayr] to have; to hold; to be; to contain; to have to
ter de/que to have to
terça-feira [**tay**rsa f**ay**ra] Tuesday
ter calor [tayr kal**oh**r] to be warm
terceiro [tirs**ay**roo] third
terceiro andar m third floor, (US) fourth floor
termas fpl [**teh**rmash] spa
terminado [termin**a**doo] over; finished
terminal m [tirmina**l**] terminus
terminar [tirmin**ar**] to finish
termo m [**tay**rmoo] vacuum flask
termómetro m [tirm**oh**mitroo] thermometer
terra f [**teh**rra] earth
terraço m [tirr**a**soo] terrace
terrível [tirr**ee**vil] terrible
tesoura f [tiz**oh**ra] scissors
testa f [**teh**shta] forehead
testemunha m/f [tishtim**oo**n-ya] witness
teu [**tay**-oo], **teus** [**tay**-oosh] your; yours
teve [tayv] he/she/it/you had
têxteis textiles
ti you
tia f [**tee**-a] aunt
tigela f [tiJ**eh**la] dish, bowl
tijolo m [tiJ**oh**loo] brick
tímido [**tee**midoo] shy
tinha [**tee**n-ya] I/he/she/it/you used to have
tinham [**tee**n-yowng] you/they used to have
tínhamos [**tee**n-yamoosh] we used to have
tinhas [**tee**n-yash] you used to have
tinta f [**tee**nta] paint; tint
tinto [**tee**ntoo] red
tinturaria f [teentoorar**ee**-a] dry-cleaner
tio m [**tee**-oo] uncle
típico [**tee**pikoo] typical
tipo m [**tee**poo] sort, type, kind
tiragem f [tir**a**Jayng] collection; edition; circulation

tirar to remove
tive [teev] I had
tivemos [tivaymoosh] we had
tiveram [tivehrowng] you/they had
tiveste [tivehsht] you had
TLP telephone company for Lisbon and Oporto
toalha f [twal-ya] towel
toalha de banho [di ban-yoo] bath towel
toalha de cara [kara] flannel
toalha de mesa [mayza] tablecloth
toalhas higiénicas fpl [twal-yaz iJ-yehnikash] sanitary towels
tocar [tookar] to touch
toda a gente [tohda a Jaynt] everyone
todas [tohdash] all; all of them
todas as vezes [aJ vayzish] every time
todo [tohdoo] all; all of it
todo o dia/o dia todo [oo dee-a] all day
todos [tohdoosh] all; all of them
todos os dias [tohdooz-ooJ dee-ash] every day, daily
para todos suitable for all age groups
toilette m [twaleht] toilet, rest room
tolo [tohloo] silly
tomada f [toomada] socket; plug; power point
tomada para a máquina de barbear [makina di barb-yar] shaving point
tomar [toomar] to take
o que vai tomar? [oo ki vī] what'll you have?
tomar antes de se deitar to be taken before going to bed
tomar a seguir às refeições to be taken after meals
tomar banho [ban-yoo] to have a bath
tomar banho de sol to sunbathe
tomar conta de [kohnta] to look after, to take care of
tomar em jejum take on an empty stomach
tomar ... vezes ao dia to be taken ... times a day
tome lá [tohm] there you are
tónico m [tonikoo] toner
tonturas: sinto tonturas [seentoo tontoorash] I feel dizzy
topo: no topo de ... [tohpoo di] at the top of ...
toque (a campainha) ring (the bell)
torcer [toorsayr] to sprain; to twist
tornar-se [toornarsi] to become
torneira f [toornayra] tap, faucet
tornozelo m [toornoozayloo] ankle
torre f [tohrr] tower
tosse f [tos] cough
tossir [tooseer] to cough
tostão coin worth one tenth of an escudo
totalmente [tootalmaynt] totally; altogether
touca de banho f [tohka di ban-

yoo] bathing cap
tourada f [tohrada] bullfight
toureiro m [tohrayroo] bullfighter
touro m [tohroo] bull
tóxico [toksikoo] toxic, poisonous
trabalhar [trabal-yar] to work
trabalho m [trabal-yoo] work
tradição f [tradisowng] tradition
tradicional [tradis-yoonal] traditional
tradução f [tradoosowng] translation
tradutor m [tradootohr], **tradutora** f [tradootohra] translator
traduzir [tradoozeer] to translate
tragédia f [traJehd-ya] disaster
trajecto m [traJehtoo] route
trancar [trankar] to lock
tranquilo [trankweeloo] peaceful
transferência f [transfiraynς-ya] transfer
trânsito m [tranzitoo] traffic
trânsito condicionado traffic congestion
trânsito fechado road blocked
trânsito nos dois sentidos two-way traffic
trânsito proibido no thoroughfare, no entry
transmissão f [tranJmisowng] transmission
traseiro (m) [trazayroo] bottom (of person); back
traumatismo m [trowmateeJmoo] concussion
travão m [travowng] brake
travão de mão [di mowng] handbrake
travar to brake
travel-cheque m [shehk] traveller's cheque
travessa f [travehsa] tray
travessia f [travisee-a] crossing
trazer [trazayr] to bring
trazer de volta [di] to bring back
três [traysh] three
trespassa-se premises for sale
treze [trayz] thirteen
trezentas [trizayntash], **trezentos** [trizayntoosh] three hundred
tribunal m [triboonal] court
tricotar [trikootar] to knit
trinta [treenta] thirty
tripulação f [tripoolasowng] crew
triste [treesht] sad
trocar [trookar] to change (money)
troco m [trohkoo] change (money)
trombose f [tromboz] thrombosis
trombose cerebral [siribral] stroke
trovão m [troovowng] thunder
trovoada f [troovwada] thunder
tu [too] you
tua [too-a], **tuas** [too-ash] your; yours
tubo de escape m [tooboo dishkap] exhaust pipe

tudo [toodoo] everything
é tudo [eh] that's all
tudo bem! [bayng] no problem!
tudo bem? how are you?
tudo incluído all-inclusive
túnel m [toonil] tunnel
turismo m [tooreeJmoo] tourist information office
turista m/f [tooreeshta] tourist

UE [oo eh] EU
úlcera f [oolsira] ulcer
último m [ooltimoo] last, latest
ultrapassar [ooltrapasar] to overtake, to pass
um [oong], **uma** [ooma] a, an; one
umas [oomash] some
uma vez [ooma vaysh] once
unha f [oon-ya] fingernail
União Europeia f [ooni-owng ay-ooroopay-a] European Union
unicamente para adultos for adults only
universidade f [oonivirsidad] university
uns [oonsh] some
urgência f [oorJayns-ya] casualty, emergencies
urgente [oorJaynt] urgent
usar [oozar] to use
uso m [oozoo] use
uso externo for external use only
utensílios de cozinha mpl [ootaynseel-yoosh di koozeen-ya] cooking utensils
útil [ootil] useful

vaca f cow
vacina f [vaseena] vaccine
vacinação f [vasinasowng] vaccination
vagão m [vagowng] carriage (on train)
vagão restaurante [rishtowrant] dining car
vai he/she/it goes; you go
vais [vīsh] you go
vale m [val] valley
vale postal internacional international money order
validação de bilhetes punch your ticket here
válido [validoo] valid
válido até ... valid until ...
valioso [val-yohzoo] valuable
valor m [valohr] value
válvula f [valvoola] valve
vamos [vamoosh] we go
vamos! let's go!
vão [vowng] you/they go
varanda f balcony
varicela f [varisehla] chickenpox
vários [var-yoosh] several
vá-se embora! [vasi aymbora] go away!
vassoura f [vasohra] broom
vazio [vazee-oo] empty
vedação f [vidasowng] fence

vedado ao trânsito no thoroughfare
vegetariana (f) [viJitar-yana], **vegetariano** (m) [viJitar-yanoo] vegetarian
veículo m [vi-eekooloo] vehicle
veículos longos long vehicles
veículos pesados heavy vehicles
veio [vay-oo] he/she/it came, he/she/it has come; you came, you have come
vela f [vehla] spark plug; sail; candle
velejar [viliJar] to sail; sailing
velho [vehl-yoo] old
velocidade f [viloosidad] speed
velocidade máxima ... km/h maximum speed ... km/h
velocímetro m [vilooseemitroo] speedometer
vem [vayng] he/she/it comes; you come
vêm you/they come
venda f [vaynda] sale
à venda [vaynda] for sale
vendedor de jornais [di Jornīsh] newsagent, news vendor
vendem-se [vayndaynsi] for sale
vender [vayndayr] to sell
vende-se [vayndi-si] for sale
veneno m [vinaynoo] poison
venenoso [vininohzoo] poisonous
venho [vayn-yoo] I come
vens [vaynsh] you come
vento m [vayntoo] wind
ventoinha f [vayntween-ya] fan (electrical)
ver [vayr] to look; to have a look; to see
Verão m [virowng] summer
verdade f [virdad] truth
de verdade? [di] really?
verdadeiro [virdadayroo] real; true
verde [vayrd] green
vergas fpl [vayrgash] wicker goods
verificar [virifikar] to check
vermelho [virmayl-yoo] red
verniz de unhas m [virneeJ doon-yash] nail varnish
vespa f [vayshpa] wasp
Véspera de Natal f [vehshpira di] Christmas Eve
véspera do dia de Ano Novo [vehshpira doo dee-a danoo nohvoo] New Year's Eve
vestiário m [visht-yar-yoo] cloakroom, checkroom
vestido m [vishteedoo] dress
vestir [vishteer] to dress
vestir-se [vishteersi] to get dressed
veterinário m [vitirinar-yoo] vet
vez f [vaysh] time
a próxima vez [prosima] next time
a última vez [ooltima] last time
esta vez [ehshta] this time
às vezes [aJ vayzish] sometimes
em vez [ayng] instead
em vez de ... [di] instead of ...

via (f) [vee-a] via; lane
via aérea: por via aérea by airmail
viagem f [v-yaJayng] journey
viagem de negócios [di nigos-yoosh] business trip
via intravenosa intravenously
viajar [v-yaJar] to travel
via oral to be taken orally
via rápida dual carriageway, divided highway
via rectal per rectum
via superfície surface mail
vida f [veeda] life
videogravador m [veed-yoogravadohr] video recorder
vidraria f [vidraree-a] glazier's
vidro m [veedroo] glass
viela f [v-yehla] lane
viemos [v-yaymoosh] we came, we have come
vieram [v-yehrowng] you/they came, you/they have come
vieste [v-yehsht] you came, you have come
vim [veeng] I came, I have come
vimos [veemoosh] we come; we saw
vindima f [vindeema] grape harvest
vindo [veendoo] come
vinha f [veen-ya] vineyard
vinte [veent] twenty
vinte e um [veenti-oong] twenty-one
viola f [v-yola] traditional Portuguese guitar
violação f [v-yoolasowng] rape
vir [veer] to come
virar [veerar] to turn; to turn off
vir de carro [veer di karroo] to drive
vire à esquerda/direita [veer-ya shkayrda/dirayta] turn left/right
vírgula f [veergoola] comma; decimal point
visita f [vizeeta] visit
visita guiada [vizeeta gee-ada] tour
visitar [vizitar] to visit
visor m [vizohr] viewfinder
vista f [veeshta] view
visto (m) [veeshtoo] visa; seen
visto que [veeshtoo ki] since
viu [vee-oo] you have seen
viúva f [v-yoova] widow
viúvo m [v-yoovoo] widower
vivenda f [vivaynda] villa
viver [vivayr] to live
vivo [veevoo] bright; alive
vizinha f [vizeen-ya], vizinho m [vizeen-yoo] neighbour
voar [v-war] to fly
você [vosay] you
você primeiro [primayroo] after you
vocês [vosaysh] you
de vocês [di] your; yours
volante m [voolant] steering wheel
com volante à direita [kong] right-hand drive
volta: por volta de ... [poor] about ..., approximately ...
voltar to go back, to get back,

to come back, to return
voltar a telefonar [voltwa telefoonar] to ring back
volto já [voltoo Ja] back in a minute
vomitar [voomitar] to be sick, to vomit
voo m [voh-oo] flight
voo de ligação [di ligasowng] connecting flight
voo directo [direhtoo] direct flight
voo doméstico [doomehshtikoo] domestic flight
voo fretado [fritadoo] charter flight
voo regular [rigoolar] scheduled flight
vou [voh] I go
voz f [vosh] voice
vulgar [voolgar] ordinary

X

xadrez m [shadraysh] chess
xarope m [sharop] cough medicine; cordial

Z

zangado [zangadoo] angry; mad
zona azul f [zohnazool] parking permit zone
zona de banhos swimming area under the surveillance of lifeguards
zona para peões pedestrian precinct
zona perigrosa danger zone

Menu Reader: Food

Essential Terms

bread o pão [**pow**ng]
butter a manteiga [mant**ay**ga]
cup a chávena [sh**a**vena]
dessert a sobremesa [sobrim**ay**za]
fish o peixe [**pay**-ish]
fork o garfo [g**a**rfoo]
glass o copo [k**o**poo]
knife a f**a**ca
main course o prato principal [pr**a**too prinsip**a**l]
meat a carne [karn]
menu a ementa [em**ay**nta]
pepper a pimenta [pim**ay**nta]
plate o prato [pr**a**too]
salad a sal**a**da
salt o sal
set menu a ementa fixa [em**ay**nta f**ee**ksa]
soup a sopa [s**oh**pa]
spoon a colher [kool-y**eh**r]
starter a entrada [ayntr**a**da]
table a mesa [m**ay**za]

another ..., please outro/**ou**tra ..., por favor [**oh**troo – poor fav**oh**r]
excuse me! (to call waiter/waitress) se faz favor! [si fash]
could I have the bill, please? pode-me dar a c**o**nta, por favor? [p**o**d-mi – poor fav**oh**r]

abóbora [ab**o**boora] pumpkin
acepipes [asip**ee**pish] hors d'œuvres
açorda de alho [as**oh**rda d**a**l-yoo] thick soup of bread and garlic
açorda de mariscos [di mar**ee**shkoosh] thick soup of bread and shellfish
açorda de miolos [m-y**o**loosh] thick soup of bread and brains
açúcar [as**oo**kar] sugar
agriões [agr-y**oy**ngsh] watercress
aipo [īpoo] celery
alcachofra [alkash**oh**fra] artichoke
alface [alf**a**s] lettuce
alheira [al-y**ay**ra] garlic sausage
alho [**a**l-yoo] garlic
alho francês [frans**ay**sh] leek
à lista [**lee**shta] à la carte
almoço [alm**oh**soo] lunch
almóndegas [alm**oh**ndigash] meatballs
alperces [alp**eh**rsish] apricots
amêijoas [am**ay**Jwash] clams
amêijoas à Bulhão Pato [am**ay**Jwaza bool-y**ow**ng p**a**too] clams cooked with fresh coriander, garlic and olive oil
amêijoas na cataplana [am**ay**Jwash] clams, ham, sausages, onions, parsley, chillies and olive oil cooked slowly in a covered pan
ameixa [am**ay**sha] plum
ameixas de Elvas [d**eh**lvash] dried plums from Elvas
ameixas secas [s**ay**kas] prunes
amêndoas [am**ay**ndwash] almonds
amendoins [amayndw**ee**nsh] peanuts
à moda de ... [di] ...-style
amoras [am**o**rash] blackberries
ananás [anan**a**sh] pineapple
anchovas [ansh**oh**vash] anchovies
anho à moda do Minho [**a**n-yoo a m**o**da doo m**ee**n-yoo] roast lamb served with rice
aniz [an**ee**sh] aniseed
anona [an**oh**na] custard apple
ao natural [ow natoor**a**l] plain
ao ponto [p**oh**ntoo] medium-rare
arroz [arr**oh**sh] rice
arroz árabe [arr**oh**z **a**rab] fried rice with nuts and dried fruit
arroz à valenciana [valayns-y**a**na] rice with chicken, pork and seafood
arroz branco [arr**oh**J br**a**nkoo] plain rice
arroz de cabidela [di kabid**eh**la] rice cooked in birds' blood
arroz de frango [fr**a**ngoo] rice with chicken
arroz de funcho [f**oo**nshoo] rice with fennel
arroz de mariscos [mar**ee**sh-koosh] a soupy dish of rice with mixed seafood

arroz de pato [pa**too**] rice with duck
arroz de polvo [**poh**lvoo] rice with octopus
arroz doce [dohs] sweet rice dessert
asa [**a**za] wing
assado [as**a**doo] roasted
atum [at**oo**ng] tuna
atum assado [as**a**doo] baked tuna
avelãs [avil**a**ngsh] hazelnuts
aves [**a**vish] poultry
azeitão [azayt**ow**ng] full fat soft goat's cheese
azeite [az**ay**t] olive oil
azeitonas [azayt**oh**nash] olives
azeitonas com pimentos [kong pim**ay**ntoosh] olives stuffed with pimentos
azeitonas recheadas [rish-y**a**dash] stuffed olives

bacalhau [bakal-y**ow**] dried salted cod
bacalhau à Brás [brash] dried cod with egg and potatoes
bacalhau à Gomes de Sá [gohmsh di] dried cod fried with onions, boiled eggs, potatoes and black olives
bacalhau assado [as**a**doo] roast dried cod
bacalhau à Zé do Pipo [zeh doo p**ee**poo] dried cod with egg sauce
bacalhau com natas [kong n**a**tash] dried cod with cream
bacalhau dourado [dohr**a**doo] dried cod baked in the oven
bacalhau grelhado [gril-y**a**doo] grilled dried cod
bacalhau na brasa [br**a**za] barbecued dried cod
bacalhau na cataplana dried cod, onion, tomato, ham, coriander, prawns and cockles cooked slowly in a covered pan
banana flambée [flamb**ay**] flambéed banana
batata assada [batatas**a**da] baked potato
batata murro [m**oo**roo] small baked potato
batata palha [p**a**l-ya] French fries
batatas [bat**a**tash] potatoes
batatas cozidas [kooz**ee**dash] boiled potatoes
batatas fritas [fr**ee**tash] chips, French fries
batatas salteadas [salt-y**a**dash] sautéed potatoes
baunilha [bown**ee**l-ya] vanilla
bavaroise [bavarw**a**z] dessert made from egg whites and cream
bem passado [bayng pas**a**doo] well-done
berbigão [birbeeg**ow**ng] shellfish similar to mussels
berinjela [bireenJ**eh**la] aubergine, eggplant
besugos [biz**oo**goosh] sea bream
beterraba [biterr**a**ba] beetroot
bifanas [beef**a**nash] pork slice

in a bread roll
bife [beef] steak
bife à cortador [koortadohr] thick tender steak
bife à portuguesa [poortoogayza] steak with mustard sauce and a fried egg
bife de alcatra [dalkatra] rump steak
bife de atum [datoong] tuna steak
bife de javali [di Javalee] wild boar steak
bife de pojadouro [pooJadohroo] type of beefsteak
bife de vaca [vaka] steak
bife de vaca com ovo a cavalo [kong ohvoo a kavaloo] steak with an egg on top
bife grelhado [gril-yadoo] grilled steak
bife tártaro [tartaroo] steak tartare
bifes de cebolada [beefsh di siboolada] thin slices of steak with onions
bifinhos de porco [beefeen-yooJ di pohrkoo] small slices of pork
bifinhos na brasa [braza] small slices of barbecued beef
bolacha [boolasha] biscuit, cookie
bola de carne [di karn] meatball
bolo [bohloo] cake
bolo de anjo [danJoo] angel cake
bolo de chocolate [shookoolat] chocolate cake
bolo de nozes [nozish] walnut cake
bolo inglês [inglaysh] sponge cake with dried fruit
bolo Rei [ray] ring-shaped cake (eaten at Christmas)
bolos e bolachas [bohlooz ee boolashash] cakes and biscuits/cookies
bomba de creme [bohmba di kraym] cream puff
borrego [boorraygoo] lamb
brioche [br-yosh] slightly sweet round bun
broa [broh-a] maize/corn bread or rye bread
broas [broh-ash] small maize/corn cakes (eaten at Christmas)

cabeça de pescada cozida [kabaysa di pishkada koozeeda] boiled head of hake
cabreiro [kabrayroo] goat's cheese
cabrito [kabreetoo] kid
cabrito assado [asadoo] roast kid
caça [kasa] game
cachola frita [kashola freeta] fried pig's heart and liver
cachorro [kashohrroo] hot dog
caldeirada [kaldayrada] fish stew
caldo [kaldoo] broth
caldo de aves [davish] poultry soup
caldo de carne [di karn] meat soup

caldo verde [vayrd] cabbage soup
camarões [kamar**oy**ngsh] prawns
canela [kan**eh**la] cinammon
canja de galinha [k**a**nJa di gal**ee**n-ya] chicken soup
caracóis [karak**oy**sh] snails
caranguejo [karang**ay**Joo] crab
carapau [karap**ow**] mackerel
carapaus de escabeche [karap**ow**J dishkab**eh**sh] marinated mackerel
carapaus fritos [karap**ow**sh fr**ee**toosh] fried mackerel
caril [kar**ee**l] curry
carne [karn] meat
carne à jardineira [Jardin**ay**ra] meat and vegetable stew
carne de cabrito [di kabr**ee**too] kid
carne de porco [di p**oh**rkoo] pork
carne de porco com amêijoas [kong am**ay**Jwash] pork with clams
carne de vaca [v**a**ka] beef
carne de vaca assada roast beef
carne de vaca guisada [geez**a**da] stewed meat
carne estufada [shtoof**a**da] stewed meat
carneiro [karn**ay**roo] mutton
carneiro assado [as**a**doo] roast mutton
carne picada [pik**a**da] minced meat
carnes [k**a**rnish] meats
carnes frias [fr**ee**-ash] selection of cold meats
caseiro [kaz**ay**roo] home-made
castanhas [kasht**a**n-yash] chestnuts
cebola [sib**oh**la] onion
cenoura [sin**oh**ra] carrot
cerejas [sir**ay**Jash] cherries
chanfana de porco [shanf**a**na di p**oh**rkoo] pork casserole
chantilly [shantil**ee**] whipped cream
charlottes [sharl**o**tsh] biscuits/ cookies with fruit and cream
cherne [shehrn] sea bream
chocos [sh**oh**koosh] cuttlefish
chouriço [shoor**ee**soo] spiced sausage
choux [shoo] cake made with choux pastry
churros [sh**oo**rrosh] long thin fritters
civet de lebre [seev**ay** di lehbr] jugged hare
cocktail de camarão [kokt**eh**l di kamar**ow**ng] prawn cocktail
codorniz [koodoorn**ee**sh] quail
codonizes fritas [koodoorn**ee**zish fr**ee**tash] fried quail
coelho [kw**ay**l-yoo] rabbit
coelho à caçadora [kasad**oh**ra] rabbit casserole with rice
coelho de escabeche [dishkab**eh**sh] marinated rabbit
coelho de fricassé [frikas**ay**] rabbit fricassee

coelho frito [**free**too] fried rabbit
coêntros [kw**ay**ntroosh] coriander
cogumelos [kogoom**eh**loosh] mushrooms
cogumelos com alho [kong **al**-yoo] mushrooms with garlic
comida congelada [koom**ee**da konJil**a**da] frozen food
comidas [koom**ee**dash] meals
compota stewed fruit
compota de laranja [di lar**a**nJa] marmalade
conquilhas [konk**ee**l-yash] baby clams
consomme [konsoom**ay**] consommé, clear meat soup
coração [kooras**ow**ng] heart
corações de alcachofra [kooras**oy**ngsh dalkash**oh**fra] artichoke hearts
corvina [koorv**ee**na] large saltwater fish
costela [koosht**eh**la] rib
costeleta [kooshtil**ay**ta] chop
costeletas de carneiro [kooshtil**ay**taJ di karn**ay**roo] lamb chops
costeletas de porco [di p**oh**rkoo] pork chops
costeletas fritas [**free**tash] fried chops
costeletas grelhadas [gril-**ya**dash] grilled chops
courgettes com creme no forno [koorJ**eh**tsh kong kraym noo f**oh**rnoo] baked courgettes/zucchini served with cream
courgettes fritas [**free**tash] fried courgettes/zucchini
couve [kohv] cabbage
couve branca com vinagre [kong vin**a**gr] white cabbage with vinegar
couve-flor [kohv flohr] cauliflower
couve-flor com molho branco no forno [kong m**oh**l-yoo br**a**nkoo noo f**oh**rnoo] cauliflower in white sauce
couve-flor com natas [n**a**tash] cauliflower with cream
couve roxa [r**oh**sha] red cabbage
couvert cover charge
couves de bruxelas [kohvsh di broosh**eh**lash] Brussels sprouts
couves de bruxelas com natas [kong n**a**tash] Brussels sprouts with cream
couves de bruxelas salteadas [salt-**ya**dash] sautéed Brussels sprouts
couves guisadas com salsichas [geez**a**dash kong sals**ee**shash] stewed cabbage with sausage
cozido [kooz**ee**doo] boiled; stewed; poached; cooked (either in a sauce or with olive oil); stew
cozido à portuguesa [poortoog**ay**za] stew made from chicken, sausage, rice, potatoes and vegetables
creme de cogumelos [kraym di kogoom**eh**loosh] cream of

mushroom soup
creme de mariscos [mar**ee**shkoosh] cream of shellfish soup
crepe de camarão [krehp di kamar**ow**ng] prawn crêpe
crepe de carne [karn] meat crêpe
crepe de cogumelos [kogoom**eh**loosh] mushroom crêpe
crepe de espinafres [dishpin**a**frish] spinach crêpe
crepe de legumes [lig**oo**mish] vegetable crêpe
crepe de pescada [pishk**a**da] hake crêpe
crepes [kr**eh**pish] crêpes, pancakes
cru/crua [kroo/kr**oo**-a] raw

damasco [dam**a**shkoo] apricot
dobrada [doobr**a**da] tripe with chickpeas
doce [dohs] jam; any sweet dish or dessert
doce de amêndoas [dam**ay**ndwash] almond dessert
doce de ovos [d**o**voosh] type of egg custard
doces regionais regional desserts
dose [doz] portion
dose para crianças [kr-y**a**nsash] children's portion
dourada [dohr**a**da] dory (saltwater fish); browned, golden brown
dourado [dohr**a**doo] browned, golden brown

éclair de café [aykl**eh**r dih kaf**eh**] coffee éclair
éclair de chantilly [shantil**ee**] whipped cream éclair
éclair de chocolate [shookool**at**] chocolate éclair
eirozes [ayr**o**zish] eels
ementa [em**ay**nta] menu
ementa fixa [f**ee**ksa] set menu
ementa turística [toor**ee**shtika] set menu
empada pie
empadão de carne [aympad**ow**ng di karn] large meat pie
empadão de peixe [paysh] large fish pie
encharcada [aynshark**a**da] dessert made from almonds and eggs
enguias [ayng**ee**-ash] eels
enguias fritas [fr**ee**tash] fried eels
ensopado de ... [aynsoop**a**doo di] ... stew
ensopado de borrego [boorr**ay**goo] lamb stew
ensopado de enguias [dayng**ee**-ash] eel stew
entradas [ayntr**a**dash] starters, appetizers
entrecosto [ayntrik**oh**shtoo] entrecôte
entrecosto com amêijoas [kong am**ay**Jwash] entrecôte with clams
entrecosto frito [fr**ee**too] fried

entrecôte
ervas [**eh**rvash] herbs
ervilhas [irv**ee**l-yash] peas
ervilhas de manteiga [di mant**ay**ga] peas in butter
ervilhas reboçadas [riboos**a**dash] peas in butter with bacon
escalope ao Madeira [shkal**o**p ow mad**ay**ra] escalope in Madeira wine
escalope de carneiro [di karn**ay**roo] mutton escalope
escalope de porco [p**oh**rkoo] pork escalope
escalope panado [pan**a**doo] breaded escalope
espadarte [shpad**a**rt] scabbard fish
espaguete à bolonhesa [shpag**eh**t a booloon-y**ay**za] spaghetti bolognese
espargos [shp**a**rgoosh] asparagus
esparregado [shparrig**a**doo] stew made from chopped green vegetables
especiaria [shpis-yar**ee**-a] spice
espetada de leitão [shpit**a**da di layt**ow**ng] sucking pig kebab
espetada de rins [reensh] kidney kebab
espetada de vitela [vit**eh**la] veal kebab
espetada mista [m**ee**shta] mixed kebab
espinafre [shpin**a**fr] spinach
espinafres gratinados [shpin**a**frish gratin**a**doosh] spinach with cheese sauce browned under the grill
espinafres salteados [salt-y**a**doosh] spinach sautéed in butter
estragão [shtrag**ow**ng] tarragon
estufado [shtoof**a**doo] stewed

faisão [fīz**ow**ng] pheasant
farinha [far**ee**n-ya] flour
farófias [far**o**f-yash] cream puff with filling made from egg whites, sugar and cinammon
farturas [fart**oo**rash] long thin fritters
fatia [fat**ee**-a] slice
fatias recheadas [fat**ee**-ash rish-y**a**dash] slices of bread with fried minced meat
favas [f**a**vash] broad beans
febras de porco [f**ay**braJ di p**oh**rkoo] thin slices of pork
feijão [fayJ**ow**ng] beans
feijoada [fayJw**a**da] bean and meat stew
feijões [fayJ**oy**ngsh] beans
feijões verdes [v**ay**rdish] French beans
fiambre [f-yambr] ham
fiambre caramelizado [karamileez**a**doo] glazed ham
fígado [f**ee**gadoo] liver
figos [f**ee**goosh] figs
figos moscatel [mooshkat**eh**l] moscatel figs
figos secos [s**ay**koosh] dried figs
filete [feel**eh**t] fillet
filete de bife com foie gras [di beef kong fwa gra] beef fillet

with foie gras
filhozes [feel-**yo**zish] sugary buns
folhado de carne [fool-**ya**doo di karn] meat in pastry
folhado de salsicha [sals**ee**sha] sausage roll
fondue de carne [fond**oo** di karn] meat fondue
fondue de chocolate [shookool**at**] chocolate fondue
fondue de queijo [**kay**Joo] cheese fondue
framboesa [frambw**ay**za] raspberry
frango [fr**a**ngoo] chicken
frango assado [frangwas**a**doo] roast chicken
frango na púcara [p**oo**kara] chicken casserole with Port and almonds
frango no churrasco [noo shoorr**a**shkoo] barbecued chicken
frango no espeto [nooshp**ay**too] spit-roasted chicken
frito [fr**ee**too] fried
frito de ... [di] fritter (usually filled with fruit)
fruta [fr**oo**ta] fruit
fruta da época [**eh**pooka] seasonal fruit
fumado [foom**a**doo] smoked
funcho [f**oo**nshoo] fennel

galantine de carne [galant**ee**n di k**a**rn] cold meat roll
galantine de coelho [di kw**ay**l-yoo] cold rabbit roll
galantine de galinha [gal**ee**n-ya] cold chicken roll
galantine de vegetais [viJitīsh] cold vegetable roll
galinha [gal**ee**n-ya] chicken
galinha de África [d**a**freeka] guinea fowl
galinha de fricassé [di frikas**ay**] chicken fricassée
gambas [g**a**mbash] prawns
gambas grelhadas [gril-**ya**dash] grilled prawns
ganso [g**a**nsoo] goose
garoupa [gar**oh**pa] fish similar to bream
gaspacho [gasp**a**shoo] chilled vegetable soup
gelado [Jil**a**doo] ice cream
gelado de baunilha [di bown**ee**l-ya] vanilla ice cream
gelado de frutas [fr**oo**tash] fruit ice cream
geleia [Jil**ay**-a] preserve
gengibre [JaynJ**ee**br] ginger
gordura [goord**oo**ra] fat
grão [growng] chickpeas
grelhado [gril-**ya**doo] grilled
groselhas [grooz**eh**l-yash] redcurrants
guisado [geez**a**doo] stewed

hamburguer com batatas fritas [amb**oo**rgir kong bat**a**tash fr**ee**tash] hamburger and chips/French fries
hamburguer com ovo [**oh**voo] hamburger with an egg
hamburguer no pão [noo powng] hamburger in a roll

hortaliças [ortaleesash] green vegetables
hortelã [ortilang] mint

iogurte [yoogoort] yoghurt
iscas fritas com batatas [eeshkash freetash kong batatash] dish of fried liver and boiled potatoes

jantar [Jantar] evening meal, dinner; supper
jardineira [Jardinayra] mixed vegetables

lagosta [lagohshta] lobster
lagosta à Americana [amirikana] lobster with tomato and onions
lagosta thermidor [tirmeedohr] lobster thermidor
lagostim [lagooshteeng] saltwater crayfish
lampreia [lampray-a] lamprey
lampreia à moda do Minho [doo meen-yoo] marinated lamprey and rice, both cooked in the juices and blood of the lamprey
lampreia de ovos [dovoosh] dessert made from eggs and sugar in the shape of a lamprey
lanche [lansh] afternoon tea
laranja [laranJa] orange
lasanha [lasan-ya] lasagne
legumes [ligoomish] vegetables
leitão assado [laytowng asadoo] roast sucking pig
leitão da Bairrada [da bīrrada] sucking pig from Bairrada
leite [layt] milk
leite creme [kraym] light custard flavoured with cinammon
limão [limowng] lemon
língua [leengwa] tongue
língua de porco [di pohrkoo] pig's tongue
língua de vaca [vaka] ox tongue
linguado [lingwadoo] sole
linguado à meunière [moon-yehr] sole dipped in flour and fried in butter
linguado frito [freetoo] fried sole
linguado grelhado [gril-yadoo] grilled sole
linguado no forno [noo fohrnoo] baked sole
lista de preços [leeshta di praysoosh] price list
lombo [lohmboo] loin
lombo de porco [di pohrkoo] loin of pork
lombo de vaca [vaka] sirloin
louro [lohroo] bay leaf
lulas [loolash] squid
lulas com natas [kong natash] stewed squid with cream
lulas fritas [freetash] fried squid
lulas guisadas [geezadash] stewed squid
lulas recheadas [rish-yadash] stuffed squid

maçã [masang] apple
maçã assada baked apple
macedónia de frutas [masidon-ya di frootash] fruit cocktail
maionese [mī-oonehz] mayonnaise
maionese de alho [dal-yoo] garlic mayonnaise
mal passado [pasadoo] rare
manjericão [manJirikowng] basil
manteiga [mantayga] butter
manteiga de anchova [danshohva] anchovy butter
manteiga queimada [kaymada] butter sauce for fish
margarina [margareena] margarine
marinada marinade
mariscos [mareeshkoosh] shellfish
marmelada [marmilada] quince jam
marmelos [marmehloosh] quinces
marmelos assados [marmehlooz asadoosh] roast quinces
massa pasta
massa de fartos [di fartoosh] choux pastry
meia desfeita [may-a dishfayta] boiled dried cod, potatoes, chickpeas and olive oil
meia dose [doz] half portion
mel [mehl] honey
melancia [milansee-a] watermelon
melão [milowng] melon
melão com presunto [kong prizoontoo] melon with ham
meloa com vinho do Porto/Madeira [miloh-a kong veen-yoo doo pohrtoo/madayra] small melon with Port or Madeira wine poured over it
melocotão [milookootowng] peach
merenda [miraynda] tea; snack
merengue [mirang] meringue
mexilhões [mishil-yoyngsh] mussels
migas à Alentejana [meegaz a alayntiJana] thick bread soup
mil folhas [meel fohl-yash] millefeuille, custard slice, (US) napoleon
miolos [m-yoloosh] brains
miolos com ovos [kong ovoosh] brains with eggs
míscaros [meeshkaroosh] mushrooms
moleja [moolayJa] soup made from pig's blood
molho [mohl-yoo] sauce
molho à Espanhola [shpan-yola] spicy onion and garlic sauce
molho ao Madeira [ow madayra] Madeira wine sauce
molho bearnaise [bayrnehz] béarnaise sauce
molho béchamel [bayshamehl] béchamel sauce, white sauce
molho branco [brankoo] white sauce
molho holandês [olandaysh] hollandaise sauce
molho mornay cheese sauce
molho mousseline [moosileen]

hollandaise sauce with cream
molho tártaro [tartaroo] tartare sauce
molho veloutée [vilootay] white sauce made from cream and egg yolks
morangos [moorangoosh] strawberries
morangos com chantilly [kong shantilee] strawberries and whipped cream
morcela [moorsehla] black pudding, blood sausage
mostarda [mooshtarda] mustard
mousse de chocolate [moos di shookoolat] chocolate mousse
mousse de fiambre [f-yambr] ham mousse
mousse de leite condensado [layt kondaynsadoo] mousse made from condensed milk

na brasa [braza] charcoal-grilled
napolitanas [napoolitanash] long flat biscuits/cookies
natas [natash] cream
natas batidas [bateedash] whipped cream
nectarina [nektareena] nectarine
nêsperas [nayshpirash] loquats (yellow fruit similar to a plum)
no churrasco [noo shoorrashkoo] barbecued
no espeto [nooshpaytoo] spit-roasted
no forno [fohrno] baked
nozes [nozish] walnuts
noz moscada [noJ mooshkada] nutmeg

óleo [ol-yoo] oil
omeleta [omilayta] omelette
omeleta com ervas [kong ehrvash] vegetable omelette
omeleta de cogumelos [di kogoomehloosh] mushroom omelette
omeleta de fiambre [f-yambr] ham omelette
omeleta de queijo [kayJoo] cheese omelette
omelete [omilayt] omelette
orelha de porco de vinaigrette [orayl-ya di pohrkoo di vinagreht] pig's ear in vinaigrette dressing
ostras [ohshtrash] oysters
ovo [ohvoo] egg
ovo com maionese [kong mī-oonehz] egg mayonnaise
ovo cozido [koozeedoo] hard-boiled egg
ovo em geleia [ayng Jilay-a] egg in aspic
ovo escalfado [shkalfadoo] poached egg
ovo estrelado [shtriladoo] fried egg
ovo quente [kaynt] soft-boiled egg
ovos mexidos [misheedoosh] scrambled eggs
ovos mexidos com tomate [kong toomat] scrambled eggs with tomato

ovos verdes [vayrdish] eggs stuffed with a mixture of egg yolks, mayonnaise and parsley

palha de ovos [pal-ya dovoosh] egg pastries
panqueca [pankehka] pancake
pão [powng] bread
pão branco [brankoo] white bread
pão de centeio [di sayntay-oo] rye bread
pão de ló de Alfazeirão [law dalfazay-rowng] sponge cake
pão de ló de Ovar [dohvar] sponge cake
pão de milho [meel-yoo] bread made from maize flour, corn bread
pão integral [intigral] wholemeal bread
pão torrado [toorradoo] toasted bread
pargo [pargoo] sea bream
pargo assado [pargwasadoo] roast bream
pargo cozido [koozeedoo] bream cooked in a sauce or with olive oil
parrilhada [pareel-yada] grilled fish
passas [pasash] raisins
pastéis [pashteh-ish] pastries
pastéis de bacalhau [di bakal-yow] dried cod fishcakes
pastéis de carne [karn] puff-pastry patties filled with meat
pastéis de Chaves [shavish] thin dainty puff-pastry patties filled with meat
pastéis de nata custard tarts
pastéis de Tentúgal [tayntoogal] filo-pastry patties with an egg yolk and sugar filling, sprinkled with sugar
pastel [pashtehl] cake; pie
pastelinhos de bacalhau [pashtileen-yoosh di bakal-yow] fishcakes made from dried cod
pataniscas [pataneeshkash] dried cod fritters
pataniscas de miolos [di m-yoloosh] brain fritters
paté de aves [patay davish] pâté made from chicken, duck or goose liver
paté de coelho [di kwayl-yoo] rabbit pâté
paté de fígado [feegadoo] liver pâté
paté de galinha [galeen-ya] chicken pâté
paté de lebre [lehbr] hare pâté
pato [patoo] duck
pato assado [asadoo] roast duck
pato com laranja [kong laranJa] duck à l'orange
peixe [paysh] fish
peixe espada [shpada] swordfish
peixe espada de escabeche [dishkabehsh] marinated swordfish
peixinhos da horta [paysheen-

yoosh da **or**ta] French bean fritters

pepino [pip**ee**noo] cucumber

pequeno almoço [pik**ay**noo alm**oh**soo] breakfast

pequeno almoço continental [kontinaynt**a**l] continental breakfast

pêra [p**ay**ra] pear

pêra abacate [abak**a**t] avocado

pêra bela helena [b**eh**layl**ay**na] pear in chocolate sauce

percebes [pirs**eh**bish] shellfish similar to barnacles

perdiz [pird**ee**sh] partridge

perdizes de escabeche [pird**ee**ziJ dishkab**eh**sh] marinated partridge

perdizes fritas [pird**ee**zish fr**ee**tash] fried partridge

perdizes na púcara [pird**ee**ziJ na p**oo**kara] partridge casserole

perna [p**eh**rna] leg

perna de carneiro assada [di karn**ay**roo] roast leg of lamb

perna de carneiro entremeada [ayntrim-y**a**da] stuffed leg of lamb

perninhas de rã [pirn**ee**n-yash di rang] frogs' legs

peru [pir**oo**] turkey

peru assado [as**a**doo] roast turkey

peru de fricassé [di frikas**ay**] turkey fricassée

peru recheado [rish-y**a**doo] stuffed turkey

pescada [pishk**a**da] hake

pescada cozida [kooz**ee**da] hake cooked in a sauce or with olive oil

pescadinhas de rabo na boca [pishkad**ee**n-yash di r**a**boo na b**oh**ka] fried whiting served with their tails in their mouths

pêssego [p**ay**sigoo] peach

pêssego careca [kar**eh**ka] nectarine

petiscos [pit**ee**shkoosh] savouries

picante [pik**a**nt] hot, spicy

pimenta [pim**ay**nta] pepper

pimenta preta [pr**ay**ta] black pepper

pimentos [pim**ay**ntoosh] peppers, capsicums

piperate [peepir**a**t] pepper stew

piri-piri [p**ee**ree-p**ee**ree] seasoning made from chillies and olive oil

polvo [p**oh**lvoo] octopus

porção [poors**ow**ng] portion

porco [p**oh**rkoo] pork

porco à alentejana [alayntij**a**na] pork cooked with clams

prato [pr**a**too] dish; course

prato do dia [doo d**ee**-a] today's special

prato especial da casa [shpis-y**a**l da k**a**za] speciality of the house

prato principal [prinsip**a**l] main course

prego [pr**eh**goo] thin slice of steak in a bread roll

prego no fiambre [noo f-y**a**mbr] steak sandwich with

sliced ham
prego no pão [noo powng] steak sandwich
prego no prato [pratoo] steak, usually served with a fried egg
presunto [prizoontoo] ham
pudim de ovos [poodeeng dovoosh] egg pudding
pudim flan [flang] crème caramel
pudim molotov [molotof] crème caramel with egg whites
puré de batata [pooray di] mashed potatoes
puré de castanhas [kashtan-yash] chestnut purée
p.v. (preço variado) [praysoo var-yadoo] price varies

queijadas de Sintra [kayJadaJ di seentra] small tarts with a filling made from milk, eggs, sugar and vanilla
queijo [kayJoo] cheese
queijo curado [kooradoo] dried matured hard white cheese
queijo da Ilha [eel-ya] strong cheese from the Azores flavoured with pepper
queijo da Serra [sehrra] goat's cheese from Serra da Estrela
queijo de cabra [di] goat's cheese
queijo de ovelha [dovayl-ya] sheep's cheese
queijo de Palmela [palmehla] small white mild dried cheese
queijo de Serpa [sehrpa] small strong dried goat's cheese
queijo fresco [frayshkoo] medium-firm mild cheese
queijos [kayJoosh] cheeses

rabanadas [rabanadash] bread dipped in beaten egg and fried, then sprinkled with sugar and cinammon
raia [rī-a] skate
refeição [rifaysowng] meal
refeição ligeira [liJayra] snack, light meal
remoulade [rimoolad] dressing with mustard and herbs
requeijão [rikayJowng] curd cheese
rillete [ree-eht] potted pork meat
rins [reensh] kidneys
rins ao Madeira [reenz ow madayra] kidneys cooked in Madeira wine
rissóis [riso-ysh] deep-fried meat patties
rissol [risol] deep-fried meat patty
rissol de camarão [di kamarowng] prawn rissole
robalo [roobaloo] rock bass
rojões [rooJoyngsh] cubes of pork
rolo de carne [rohloo di karn] meat loaf
rosmaninho [rooJmaneen-yoo] rosemary

sabayon [saba-yohng] dessert

made from egg yolks and white wine
sal salt
salada salad
salada de agriões [dagr-**yoy**ngsh] watercress salad
salada de alface [dalf**as**] green salad
salada de atum [dat**oo**ng] tuna salad
salada de chicória [di shik**o**r-ya] chicory salad
salada de frutas [fr**oo**tash] fruit salad
salada de lagosta [lag**oh**shta] lobster salad
salada de ovas [d**o**vash] fish roe salad
salada de tomate [di toom**a**t] tomato salad
salada mista [m**ee**shta] mixed salad
salada russa [r**oo**sa] Russian salad, salad of diced vegetables in mayonnaise
salgado [salg**a**doo] savoury, salty
salmão [salm**ow**ng] salmon
salmão fumado [foom**a**doo] smoked salmon
salmonete [salmoon**ayt**] red mullet
salmonetes grelhados [salmoon**ay**tsh gril-y**a**doosh] grilled red mullet
salsa parsley
salsicha [sals**ee**sha] sausage
salsichas de cocktail [sals**ee**shaJ di kokt**eh**l] cocktail sausages
salsichas de peru [pir**oo**] turkey sausages
salsichas de porco [p**oh**rkoo] pork sausages
salteado [salt-y**a**doo] sautéed
sandes [s**a**ndish] sandwich
sandes de fiambre [di f-y**a**mbr] ham sandwich
sandes de lombo [l**oh**mboo] steak sandwich
sandes de paio [p**ī**-oo] sausage sandwich
sandes de presunto [priz**oo**ntoo] ham sandwich
sandes de queijo [k**ay**Joo] cheese sandwich
sandes mista [m**ee**shta] mixed sandwich, usually ham and cheese
santola spider crab
santola gratinada [gratin**a**da] spider crab with cheese sauce browned under the grill
sapateira [sapat**ay**ra] spider crab
sarda mackerel
sardinha [sard**ee**n-ya] sardine
sardinhas assadas [sard**ee**n-yaz as**a**dash] roast sardines
selecção de queijos [silehs**ow**ng di k**ay**Joosh] selection of cheeses
sobremesas [sobrim**ay**zash] desserts
solha [s**oh**l-ya] flounder
solha assada no forno [noo f**oh**rnoo] baked flounder
solha frita [fr**ee**ta] fried

flounder
solha recheada [rish-y**a**da] stuffed flounder
sonho [s**oh**n-yoo] type of doughnut
sopa [s**oh**pa] soup
sopa à alentejana [alayntiJ**a**na] bread soup with a poached egg on top
sopa de agriões [dagr-y**oy**ngsh] watercress soup
sopa de alho francês [d**a**l-yoo frans**ay**sh] leek soup
sopa de camarão [kamar**ow**ng] prawn soup
sopa de caranguejo [karang**ay**Joo] crab soup
sopa de cebola gratinada [sib**oh**la] French onion soup with melted cheese on top
sopa de cogumelos [kogoom**eh**loosh] mushroom soup
sopa de espargos [dishp**a**rgoosh] asparagus soup
sopa de feijão verde [fayJ**ow**ng vayrd] green bean soup
sopa de grão [gr**ow**ng] chickpea soup
sopa de lagosta [lag**oh**shta] lobster soup
sopa de legumes [lig**oo**mish] vegetable soup
sopa de mariscos [mar**ee**shkoosh] shellfish soup
sopa de ostras [d**oh**shtrash] oyster soup
sopa de panela [di pan**eh**la] egg-based dessert
sopa de pão e coentros [powng ee kw**ay**ntroosh] bread and coriander soup
sopa de pedra [p**eh**dra] thick vegetable soup
sopa de peixe [paysh] fish soup
sopa de rabo de boi [r**a**boo di boy] oxtail soup
sopa de tartaruga [tartar**oo**ga] turtle soup
sopa do dia [doo d**ee**-a] soup of the day
sopa dourada [dohr**a**da] egg-based dessert
sopa e cozido [s**oh**pī kooz**ee**doo] meat stew
sopa juliana [s**oh**pa Jool-y**a**na] vegetable soup
sopas [s**oh**pash] soups
soufflé de camarão [soofl**ay** di kamar**ow**ng] prawn soufflé
soufflé de chocolate [shookool**a**t] chocolate soufflé
soufflé de cogumelos [kogoom**eh**loosh] mushroom soufflé
soufflé de espinafres [dishpin**a**frish] spinach soufflé
soufflé de peixe [paysh] fish soufflé
soufflé de queijo [k**ay**Joo] cheese soufflé
soufflé gelado [Jil**a**doo] ice-cream soufflé

tarte de amêndoas [tart dam**ay**ndwash] almond tart
tarte de cogumelos [di

kogoomehloosh] mushroom quiche
tarte de limão [limowng] lemon tart
tarte de maçã [masang] apple tart
taxa de serviço [tasha di sirveesoo] service charge
tempero da salada [taympayroo da salada] salad dressing
tomar [toomar] fresh soft goat's cheese
tomate [toomat] tomato
tomates recheados [toomatish rish-yadoosh] stuffed tomatoes
tomilho [toomeel-yoo] thyme
toranja [tooranJa] grapefruit
torrada [toorrada] toast
torresmos [toorrayJmoosh] small fried rashers of bacon
torta tart
torta de maçã [masang] apple pie
torta de nozes [di nozish] walnut tart
tortilha [toorteel-ya] Spanish-style omelette with potato
tosta [toshta] toasted sandwich
tosta mista [meeshta] toasted ham and cheese sandwich
toucinho do céu [tooseen-yoo doo seh-oo] kind of dessert made from eggs, sugar and almonds
tripas [treepash] tripe
tripas à moda do Porto [treepaza moda doo pohrtoo] tripe with beans and vegetables
trufas de chocolate [troofaJ di shookoolat] chocolate truffles
truta [troota] trout
truta assada no forno [noo fohrnoo] baked trout
truta cozida [koozeeda] trout cooked in a sauce or with olive oil
truta frita [freeta] fried trout

uvas [oovash] grapes
uvas brancas [oovaJ brankash] green grapes
uvas moscatel [mooshkatehl] muscatel grapes
uvas pretas [oovaJ praytash] black grapes

veado assado [v-yadoo asadoo] roast venison
vieiras recheadas [v-yayrash rish-yadash] scallops filled with seafood
vinagre [vinagr] vinegar
vinagre de estragão [dishtragowng] tarragon vinegar
vitela [vitehla] veal

Menu Reader: Drink

Essential Terms

beer a cerveja [sir**vay**Ja]
bottle a garrafa
brandy o brandy
coffee o café [ka**feh**]
a cup of ... uma chávena de ... [**oo**ma sh**a**vena di]
gin o gin [Jeeng]
gin and tonic um gin-tónico [oong Jeeng **to**nikoo]
glass o copo [**ko**poo]
a glass of ... um copo de ... [oong **ko**poo di]
milk o leite [layt]
mineral water a água mineral [**a**gwa]
orange juice o sumo de laranja [**soo**moo di lar**an**Ja]
port o vinho do Porto [**vee**n-yoo doo p**oh**rtoo]
red wine o vinho tinto [**tee**ntoo]
rosé rosé [roo**zay**]
soda (water) a soda
soft drink a bebida não alcoólica [bib**ee**da nowng alko-**o**leeka]
sugar o açúcar [as**oo**kar]
tea o chá [sha]
tonic (water) a água tónica [**a**gwa]
vodka o vodka
water a água [**a**gwa]
whisky o whisky [**wee**shkee]
white wine o vinho branco [**vee**n-yoo br**a**nkoo]
wine o vinho [**vee**n-yoo]
wine list a lista dos vinhos [**lee**shta dooJ **vee**n-yoosh]

another ..., please outro/outra ..., por favor [**oh**troo – poor fav**ohr**]

açúcar [as**oo**kar] sugar
água mineral [**a**gwa miner**al**] mineral water
aguardente [agward**ay**nt] clear spirit/brandy (literally: 'firewater'), distilled from wine or grape skins
aguardente de figo [**fee**goo] fig brandy
aguardente de pêra [di p**ay**ra] brandy with a pear or pears in the bottle
aguardentes bagaceiras [agward**ay**ntish bagas**ay**rash] clear spirit/brandy distilled from grape skins
aguardentes velhas [v**eh**l-yash] matured brandies
aguardentes velhas ou preparadas [v**eh**l-yaz oh prepar**a**dash] brandies matured in oak
álcool [**a**lko-ol] alcohol
amêndoa amarga [am**ay**ndwa am**a**rga] bitter almond liqueur
aperitivo [apirit**ee**voo] aperitif

bagaço [bag**a**soo] clear spirit/brandy (literally: 'firewater'), distilled from grape skins
Bairrada [bīrr**a**da] region producing fruity red wines
batido de leite [bat**ee**doo di layt] milkshake
bebida [bib**ee**da] drink
bica [b**ee**ka] small black espresso-type coffee
branco [br**a**nkoo] white
bruto [br**oo**too] extra-dry
Bual [boo-**al**] medium-sweet Madeira wine
Bucelas® [boos**eh**lash] crisp dry white wine from the Estremadura area

cacau [kak**ow**] cocoa
café [kaf**eh**] small black espresso-type coffee
café com leite [kong layt] white coffee, coffee with milk
café com pingo [p**ee**ngoo] espresso with brandy
café duplo [d**oo**ploo] two espressos in the same cup
café glacé [glas**ay**] iced coffee
café instantâneo [inshtant**a**n-yoo] instant coffee
caneca [kan**eh**ka] half-litre
capilé [kapil**eh**] drink made from water, sugar and syrup
carapinhada de café [karapeen-y**a**da di kaf**eh**] coffee drink with crushed ice
carapinhada de chocolate [shookool**a**t] chocolate drink with crushed ice
carapinhada de groselha [grooz**eh**l-ya] redcurrant drink with crushed ice
carapinhada de morango [moor**a**ngoo] strawberry drink with crushed ice
carioca [kar-y**o**ka] small weak black coffee
cerveja [sirv**ay**Ja] beer
cerveja branca [br**a**nka] lager

cerveja de pressão [di prisowng] draught beer
cerveja preta [prayta] bitter, dark beer
chá [sha] tea
chá com leite [kong layt] tea with milk
chá com limão [limowng] lemon tea
chá com mel [mehl] tea with honey
chá de limão [di limowng] infusion of hot water with a lemon rind
chá de lucialima [loos-yaleema] herb tea
chá de mentol mint tea
chá de tília [teel-ya] linden blossom tea
champanhe [shampan-yi] champagne
chocolate glacé [shookoolat glasay] iced chocolate
chocolate quente [kaynt] hot chocolate
cidra [seedra] cider
cimbalino [simbaleenoo] small espresso
clarete [klarayt] claret
Colares [koolarish] table wine from the Colares region
com gás [kong gash] carbonated
com gelo [Jayloo] with ice, on the rocks
conhaque [koon-yak] cognac, brandy
Constantino® [konshtanteenoo] Portuguese brandy
cubo de gelo [kooboo di Jayloo] ice cube

Dão® [downg] red table wine from the Dão region
descafeinado [dishkafaynadoo] decaffeinated
doce [dohs] sweet (usually very sweet)

espumante [shpoomant] sparkling
espumantes naturais [shpoomantish natoorīsh] sparkling wine made by the champagne method
expresso [shprehsoo] espresso

figo [feegoo] fig brandy

galão [galowng] large weak milky coffee, served in a tall glass
garoto [garohtoo] small coffee with milk
garrafa bottle
garrafeira [garrafayra] aged red wine set aside by the producer in years of exceptional quality
gasoso [gazohzoo] fizzy
gelo [Jayloo] ice
ginja [JeenJa], **ginjinha** [JeenJeen-ya] brandy with sugar and cherries added

imperial [eempir-yal] regular glass size for drinking beer (about/litre)

italiana [ital-**ya**na] half a very strong espresso

jarro [Jarroo] jug

Lagoa® [lag**oh**-a] table wine from the Algarve

leite [layt] milk

licor [lik**ohr**] liqueur; sweet flavoured spirit

Licor Beirão® [bayr**ow**ng] cognac with herbs

licor de medronho [di midr**oh**n-yoo] berry liqueur

licor de ovo [d**oh**voo] advocaat

licor de pêras [di p**ay**rash] pear liqueur

licor de whisky [w**ee**shkee] whisky liqueur

limonada [limoon**a**da] fresh lemon juice with water and sugar

lista de preços [l**ee**shta di pr**ay**soosh] price list

lista dos vinhos [dooJ v**ee**n-yoosh] wine list

Macieira® [masi-**ay**ra] Portuguese brandy

Madeira [mad**ay**ra] wine-producing region; sweet and dry fortified wines

maduro [mad**oo**roo] mature

Malvasia [malvas**ee**-a] Malmsey wine, a sweet heavy Madeira wine

Mateus Rosé® [mat**ay**-oosh rooz**ay**] sweet rosé wine

mazagrin [mazagr**a**ng] iced coffee with lemon

meia de leite [m**ay**-a di layt] large white coffee

meia garrafa half-bottle

meio seco [m**ay**-oo s**ay**koo] medium-dry (usually fairly sweet)

morena [moor**ay**na] mixture of lager and bitter

moscatel [mooshkat**eh**l] muscatel wine

não alcoólico [nowng alko-**o**leekoo] non-alcoholic

pingo [p**ee**ngoo] small coffee with milk

ponche [pohnsh] punch

pré-pagamento pay in advance

região demarcada wine-producing region subject to official controls

Reguengos [rig**ay**ngoosh] table wine from Alentejo

reserva [riz**eh**rva] aged wine set aside by the producer in years of exceptional quality

Sagres® [s**a**grish] popular brand of lager

Sagres Europa® [sagr**i**z ay-oor**o**pa] brand of lager

Sagres Preta® [pr**ay**ta] dark beer resembling British brown ale

saquinhos de chá [sak**ee**n-yooJ di sha] teabags

seco [saykoo] dry
selo de garantia seal of guarantee
sem gás [sayng gash] still
sem gelo [Jayloo] without ice
Sercial [sirsee-al] the driest variety of Madeira wine
sirva gelado served chilled
sirva-se à temperatura ambiente serve at room temperature
sirva-se fresco serve cool
sumo de laranja [soomoo di laranJa] orange juice
sumo de lima [leema] lime juice
sumo de limão [limowng] lemon juice
sumo de maçã [masang] apple juice
sumo de tomate [toomat] tomato juice
Sumol® [soomol] fizzy fruit juice
Super Bock® brand of lager

tarifas de consumo price list
Tavel® [tavehl] rosé wine
tinto [teentoo] red
Tri Naranjus® [treenaranJoosh] brand name for a range of fruit drinks

Valpaços® [valpasoosh] table wine from Trás-os-Montes
velha [vehl-ya] old, mature
velhíssima [vehl-yeesima] very old (spirits)
Verdelho [virdayl-yoo] a medium-dry Madeira wine
vermute [vermoot] vermouth
vinho [veen-yoo] wine
vinho branco [brankoo] white wine
vinho da casa [kaza] house wine
vinho da Madeira [madayra] Madeira wine
vinho de aperitivo [dapiriteevoo] aperitif
vinho de mesa [di mayza] table wine
vinho de Xerêz [shiraysh] sherry
vinho do Porto [doo pohrtoo] port
vinho espumante [shpoomant] sparkling wine
vinho moscatel [mooshkatehl] muscatel wine
vinho rosé [roozay] rosé wine
vinho tinto [teentoo] red wine
vinho verde [vayrd] young, slightly sparkling white, red, or rosé wine produced in the Minho

whisky de malte [weeshkee di malt] malt whisky

xarope [sharop] cordial, concentrated juice
xarope de groselha [di groozehl-ya] redcurrant cordial
xarope de morango [moorangoo] strawberry cordial